Improving Software Quality

WILEY SERIES IN
SOFTWARE ENGINEERING PRACTICE

SERIES EDITORS:

Patrick A.V. Hall, The Open University, UK
Martyn A. Ould, Praxis Systems plc, UK
William E. Riddle, Software Design & Analysis, Inc., USA

Fletcher J. Buckley • Implementing Software Engineering Practices

John J. Marciniak and Donald J. Reifer • Software Acquisition Management

John S. Hares • SSADM for the Advanced Practitioner

Martyn A. Ould • Strategies for Software Engineering: The Management of Risk and Quality

David P. Youll • Making Software Development Visible: Effective Project Control

Charles P. Hollocker • Software Reviews and Audits Handbook

John S. Hares • Information Engineering for the Advanced Practitioner

David Whitgift • Methods and Tools for Software Configuration Management

Robert L. Baber • Error-Free Software

Charles R. Symons • Software Sizing and Estimating: MKII FPA (Function Point Analysis)

H. Ronald Berlack • Software Configuration Management

Ken Shumate and Marilyn Keller • Software Specification & Design: A Disciplined Approach for Real-Time Systems

L. Jay Arthur • Rapid Evolutionary Development: Requirements, Prototyping, & Software Creation

Michael Dyer • The Cleanroom Approach to Quality Software Development

L. Jay Arthur • Improving Software Quality: An Insider's Guide to TQM

Jean-Paul Calvez • Embedded Real-Time Systems: A Specification and Design Methodology

Donald J. Reifer • Managing Software Reuse

P. Grant Rule • A Field Guide to JSD

Keith Edwards • Real-Time Structured Methods: Systems Analysis

Improving Software Quality
An Insider's Guide to TQM

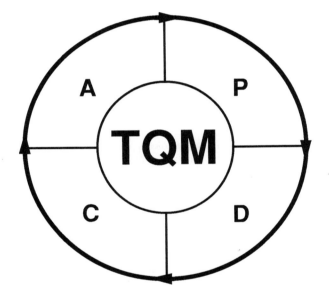

LOWELL JAY ARTHUR

John Wiley & Sons, Inc.
New York / Chichester / Brisbane / Toronto / Singapore

Library of Congress Cataloging-in-Publication Data

Arthur, Lowell Jay
    Improving software quality : an insider's guide to TQM / Lowell
Jay Arthur.
       p. cm. — (Wiley series in software engineering practice)
    Includes bibliographical references and index.
    ISBN 0-471-57804-5
    1. Computer software—Quality control. 2. Total quality
management. I. Title. II. Series.
QA76.76.Q35A3 1992
005.1'068'5—dc20   92-23057
                                  CIP

Printed in the United States of America
10 9 8 7 6 5 4 3 2 1

Contents

14   Software Evolution   247

Preface

Shades of Ayn Rand's *Atlas Shrugged*. Across the nation and around the solar system, software systems—those little strings of ones and zeros that make computers jump through hoops—are missing the hoop with the accuracy of a stupid pet trick on David Letterman.

At 2:21 PM on January 15th, at the height of the afternoon calling period, a 4ESS switching system on the lower end of Manhattan noticed a minor hardware fault—a problem between the switch and the signaling network. The 4ESS promptly took itself out of the network and, as a kindness, sent messages about its shutdown to all of its neighboring switches so that they would route calls around it. Within seconds, the Manhattan switch came back on-line and sent still more messages to its friends and neighbors. Like tourist postcards that get delivered on the same day, the receiving switches were still processing the first message when they got the second. They became confused, noticed they were confused and checked themselves into the clinic for repair. But before they shut down to reinitialize, they sent out similar messages to their neighbors.

Like an epidemic of influenza, the messages swept across the nation's switching machines. No sooner would one machine get sick and recover than it would receive a barrage of messages from other sick companions and it would fall ill again. The Manhattan switch began to feel guilty. People also began to feel ill.

Telemarketing companies around the country turned pale and sat in dazed silence as people suddenly stopped calling. Fortune 500 companies found it difficult if not impossible to reach out and touch someone. Tempers flared. Faces twisted in frustration.

In the network operations center in Bedminster, N.J. and the technical support center in Lisle, Ill., massive computerized maps display the condition of AT&T's telephone network. Lines on the maps turned an angry red, slashing across the nation, spreading out from Manhattan like a web. The network engineers began to turn green. They followed the standard procedures for correcting problems; they invented new ones; but for the first time in AT&T's history, nothing worked.

The 4ESS switches were designed to handle 700,000 calls an hour. For almost nine hours, the vast array of 114 4ESS switches—the primary switch in the network—managed to handle only half that many. Long-distance, overseas, and 800 traffic were all affected. Toll-free 800 services had the most difficulty. Chaos gripped the network and its customers. Fortunately for AT&T, it was Martin Luther King Jr.'s birthday, a national holiday—many government agencies and businesses were closed.

A tiny software bug in the December release of the 4ESS switching system caused the error. AT&T reverted to the old version of the software and installed a corrected version on January 20th, but the damage was done. Large companies that depend on long-distance services, especially 800 services, may well seek alternative suppliers. AT&T's Teflon image was gone.

Ten days later, the Government Printing Office in Washington, D.C. narrowly averted another nationwide epidemic. Like a street addict unaware of their disease, the GPO was handling the processing and distribution of two floppy disks for its dealer, the U.S. Census Bureau. The disks would allow libraries across the nation to retrieve data from the Census Bureau. On January 25th, the GPO was in the process of mailing these out to 772 locations across the country when it learned that one of the disks contained the Jerusalem virus—a software program designed to damage computers.

Also known as the Friday the 13th virus, the Jerusalem virus infects an MS-DOS computer's operating system and programs, causing them to expand like a case of elephantiasis that clogs the computer's memory. The infected system slows dramatically and its data can be destroyed.

The GPO halted the mailing and rounded up the few wayward disks before much damage was done. A close call.

A few days later, the Galileo spacecraft—named after an Italian astronomer who was almost burned at the stake for his beliefs—took a hard swing around Venus on its way to Jupiter. The electronic eye began to snap uncontrollably when the software controlling it went on a rampage as the 2.8 ton cyclops swooped within 10,000 miles of the planet. The camera took 16 pictures of Venus and then, for five hours that Saturday morning as the spacecraft completed its first "gravity assist maneuver", the camera shutter fluttered like a strobe. 450 times it opened to gaze at the planet below and then clicked shut as if offended by what it saw. Could it be the Jerusalem virus, they wondered? Who knows? By late afternoon, NASA engineers at the Jet Propulsion Laboratory in Pasadena had corrected the software flaw and the machine took 38 more souvenir photos of Venus as it turned back toward Earth.

The spacecraft gained 5,000 miles-per-hour using the gravity of Venus to sling it back toward Earth, where our planet's gravitational pull will accelerate it toward its encounter with Jupiter in 1995. Let's hope the three-ton, software-controlled bullet is on course. And if it is off course, let's hope that stupid switching machine in lower Manhattan gets what it deserves.

Software problems buzz around us like killer bees just waiting for Murphy's law to take hold and something unspeakable to happen. Compare this to the alternative: A group working on a large data base system uses simple quality tools to identify the reasons that a sort-intensive program runs for almost six hours on an IBM mainframe. The root cause, the group discovers, is the low level of main memory given to the sort, only 3 Mb—a previous limit established by the hardware and software. The group consults with the sort vendor and raises the limit to the new maximum, 12 Mb, and the program run times decrease from six hours to four. This change saves the customer money and reduces the opportunity for system failures and operator interventions that have often caused extensive rework to rerun the program. The group shares this information with other groups that have similar, large sort programs. Within a few months, based on the lessons learned from this group's work, *all* major systems are running more quickly which reduces the chance for error and postpones the requirement for new hardware which dramatically reduces costs.

Another group handles an on-line system that is down over 100 hours per month to handle data base reorganizations on hundreds of data base tables. The average time to reorganize a data base is just under an hour. Using simple tools and analysis the team determines a variety of countermeasures and implements them. In just a few months, the average time to reorganize these data bases has dropped to less than 20 minutes, and the system's availability has increased by 50 hours a month. The customer, needless to say, is delighted. Other operations groups are appraised of the changes and *other* on-line systems begin to reduce their down time for data base reorganizations.

Another group analyzes the annual failures in a large system. A few programs surface as the major contributors. Further investigation reveals that a few key modules in these programs, one data base, and the operations run book are the key contributors to the failure rate. The group reengineers the key modules and the data base. The run book is revised for clarity and readability. In succeeding months, the failure rate falls dramatically, reducing overtime and rework. Heartened by the results, the group begins to enthusiastically work on analyzing other programs and data bases that have become the new leaders in failure rates. More work begins to flow through the enhancement process. Again the customer is delighted and other groups begin to analyze their failure rates and clean up their systems.

During the 1990s, *quality improvement* will deliver tremendous personal and corporate advantage while simultaneously draining the lifeblood of those who are unprepared. You can sense it all around you, a software crisis: your bank statement's not right, the PC software has glitches, and the software you've written keeps you up nights. Everyone can feel the problem, but they can't define it. Most software engineers believe there is a crisis, but they haven't been able to figure out what to do to change it.

"The problem is quality!" they cry. Nonsense, quality is the solution to your problem.

In *The Structure of Scientific Revolutions*, Thomas Kuhn discovered that our current problem-solving processes are continually being replaced by newly developed processes that assist us in solving problems that were outside of our reach with the old process. In software, for example, there have been moves from process-oriented structured programming to data-oriented information engineering to data-*and*-process-focused, object-oriented programming. Each of these is a powerful tool for solving a particular class of problems, but not so great for others. In effect, new problem-solving processes are constantly being developed to solve new problems.

Quality improvement (QI) is the next problem-solving process that will have to be embraced to succeed at creating and evolving software. The basic seven QI tools will solve a great number of problems. One of the challenges for companies that get involved with quality improvement is that the easiest problems are always solved first with these tools. As you eliminate the "low hanging fruit," the problem-solving becomes more difficult. When the original seven QI tools begin to fail to solve the increasing complexity of problems that remained, the next seven QI tools need to be implemented. And I am sure, based on Kuhn's arguments, that there are seven beyond those and seven more beyond those, or some completely new and unique process that hasn't even been thought of yet. Learning these seven tools will only help you level the playing field, and then you will need to continue to learn and apply new techniques to maintain an advantage.

Steps to Quality

So why should you consider getting involved with quality improvement? Because it's not the "new" fad or panacea; it's actually over 70 years old. It might surprise you to learn that quality concepts were invented at Bell Labs in the 1920s and exported to Japan after the war. Many people say: "I thought I was already doing a good job—the best job I know how. Why do I need to improve?" And they are right, they have been doing a good job or their company wouldn't be in business, but good just isn't good enough anymore. If you aren't continuously improving your skills and ability to produce better quality products and services faster than ever before at lower cost, then you may not have a job much longer. Most industries have gone through several steps in their search for quality:

1. A feeling of complacency and market dominance.
2. An awareness of the importance of quality as market share erodes to firms that supply higher quality.
3. Slogans: Work harder, Do better. Do the right things right. A search for "silver bullet" solutions.
4. Massive inspection and testing efforts to *detect* errors in products.
5. A shift to defect *prevention* that focuses on *the process*, not the product, using quality improvement techniques.
6. Quality becomes everybody's job, and, overall, it is *management's responsibility*.

Software engineering is stuck somewhere between the search for magic solutions (Computer-aided software engineering) and massive inspection/testing which consumes 50 percent of the software life cycle (Brooks 1976). Unfortunately, most organizations will wait until their survival is in jeopardy before taking action.

New Paradigm

To survive and thrive in the information economy, we need to begin moving toward defect *prevention*, as opposed to defect *detection*. To accomplish this, we need to:

- Educate software engineers in a few basic graphical tools and methods to help them identify problems in the process.
- Inspect enough of their work to determine if their processes are stable—in *statistical process control* (SPC). If they are, the quality

of the software they produce cannot improve without changes in the process.

- Investigate ways to correct the process, implement them, and then measure the results to determine the effects of the change.
- Reduce inspections by using the information gathered from them to simplify and improve the methods for requirements, design, and code development to the point that we prevent most errors. We will no longer need 100 percent walkthroughs and inspections, just enough to establish and maintain SPC.

No Testing Group

We will not need an independent testing group. Software engineers will be responsible for the quality of their products. Each engineer should view their work products—requirements, design, code, whatever—as having a customer and continuously evolve their product to meet the needs of that customer. A designer's customer, for example, might be a coder.

The final customer is the end user. They know quality when they see it, and so will you. Simply put, software engineers and managers need to shift their focus from finding and fixing defects in the product to preventing defects from ever slipping into the product. This requires finding and fixing defects in the *process*. Doing so eliminates the need for 100 percent inspection and independent verification. Each software engineer becomes responsible for the quality of their product. *Management* becomes responsible for engineering changes in the process that will prevent defects and reduce variation in the end product.

In other industries this shift in mental attitude, from fixing symptoms to fixing root causes, has resulted in a 30 percent reduction in defects. Costs are reduced because there are fewer tests and less debugging and rework; each person is his or her own quality consultant. On one project that I'm aware of, for example, 30 percent of everyone's time was consumed by design and requirements rework.

Look at how we build software today: 50 percent of the costs are for testing. In other words, there is one inspector for every developer. Let me state this clearly: *We plan for defects*. And we are pathetic at correcting these defects: a programmer has a 50–50 chance of repairing one. Hours of rework are associated with each fix.

And we haven't gotten any better. On the average, an application programmer can produce 10 to 15 debugged statements per day. It doesn't matter if they're coding in assembler or FOCUS. Deming would say that the *process* is in *statistical control*: our software development and maintenance processes only allow us to *build 10 lines per day* (probably with at least one defect).

We've tried everything to change this: new tools, new methodologies, magic elixirs, but nothing works; productivity and quality don't improve. We continue to *manufacture* defects.

Existing software processes *cause* over 85 percent of our defects. These process-oriented bugs have *common causes*. The other 15 percent of our total defects have special causes—people, unreliable hardware, unmaintainable existing systems, and so on. Most bugs are caused by a failure to adhere *closely* to the structured methodologies. This restates what Deming says: defects are caused by the process, not people.

How do we get better? Fact- and data-based graphs can help you identify the common and special causes of defects. Once special causes are identified and corrected, nothing will affect productivity or quality except a change in *the process*. Deming is fond of saying that quality is everyone's job, but it's management's responsibility. Management is responsible for changing the process. Having eliminated special causes of defects, you can use Pareto analysis to identify the most costly defects and their *common causes*. Knowing this, management can use programmer or analyst suggestions to eliminate common causes of defects.

Common causes are removed by *reducing variation*. Variations in people can be narrowed through training and education. Variations in work products can be reduced through changes in the process or tools or standards. This is perhaps why Yourdon proclaimed 50 lines of code as the maximum size for a module: it reduces variation. Changes in quality and productivity require a simple, yet difficult, shift in focus.

We must shift from defect *detection* to defect *prevention*, from symptoms to root causes, from problem avoidance to problem affection, from products to processes.

As Peters said in *In Search of Excellence*: successful companies do many things just a little bit better. We can do this through process changes that eliminate common and special causes of defects. We cannot achieve these changes with magic wands or slogans or quotas or objectives. Quality improvement is a continuous process. It is not another quick-fix program. It is work. To accomplish this transformation, we all need to embrace Deming's 14 points. I've rearranged them as follows:

Adopt a new philosophy:

- Create a constancy of purpose toward quality and continuous improvement.
- Institute leadership instead of management by numbers.

- Drive out fear so that everyone may work effectively.
- Break down barriers between departments and work groups.
- Eliminate slogans, work quotas, and management by numbers. Substitute leadership.
- Remove barriers that rob workers (management, professional, and craft) of pride of workmanship.
- Cease dependence on inspection to find defects . . . prevent them.
- Refuse to award business on the basis of lowest cost. Instead, minimize total cost—purchase price plus maintenance.

There is no one-size-fits-all quality improvement process, but this book will present a good place to start. We are flying blind in the vortex of the software crisis. Without a quality focus, there can be no measurable change in productivity or quality.

Put everyone to work on the company's quality transformation. Quality is *everyone's job*. The transformation will take time and effort, but every day we do nothing puts our competition one day farther ahead.

During the 1990s, quality will deliver tremendous personal and corporate advantage while simultaneously draining the life-blood of those who are unprepared. Quality has been described as "the systematic application of common sense." Quality means that you serve your customers so well that they return time after time for the next product they need. If you want to:

- surprise and delight software users
- be more productive
- produce better quality software
- and explore new technologies

then you need to discover quality improvement.

If you don't discover quality improvement, prepare for what the Japanese call "the death of a thousand cuts." No single blow will kill your company; the accumulated nicks and cuts of advances by your competition will. If you don't discover quality improvement:

- your competitors will
- your customers will desert you
- productivity and quality will decline relative to the competition
- funding for new technology will vanish

Quality improvement will be part of your future. Will you embrace it now or wait until your competition forces you to? Which would you prefer? To maximize your competitive advantage or risk the death of a thousand cuts? The choice is up to you.

About the Author

Lowell Jay Arthur has over 20 years experience in the creation and evolution of software. He has led and facilitated software quality improvement teams and their management support teams. He is a certified instruction of the Deming Prize-winning Florida Power and Light quality improvement process and a Master Practitioner of Neuro-Linguistic Programming. He has conducted SEI software process assessments and implemented extensive software measurement processes. He is the author of *Programmer Productivity, Software Evolution—The Software Maintenance Challenge, UNIX Shell Programming (2nd)*, and *Rapid Evolutionary Development*. He has a B.S. in System Engineering and an M.S. in Operations Research.

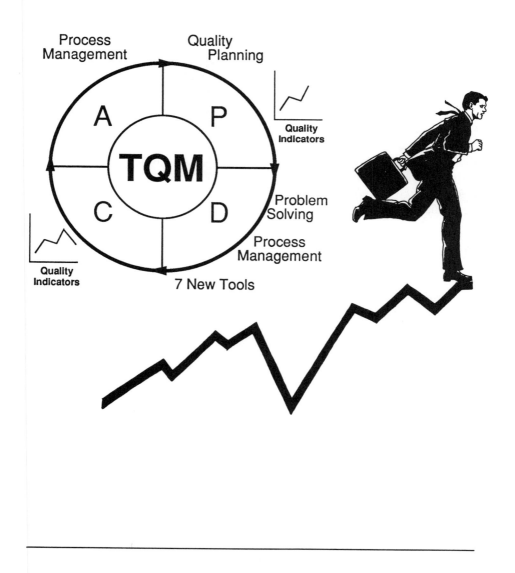

CHAPTER 1

Introduction to Software Quality

Improve constantly and forever the system of production and service.
—*W. Edwards Deming*

What is quality improvement? Putting out fires and removing individual defects from software is not quality improvement. Customers want better quality, faster, and at a lower cost. Most information system (IS) organizations aim for delivery of software on a specific due date. Unfortunately, this usually only means that the customer receives a *defective* product *on time*. In today's climate, the focus is on cost cutting because of a misguided belief that only the lowest cost provider will survive. Cutting costs often slashes quality leading to customer dissatisfaction with a poor quality product at a lower *initial* cost but a higher total cost. It is possible to deliver high quality software on time and at a lower cost, but not in the chaotic ways that we often employ today. We must begin making quality software products that satisfy our customers first, and then continuously reduce the time and cost to make those high quality products through better management, processes, and materials.

Quality demands that we fix fewer problems, but that they are all high leverage problems. In most organizations, when a problem occurs, we react by fixing the problem whether it is important or not. The only criteria seems to be how loudly the customer screams. Quality demands that the whole organization learn how to fix problems more quickly and effectively. Quality also demands that we not only fix the observable symptoms of the problem—a program failure—but shift the bulk of our

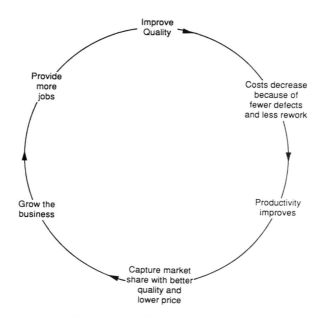

Figure 1.1 The Deming Chain

problem solving efforts to the root causes of the problem—defects in the process that produced or enhanced the program in the first place. IS must stop fighting the fires, ignore the immediate crisis, and begin preventing fires by correcting the way software is created and evolved. A healthy organization will spend 80 percent of its problem solving effort on preventing problems, while a poor-performing, reactive organization will spend 90 percent of its time on fixing symptoms instead of causes (Sirkin 1990). In an IS organization that learns from its mistakes, prevention is the order of the day. Preventing defects, problems and rework frees everyone to concentrate on adding value for the customer.

Quality improvement is an adventure of continuous discovery into the root causes of product and service failures—fire prevention, not fire fighting. The reason that we want to improve software quality continuously is expressed in the Deming chain (Figure 1.1): improving quality leads to lower costs from less debugging and rework, which causes productivity to improve, which increases the demand for your software development and maintenance skills, which causes the company or department to grow in size and profitability. The flip side of this is that static or lower quality will lead to the wholesale desertion of your customers, loss of funding, staffing cuts, and reduced market share. The choice is up to you.

It is not uncommon to find an MIS department with no formal quality program, whose quality costs are 30 percent or even 50 percent of the annual MIS budget. This is a very expensive and slow way to build software.
—Richard Zultner

Jobs are guaranteed by customers, not by the company. Improving software quality is the key to achieving competitive advantage in the *information economy*. Improving software quality involves every employee—manager, analyst, and programmer—in the continuous and ongoing improvement of every aspect of software creation and evolution. This book will help you discover the proven methods to establish and support continuous quality improvement, a.k.a. Total Quality Management (TQM), in a software development and maintenance environment.

Kaizen is the Japanese concept that describes the continuous, never-ending improvement of processes—management, software development, and software evolution. As Masaaki Imai (Imai 1986) describes it, *kaizen* is the "process-oriented way of thinking versus the West's innovation- and results-oriented thinking." Innovation and results-oriented thinking are not *wrong*, but like a weight lifter that only exercises one side of the body, we are underdeveloped in the area of *kaizen*.

Nothing concentrates a man's mind so wonderfully as the prospect of being hanged in the morning.
—Samuel Johnson

Survival depends on quality. Let me offer you some startling statistics. Current industry literature has identified that typical U.S. business software will incur 3–4 defects per thousand lines of code (KLOC) or 3,000 defects per million lines of code. The space shuttle has only 70 defects per million lines using *known software techniques*. Fujitsu currently encounters only 10 defects per million lines. This low level of defects has made system testing so expensive (per defect found) that it has been dropped from their software process. Motorola has an effort underway to reach 3.4 defects per million lines and expect to reach it by 1994.

We must learn to attack the disease, not the symptoms; the process, not the defects. Cold remedies attack the symptoms of colds, not the cold virus itself. Hands transfer cold viruses to our mucus membranes. Routinely washing your hands prevents the transmission of cold viruses during cold season. Changing the software creation and evolution process will prevent the transmission of viruses from one step to another.

The difference between 3000 defects per million and 3.4 defects per million cannot be found in the type of CASE tools used, but rather in the process used. The rigor with which we train everyone to reach the same level of skill and apply the process will determine our quality and productivity. The only way that this level of errors can be reduced is through a process of continuous improvement.

Stop paving the cow paths.

—Michael Hammer (1990)

W. Edwards Deming (Deming 1985) suggests that any process (including software) that is not under some form of quality management wastes 25 to 40 percent of all effort and expenditures. Looking at the debugging industry that threatens the creation and evolution of all software projects, you have to address not only the technological aspects of software engineering (i.e., CASE—Computer Aided Software Engineering), but the *process* issues as well. Before you can automate software engineering, you must first define and streamline the software process.

CUSTOMER SATISFACTION

Quality improvement has one main focus: customer satisfaction. Quality aligns the business with the present and future needs and expectations of the customer. Where the old definition of quality suggested that meeting the customer's requirements was enough, today's definition demands that we not only meet their needs, but surprise and delight them above and beyond their expectations. Customer satisfaction has many aspects; here are just a few key ones:

- Quality—conformance to customer valid requirements
- Cost—as low as possible within conformance to customer requirements
- Delivery—availability and reliability of information systems where and when required
- Timeliness—on schedule

A dissatisfied customer is a terrorist. A dissatisfied customer will tell an average of 16 other people about their problems. A satisfied customer will tell eight (Deming 1986, pg. 122).

CONTINUOUS IMPROVEMENT

We shall build good ships here; at a profit if we can, at a loss if we must, but always good ships.

—Collis P. Huntington (1860)

Continuous improvement is not new. Virtually all advances in human evolution have benefited from continuous improvements. It is only in the last 40 years that champions like W. Edwards Deming and J. M. Juran have hammered some discipline into this evolutionary process.

Continuous improvements come from two main sources: innovation (revolution) and continuous improvement (evolution, a.k.a. *kaizen*). Revolution is the founding metaphor of America, so it comes as no surprise that the U.S. has relied on innovations to sustain competitive advantage world-wide. Similarly, the industrial revolution's primary metaphor was the *machine*. We have come to depend on machines to extend our abilities. In many cases, we have become so enamored with the machine that we have forgotten the role that effective and efficient processes play in the rapid creation and evolution of products and services.

Where innovation used to be sufficient to sustain competitive advantage, it is no longer good enough. To beat the competition, we must be able to innovate *and* then sustain and improve that initial innovation. We must also generate revolutionary levels of improvement through the use of incremental, evolutionary processes. The currently dominant way to attain this is called continuous quality improvement, and it is as applicable to software as it is to manufacturing. You and your co-workers may be excellent at innovation, but unless you also become excellent at evolution, kaizen, and continuous improvement, you are in trouble because the people who can incorporate your innovations, sustain the improvement, and then continue to grow beyond the original idea will bury you in the competitive marketplace.

There are a few key elements about quality that need to be understood:

- Quality is a market-based strategy. Quality creates and maintains market share, even inside a company.
- Quality depends on the process used to create a product, whether that product is hardware, software, or that elusive factor—management.
- Quality is customer-driven. They demand high quality and without it, they won't continue using your service or product. Higher quality results in increased productivity, profits, and market share (Figure 1.1). Higher quality results in lower unit costs and failure costs.
- Quality must be woven into the fabric of the system as it is created. It cannot be tested in.

With the arrival of the information economy, customers have begun to demand software quality. Market demand for quality will drive radical changes in the software industry and this is good. Unfortunately, most ideas of what constitutes software quality are sadly misguided. There are many myths about quality:

- Software failures are unavoidable
- Testing delivers quality
- Quality costs money

Defects are not free. Somebody makes them, and gets paid for making them.
            —*W. Edwards Deming (1986, pg. 11)*

Current software development processes produce two products: *software* (code, documentation, etc.) and *defects* (causing rework, waste, loss of productivity, higher costs).

The cost of finding and removing these defects is 50 percent of all software costs (Brooks 1975). This exorbitant cost has become chronic because *we have designed the software process to deliver defects as well as software. The current method* of finding these defects focuses only on *controlling* defects, not preventing them.

Quality has encountered a number of metaphors: quality is free; quality is conformance to valid customer requirements, quality is zero defects, and quality is a journey not a destination. As you will discover in the pages that follow, quality is a never-ending adventure into excellence and mastery.

Known software techniques make defect-free software possible. Most software professionals, however, avoid doing the things required to achieve zero-defect software. "Too much structure," they proclaim. "Too much bureaucracy."

Most software companies foolishly base their defect efforts on finding bugs once they're in the software. The number of defects that slip through testing depends on the number of defects *in the software when it is delivered for testing*. The number of defects in the software when delivered to testing is a direct function of the quality of the process used to create the software. Testing can only uncover 70 percent of the latent defects in the code. Inspections can remove 80 to 90 percent of the defects before testing, but a good process will prevent defects from ever entering the product.

SOFTWARE MASTERY

In George Leonard's book, *Mastery*, he describes the four types of learners—dabblers, hackers, compulsives, and masters (Figure 1.2).

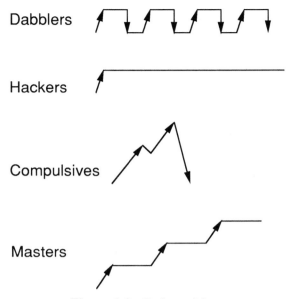

Figure 1.2 Paths to Mastery

Dabblers go from one thing to another, never resting long enough to become proficient at any one thing. Dabblers go from one methodology to the next, from one CASE tool to the next, from one language to the next, and from one job to the next. They never stay involved with one thing long enough to become excellent.

Hackers develop a low level of proficiency and then are content to stay mediocre the rest of their lives. All software "hackers" fall into this category. The programmer whose programs are always in trouble; the software "genius" who runs around fighting fires; and the manager who puts up with this type of behavior are all hackers. The future belongs to those who continuously improve their skills and abilities. Those who are content with basic levels of skill will suffer from low pay and poor working conditions.

Compulsives are not content to be on the plateau of learning. They push and push, trying harder and harder to do better. They leave work only to go home and program on their personal computer. They cram course after course into their lives. Ultimately, they just burn out.

Masters, on the other hand, know that the path to mastery is a journey. To become a master, they must always have a "beginner's mind" that is open and receptive to new learnings. They rise to the first level of skill and then they are ready to practice until they experience the next burst of learning and rise to a new level. Mastery is the path of *kaizen*—continuous incremental improvement in our skills and abilities. Masters recognize and understand *kaizen* and PDCA because they have done it all of their lives to achieve mastery.

> *Most people have spent their lives reinventing the wheel, then refusing to concede that it's out of round.*
>
> —*George Leonard*

There are five keys to software mastery—instruction, practice, surrender, intent, and pushing the envelope.

- Get instruction. Quality begins with training and ends with training.
- Practice. Learning the quality tools requires practice.
- Suspend your disbelief about what will or won't work, and surrender to your practice.
- Develop a clear intent to be the best. Intent is not *hope*. Hope offers only the flimsy wish to become excellent. Intent is a clear, definite desire and direction.
- Take a risk, push the outside of the envelope. Once firmly grounded in the basics, masters push the limits of what they know to enable them to learn more about what works and what doesn't.

THE THREE COMPONENTS OF QUALITY

Total quality management (Figure 1.3) has three key components—planning, problem-solving, and process management. Quality, as this diagram shows, begins with the customer's requirements (the voice of the customer) and ends with a satisfied or delighted customer. Quality planning (Chapter 2) identifies, at a high level, the customer's requirements for quality software systems—reliability, cycle time, defect rate, and costs. Quality planning uses the seven management and planning tools of TQM (Chapter 9) to gather the "voice of the customer" and translate these qualitative requirements into specific activities that IS does to meet or exceed these requirements. Quality function deployment (QFD) maps these customer requirements to IS actions. QFD helps us identify the *right things* to work on and measurements of those key areas for improvement. Knowing what needs to be improved to satisfy the customer, we can *deploy* improvement projects using the quality improvement problem-solving process (PDCA—plan, do, check, act) or

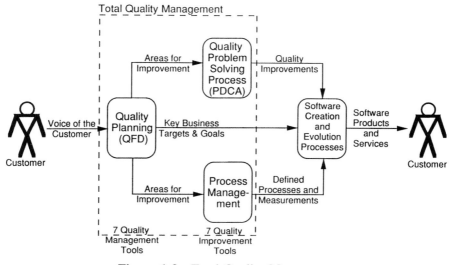

Figure 1.3   Total Quality Management

process management. Both key functions use the original seven quality improvement tools to define, measure, and analyze the software process and its stability and capability. PDCA and process management help us continually improve to ensure that we do the *right things right*.

Figure 1.4 shows a more detailed version of the TQM process. First IS gathers the voice of the customer and voice of the business to establish IS quality objectives. These objectives drive an implementation plan for quality improvement activities. From these objectives we train employees in process management and the problem-solving process, and initiate quality teams. If the process is already measured and defined, we can initiate a quality improvement team to improve the process. If the process is poorly defined or understood, then we use process management to define and measure the process. Although not shown on this flowchart, many software processes can benefit from *benchmarking* (borrowing with honor) to establish proven processes for software. Chapters 13 and 14, for example, describe processes for software creation and evolution that really work. New quality teams will need extensive coaching and support from management to be successful. Just reading a book or taking a course is rarely enough to allow success. Then, as the team moves through the process, the quality council will review their progress and assist the team in getting on track with their problem-solving effort. Once the team has a proven solution to a quality problem, they will need

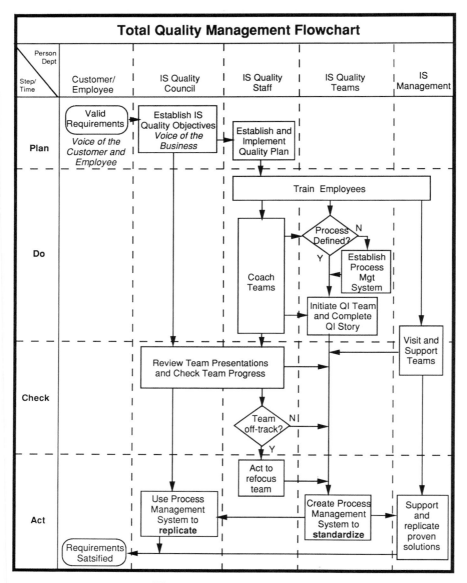

Figure 1.4   TQM Flowchart

to develop a process management system to standardize it, and then the quality council and IS management will act to multiply the benefits of the improvement by replicating the improved process across IS. All three activities fit together in a system of continuous improvement.

Quality planning is more qualitative than quantitative—focusing on understanding customer needs and translating them into quantitative objectives. Problem solving and process management are much more quantitative—focusing on measurement and analysis to drive improvements in quality and productivity. Quality planning helps us direct the improvement of our software processes to maximize the effectiveness. Used in concert, these three elements of TQM rapidly drive the software process toward excellence and mastery.

Quality Planning—Ready, *Aim*

Quality planning, or policy deployment as it is also called, is led by top management. By evaluating the "voice of the customer, business, and employees" through surveys, focus groups, and other data collection instruments, top management identifies the three to five top concerns of their customers (including employees). From these top priorities, top management negotiates with the management hierarchy to establish targets, goals, and plans for achieving breakthrough improvement in each of these areas of customer satisfaction. They do so by:

- Leading the quality improvement effort
- Establishing quality policies for "breakthroughs" in software quality and productivity
- Establishing the supporting structures—recognition, reward, training, and so on—required to reach the quality objectives.

Once these objectives are established, many people ask: "What process should I use to achieve them?" The answer lies in Appendix A—a decision process for choosing quality tools and processes.

Problem Solving with Quality Teams—Fire

Quality teams must begin to learn the problem-solving process—PDCA. Functional teams of 7 ± 2 employees begin to improve customer satisfaction by eliminating the root cause of problems in their work. Requirements analysts would identify the root causes of missing or incorrect requirements. Design analysts would identify the root causes of missing, incorrect, or difficult to interpret program specifications. Coders would identify the root causes of coding errors and defects. Testers would identify the root causes of bugs slipping through their net of test cases. Quality teams operate through the application of the problem-solving process to achieve:

- **Kaizen**—continuous, incremental improvement of all key aspects of work

- **Innovation and breakthrough**—dramatic improvement through focusing many teams on a few key success elements

Software quality teams often find that before they can begin to improve the process, they have to have it defined and measured in a way that supports continuous improvement. Process management is the key to defining and measuring processes.

Process Management

Every software process involves many repetitive work activities—design, code, test, document, and so on. Process management recognizes that each of these work activities have "internal customers" who have valid requirements for what they receive. Process management defines the process for doing each work activity and ways to measure and ensure that the process is delivering the "external customer's" needs and expectations. Process management creates a system for continuously monitoring and improving every method and procedure within the software life cycle. Process management helps us lay the ground work for the life cycle of life cycles—continuous quality improvement.

THE LIFE CYCLE OF LIFE CYCLES—PDCA: PLAN, DO, CHECK, AND ACT

Most software departments that have been in business for any length of time are probably at least successful in *planning* and *doing* software. They may even be good at *checking* and *acting* to improve it, but they have no understanding of how to check the process and act to improve *how* software is created or evolved.

When we create software, we start by planning (requirements and design). Then we shift to doing (coding). Next we check (testing) and then we act to improve (debugging). In software evolution, we begin with a change request and follow essentially the same cycle. We often use inspections or walkthroughs to identify defects between steps of the software life cycle, but we rarely use the defect information gathered during inspections and testing to identify the root causes of problems in the requirements, design, or coding process that led to the errors in the first place.

To begin to understand the importance of quality in software, we can look at the key software qualities:

1. *Flexibility* for continuous evolution to match the changing market
2. *Maintainability* for quick repair and replacement

3. *Reusability* for optimal productivity and quality
4. *Integration* for coupling one product to another
5. *Consistency* for ease of learning and use
6. *Usability* for optimal user productivity
7. *Reliability* for optimal system productivity

Within this framework, one meaningful software quality goal is the absence of defects. The only way to assure zero defects is to avoid putting them into the product. The only way to avoid putting them in the product is to improve the process in such a way that you prevent them from slipping in at each stage of its creation.

Quality is not just the absence of defects. From the customer's perspective, quality means the presence of value as well as the absence of defects. Customers want long-term value that saves them time and effort and frustration. Quality is not only in the product, but also in every service you deliver—from developing requirements to fixing bugs—and the relationship you establish with the customer.

Quality does cost money, but delivering a quality product costs far less than delivering a shoddy product. The "invisible" costs of software failure—downtime, rework, and possible warranty charges—vastly outweigh the cost of delivering quality. There are three "costs" of quality:

- *Failure* costs arise when software (i.e., requirements, designs, code, or data) fails before or after release. Failures and faults require analysis, debugging, rework, retest, and reinstallation—the costs of failure.
- *Appraisal* costs include the costs of inspecting or testing the software prior to release to find defects. In good companies, this cost is as low as 25 percent of the total cost; in poor companies, appraisal costs can run as high as 50 percent.
- *Prevention* costs include the costs of training, and the application of the methods and tools to prevent defects through the application of optimal software processes and continuous quality improvement.

Perhaps the question is not "What does quality cost?" but "How much does good quality save?" For the period 1965 to 1985, Deming Prize-winning companies increased sales and profits by 14 percent, 2 percent higher than other Japanese companies and 6 percent higher than American companies (Hudiburg 1991).

The company that can deliver quality software in the 1990s will not suffer a lack of work or customer disdain. It takes eight times as much investment to get a new customer as it does to keep an old one. Quality keeps them coming back. Quality is:

- A systematic process for continuous improvement, not a function or a department
- Everybody's job, not just a few specialists
- Applicable to all activities, not just manufacturing
- What the buyer wants and needs, not what suppliers want to provide
- The continuous application of quality improvement techniques, not a periodic quality inquisition
- The foundation for planning, creating, and automating all processes

Quality improvement is not without its problems. What are the pitfalls of quality improvement? Typically, they are a lack of:

- Understanding quality and its benefits at all levels in the organization. For everyone to be involved in quality, everyone must understand the "whys" and "how tos" of continuous quality improvement. This amount of training requires a significant investment and takes time. There will be times when part of the organization doesn't understand this new quality thing, and they will actively resist. Even after everyone is trained, there will still be some arch-enemies of quality. Cultural change takes time, and U.S. management is notoriously impatient.
- Acceptance of where you are and where you need to go. "I'm already doing a quality job, aren't I?" Denial occurs at all levels in the organization. Yes, we are getting by, and no, we are nowhere near software mastery. It will take several years to reach a point where employees at all levels are willing to admit that we aren't very good at this process called software.
- Involvement, on a personal level, with quality improvement. "I'm too busy." "Let the quality department handle that." To become excellent at software development, everyone must get involved on an ongoing basis with quality improvement. Unfortunately, with our sights still set on the results of the process rather than the process itself, this transformation will take time.
- Support for quality improvement (investment, resources, time). Most companies only start moving toward quality improvement after they have exhausted all of the alternatives in their old bag of tricks and the pain of lost market share is bearing down on them. Look no farther than the American auto industry and Xerox for examples. We

wait until the pain is too great and then we turn to quality. Of course, by then there is little time or money to embark on a vast retraining effort. Many companies will go under. The time to invest is *before* you get in trouble, and most software organizations are already feeling the pinch. Many large corporations in the 1990s will outsource their data processing development and maintenance to consulting firms who can do it better, faster, and cheaper.

- Expectations, goals, and objectives for quality improvement. Employees and managers alike are still looking for the panacea and they think that quality improvement is the answer. Unfortunately, the problems that have been bothering you have been around a long time and it will take time to dispatch them. During the quality start-up process, improvement teams will try to tackle world hunger problems and simply become frustrated instead of solving smaller issues that are components of the larger issue. You eat the elephant one bite at a time.

- Recognition and reward for success. In America, we reward people for results, especially revolutionary results. Quality improvement must reward the process of evolutionary improvement, not the results generated. The story that comes to mind is of one Japanese auto manufacturer that gave their top honors to a team in the company cafeteria that reduced the amount of tea consumption by simply measuring and observing consumption patterns during lunch.

All of these potential problems revolve around the people that will use the quality improvement and software processes.

People

The industrial revolution created a paradigm that people are just factors of production. People are no longer just factors in production; *people are the production* when it comes to software. Technology isn't the barrier to software excellence, change is the barrier. Change only occurs through training that involves the eyes, ears, and bodies of software developers and maintainers and managers.

A major weakness in software lies in the way people cooperate, manage, and organize themselves. Often, the goals of developers, customers, project managers, maintainers, operators, and management are in conflict. The winners and the losers of the 90s will be separated by mentality and attitude, not nationality.

Using the quality improvement process, employees at all levels can improve their jobs. It doesn't matter if they save $100,000 or $100; every contribution is important to the company's longevity and profitability. More important than the money saved is the employees' feeling of pride in improving their job. When employees feel better, their morale is better, they perform better, they improve more processes, they produce better quality, and the savings mount like compound interest.

Process

There never seems to be time to do it right, but customers, managers, and technicians always seem to suggest that there will be time to do a system over again. These ridiculous notions waste your most precious commodity—time. There is never time to recreate a poorly built system, but organizations do so. Software, unlike houses or machinery, simply doesn't wear out. Here again, the construction paradigm has gotten us into trouble. In America, we tear down old buildings and put up new ones or we sell our old clunker and buy a new car but there is no reason to replace software. It will run forever given that the hardware can be maintained to support it.

To succeed at software evolution, prototypers and managers alike must shift from the mistaken belief that you can buy a replacement system. Mass production has convinced us that we can buy replacement products easily and effortlessly. Unfortunately, we only produce software by custom development. (Isn't it odd that "custom" is the first portion of "customer?")

> *There is no silver bullet.*
>
> *—Fred Brooks*

There appear to be two theories about how to improve software quality and productivity. The *Silver Bullet* theory focuses on major innovations to improve productivity and quality. Silver bullets are very American, but occur infrequently, like miracles. *Continuous Improvement* focuses on slow, steady improvement that incorporates innovations as they arise. It is usually done every day by everyone. It relies on the small win.

Software departments must learn to create the right systems (the ones of most value) and then to create the systems in the right way (Figure 1.5). We often attain unanimous agreement to create a system, and then develop it in ways that result in a system that none of us wants. The user may not know exactly what they want or what IS can deliver. Consequently short cuts are taken, requirements missed, and objectives overlooked. Any way you look at it, creating the wrong system is a waste of everyone's time. Creating the right system, even if it's done marginally,

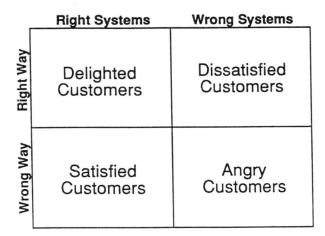

Figure 1.5   Right Systems, Right Way

is often a success. Done the "right way" with minimum cycle time, defect rate, and cost, it will surprise and delight your customer.

In the past, Information Systems (IS) departments have depended on their gurus to take them from conception to delivered product. To rise out of the chaos of these ad hoc projects, IS must shift to software processes that are both rapid and effective. IS must focus on preventing defects rather than detecting and correcting them through software testing. Prevention focuses on integrating quality into the software process through planning, evolutionary analysis and design, acquisition of support tools that prevent errors and variation. Prevention requires training for all developers in new techniques and tools. To prevent errors, there must be a written process for Rapid Evolutionary Development™ and continuous Software Evolution™ of the resulting initial system (Arthur 1992 & 1988).

The first portion of the evolutionary process focuses on software creation that uses a rapid prototyping methodology emphasizing reuse of data, program components, and parts—the knowledge, organs, and cells of the system. Like matter, which has reusable parts—electron, neutrons, protons, and other subatomic particles—and music that reuses notes to form compositions, software must do the same. To succeed at Software Evolution, IS must follow the natural order of the universe and begin to reuse components that consist of smaller software parts or cells. Successful reuse programs begin with pools of data as the knowledge base, and evolve to include the various code, modules, programs, and subsystems that process the underlying data into information. Any attempt to begin with processing first will ultimately have to retrace some steps to create the data bases necessary for the company to improve and evolve.

The second portion of evolutionary process focuses on what has been called maintenance—Software Evolution. Software Evolution structures the customer's change requests and problem reports into scheduled system releases that maximize productivity through grouping changes by interim product—data, program, or documentation—and through the ability to schedule and rigorously test each of these as it is changed. The evolutionary maintenance methodology establishes a way to grow a system from its infancy into adulthood through small, incremental, evolutionary enhancement steps and genetic or surgical repairs. Where maintenance once consumed 80 percent of the IS budget, evolution will consume less than 50 percent. The remainder of the budget can be used to deliver new systems and functions via the Rapid Evolutionary Development process.

Technology

Until you pick a methodology for both development and maintenance, you can hardly expect to choose effective tools to automate either. There are, however, some tools that are essential regardless of environment.

Most companies are still mired in the tar pit of chaos. To reach the next level of software excellence, IS must have a mechanism to manage change to the evolving software system, change and configuration management. Change management tracks requested incremental improvements to the system. Configuration management controls and tracks changes to the actual system components—data, code, and documentation.

Software editors, compilers, debuggers, and so on are all necessary. Electronic communication—E-Mail, voice mail, and video—are all excellent facilities to help in moving the project forward through the transmission of enormous amounts of information. Wherever possible, video is preferable to voice mail because it carries as close to 100 percent of human communication channel as possible. Voice is preferable to E-mail because it carries almost 50 percent of the human channel, while E-mail carries only seven percent.

The third step on the path to software excellence—a defined process—can be automated through the use of appropriate tools that match the process. At this point, CASE tools become useful. Without a proven process, however, they are largely a waste of money. Unless they can mate with other tools, they are mainly useless.

The most common failing of any IS department has been the wholesale introduction of CASE tools or methods without proper training to enable the IS staff to use them effectively. Very few people have the curiosity to open a new tool and just dive in and swim around for a while to learn how to use it. If the tool isn't intuitively obvious, most people will just abandon it and move back to the way they know that works. Then IS management wonders why they haven't received the big bang the vendor suggested would be forthcoming from the implementation of this new tool kit. Small wonder.

One bad experience with a new CASE tool can sour a department's taste for new tools as well, especially when there is no methodology framework to hang it on. IS staff spot a new disaster forming quickly and move to the side to watch the fireworks.

The key to technology excellence and rapid response is integration, not alienation.

The next step—software measurement—is the checking step of the PDCA cycle. IS prototypers and managers must be able to check the process and tools through the use of software metrics if there is to be any hope of improvement. Through measurement, system evolutionists can spot the 20 percent of the system that are generating 80 percent of the costs and figure out the actions required to reduce the expense. Re-engineering and restructuring tools will automate most of the genetic re-engineering required to bring the data or code back into balance with the rest of the system. These tools can improve productivity and quality by 10 to 35 percent. Through measurement, a prototyper can also tell if an evolving data structure or a module of code is growing too large to be maintained by mere mortals. Measurement helps you know where you are historically. Comparing yourself to others, however, is a sure method for an early suicide.

The fifth and highest level of software excellence applies the basic seven quality improvement tools and the seven management and planning tools. The seven basic quality improvement tools focus on data and offer the implements necessary to solve almost any process problem an IS department will ever uncover. These tools are easily created manually and there are many tools to help the apprentice quality improvement person automate the development of pareto charts, scatter diagrams, histograms, and similar graphics. The seven management and planning tools help support quality planning and the deployment of quality improvement projects.

The seven basic tools drive the quality revolution—flowcharts, check-sheets, pareto diagrams, cause and effect diagrams, histograms, scatter diagrams, and control charts. For the next few pages we will look at a few that can dramatically improve your customer's perception of the system even before the first design is drawn or the first line of code compiled. We accomplish this shift by turning our emphasis to the user's processes and using the quality tools to tune the process first, then automate it.

At the highest level (Figure 1.6), you need to know the whole chain of *customers* and *suppliers*. Then you can begin to define the user's internal process using *process management* (Chapter 11). Then, you can begin to help the customer identify the "value-added" steps in the process and the steps that don't add any value. By removing the wasted steps and wait time from a process, it can often be shortened by 50 percent or more. This also simplifies automation, because only the value-added steps need to be automated.

In other cases, there will be complex feedback loops that can be simplified and whole steps that can be eliminated. Simplifying the user's process will help you simplify the actual creation of the system. It also helps your customer understand their requirements better before you begin the Rapid Evolutionary Development process.

Recommendations for Action

In his book, *Planning for Quality*, J. M. Juran identifies the "Quality Trilogy:"

Quality Planning	Planning for quality (management's job)
Quality Management	Defect *prevention* and continuous improvement
Quality Control	Defect *detection* and removal

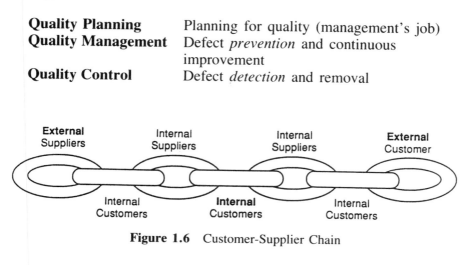

External Suppliers   Internal Suppliers   Internal Suppliers   External Customer

Internal Customers   **Internal Customers**   Internal Customers

Figure 1.6 Customer-Supplier Chain

This book addresses all three of these subjects. To begin to achieve quality, we must address each of these three key elements.

1. We must commit to developing quality awareness and skills in our personnel. All quality improvements begin with training. All managers must attend *Quality* education and begin planning for *Total Quality Management.* To succeed at quality requires leadership. All managers will benefit from learning the seven management and planning tools. The technical staff need training in process management and problem-solving.
   - Quality Awareness—familiarity with TQM
   - Quality Team training—for specific quality teams
   - Quality Consultant training—for quality consultants
   - Process Management training—to define processes and measurements
   - Quality Planning—for managers

2. We must commit to quality management—the *prevention* of defects. We must develop methods and tools for defect prevention and continuous improvement. We need to implement a *Quality Improvement* process to:
   - Identify improvements in our management and technical processes
   - Implement those improvements to prevent defects, reduce costs, and increase productivity and quality
   - Implement measurements to evaluate the effectiveness of improvements

3. We must intensify our existing commitment to quality control. Inspections should be required for all work products—requirements, designs, code, test cases, user documentation, etc. Since computer testing alone is only 70 percent efficient (leaving 30 percent) of the bugs in the code, inspections of all work products are essential to raise defect removal efficiency to 95 percent (Capers Jones). We must then use the data gathered from the inspections to improve our processes.

4. We must establish a group that continuously implements and improves quality. It is not possible to make one group responsible for quality, but it is possible to create a group that *is* responsible for implementing the Quality Trilogy—Quality Planning, Quality Control, and Quality Management. These three processes are the

keys to high productivity and dramatically reduced costs. Quality is a low-risk investment that pays huge dividends.

5. We must establish minimum training requirements. To maximize effectiveness, training must be delivered when needed—Just in Time Training(JITT); about a problem the participant needs to resolve, not some artificial one; and flexible to leverage existing knowledge (e.g., how is Object-oriented programming like Structured programming?).

To maximize Return on Investment (ROI), training must increase a participant's skills by at least an order of magnitude, ensure that the participant retains these skills. and deliver a solution to an existing business problem.

To minimize time away from the office, training needs to be done on an ''outpatient'' basis. This will require the participant to:

- Do some pre-course work—reading, problem selection, video, whatever
- Attend the training (initially instructor led, trending to CAI/ Interactive video with an AI copilot)
- Complete the course by resolving the business problem they've prepared
- Document and share their success
- Feedback into the training curriculum to improve the existing course

To maximize both quality and productivity during software creation and evolution shop, you will need to:

- **apply the quality improvement process** including *assessment* for gathering data about our current sophistication and *measurement* to evaluate our progress
- **organize for quality**
- **expand your training commitment**
- **create an optimum environment** for software work that includes and rewards excellence in both development and maintenance

Through the application of assessment, measurement, training, and the quality improvement process, you can expect to be in the top 5 percent in 5 to 10 years. Without this investment in continuous improvement, there is every likelihood that a competitor will overrun you before the turn of the century.

SUMMARY

These ideas are not new, but in our flutter from one silver bullet to the next, in our search for a savior or a magic wand, we have overlooked the obvious or pooh-poohed them as too simple. We must become more like the tortoise and less like the hare; we must seek continuous progress toward our goal. Then, in our journey, if we run across a silver bullet or a magic wand, we'll know what to do with it.

To climb to the top of the stairway to software excellence, we must implement the following key elements of people, process, and technology:

- **People** We must establish several key specialist groups:
- Quality improvement specialists to get quality rolling
- A process team to improve our processes
- A reengineering team to continuously improve our software and data
- A measurement team to see how we're doing
- An estimating team to improve our estimates

- **Process** We need methods that must be continuously improved to reduce our time-to-market for applications, products, and services:
- A flexible development methodology
- A defined evolution methodology

- **Technology** We need:
- A full-blown maintenance workbench including re-engineering tools
- A fully integrated development workbench that supports the methodology
- A change management system
- A suite of measurement tools

This is not to say that these efforts are not underway in one form or another throughout software organizations, but they have little common direction and are often derailed by the needs of special interests. Again,

The Quest for
Total Quality Management

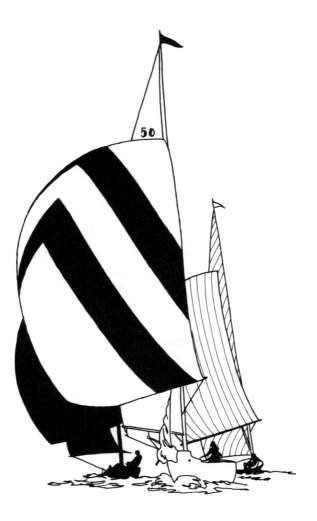

An adventure of continuous discovery.
A race without a finish line.

we need an inspiring vision, the commitment, and the resources to get there. It will not be cheap, but it will be worth it.

The typical organization without quality wastes 25 to 40 percent of its expenses on the costs of poor quality. Best companies can cut this to 5 percent. You want to cut costs? Quality offers you the way. You want to increase revenues? Quality is also the way.

Software quality improvement is not a panacea. It is an evolutionary step on the path toward software excellence. It relies on many existing methods and tools to ensure its success. Fortunately, these skills give it the ability to adapt to its environment and learn from its mistakes. May you be surprised and delighted by how quickly software quality improvement leads you to new heights of software creation and evolution.

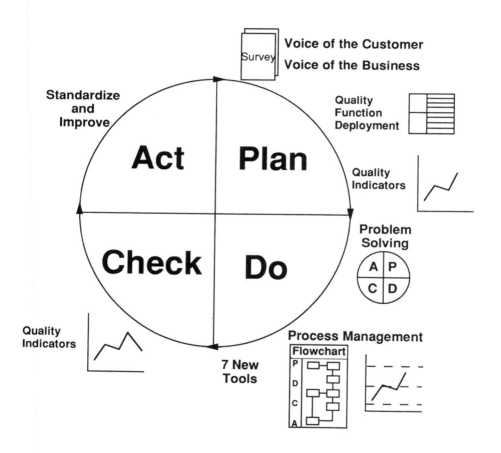

CHAPTER 2

Quality Planning—
"Doing the Right Things"

I don't worry whether something is cheap or expensive. I only worry if it is good. If it is good enough, the public will pay you back for it.
—Walt Disney
(Walt Disney, An American Original, Bob Thomas,
Simon & Schuster, 1976.)

The best kept secret of quality improvement is that evolutionary improvements can be focused in such a way as to deliver revolutionary, breakthrough improvements in quality, productivity, and customer satisfaction. In a country that thrives on revolutionary improvements—and innovations—it's a little hard for most people to grasp that revolutionary improvement also can be obtained by using *kaizen*—many incremental improvements—and directing them toward a specific target. The method to accomplish this feat is called quality planning or policy deployment.

Sports analogies, in spite of their somewhat sexist background, are useful ways to understand policy deployment. For those people who follow baseball, we've all thrilled at the occasional home run, but games are invariably won by singles, doubles, and runs batted in. In football, we get excited when the quarterback connects with a "long bomb," but the running game and short passes win most ball games. In essence, one great play will not win the game, nor will one great innovation deliver competitive advantage. Only continuous incremental improvements *supplemented* by an occasional innovation can sustain competitive advantage in the 1990s.

Policy deployment is a strategic planning and management system for achieving revolutionary improvements through *kaizen*. Quality planning focuses on improving key processes in every functional area to optimize the quality of products and services. Policy deployment relies on:

- Top management to identify the vital few quality elements to work on
- Middle management to deploy improvement efforts to focus on the vital few
- All employees to embrace and institute the improvements developed

Quality planning requires that we follow the leadership principles of Norman Schwartzkopf (Inc 1991):

- *You must have clear goals.* Set objectives and guide their achievement.
  - —Reduce customer dissatisfaction
  - —Reduce system unavailability
  - —Increase reliability
  - —Reduce repair and rework costs
  - —Reduce software cycle times
- *Give yourself a clear agenda.* Identify the five $(7 - 2)$ most important issues from your customers point of view and work on them *every day*.
- *Set high standards.* Set challenging objectives and targets for each of the five important issues (e.g., a ten-fold improvement in reliability or a 50 percent reduction in rework).
- *When in charge, take command.* Decisions elicit new information. The best policy is to decide, monitor the results, and change course if necessary.
  - —Create a feedback system to link the objectives to operations
  - —Create a systematic way of deploying corporate objectives that every employee can understand and use, and that enlists the problem solving skills and knowledge of every employee.
- *People come to work to succeed.*
  - —Focus all employees on analyzing and improving processes *over time*.
  - —Apply quality improvement tools to all strategic and tactical issues.

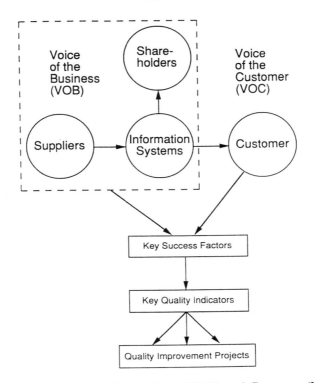

Figure 2.1   Voice of the Business (VOB) and Customer (VOC)

- *Do what's right.* "You *always* know the right thing to do. The hard part is doing it."

The purpose of business is to identify and satisfy a customer. This means that you have to gather the needs and expectations of your customer and the business (Figure 2.1), identify the 7 ± 2 most important items to work on, and then start solving them in order of importance. The focus has been on business priorities, not customers and employees. The voice of the business (VOB) and voice of the customer (VOC) give quality planning a more balanced approach.

Quality planning has seven steps (Figure 2.2):

1. Identifying the various customer groups served by the company and separating them into groups for analysis.
2. Gathering the voice of the customer through formal, ongoing customer surveys, focus groups, or one-on-one interviews to gather requirements. Both direct and indirect customer needs

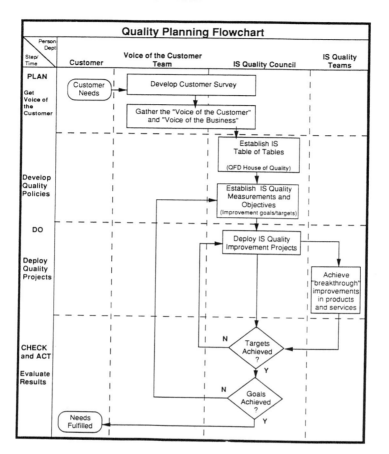

Figure 2.2 Quality Planning Process

must be determined using factual data gathered from customers, not the internal employees gut feel. There can be both direct customers who purchase the product or service, and indirect customers like the government who have requirements for payroll witholding. The voice of the business gathers the needs of suppliers, employees, and shareholders.

3. Evaluating and ranking the customer's needs, expectations, and desires to identify the key success factors. Relating customer requirements to specific quality elements like customer service, reliability, or on-time delivery through Quality Function Deployment and the "House of Quality."

4. Developing an overall ranking of the quality elements and developing measurements to evaluate them. Setting quality objectives

and targets for improvement that will help ensure that the company focuses on the key items that are important from the customer's point of view.

5. Prioritizing quality improvement work to meet the vital needs of the customer and deploying quality improvement projects to reach the goals and objectives set by the quality council.
6. Achieving breakthrough improvements in defect rate, cycle time, and cost by applying process management, quality problem solving, and benchmarking to the key business issues facing IS.
7. Checking the progress toward the goals and targets established in step 4 and taking action to deploy more improvement projects or "raise the bar" in terms of targets and goals.

Quality planning uses quality improvement in a top-down, strategic fashion to greatly enhance corporate quality, productivity, and profitability. By first surveying our customers and listening to their needs and expectations, we can figure out their hot buttons. In a software environment, these are typically reliability (i.e., defect rate or availability), system response time, cost, and responsiveness (i.e., cycle time) for emergencies, enhancement requests, and creation of new systems. Then, using data, we can begin to pull apart the components of each issue and initiate quality improvement teams to tackle each aspect of each hot button to reach our targets for improvement. As these teams examine and resolve the root causes of these problems, the force of not one, but many incremental improvements are brought to bear on the customer's requirements. Revolutionary improvements are possible. You may hear heroic goals like: "Cut the cost of software development by 50 percent in the next four years." Quality planning is the way it is going to happen—focusing effort on the vital issues of the business, not scattering them across the board as most companies do now.

Many companies feel that they are focused on the "vital few" issues, but unless they have surveyed and resurveyed their customers to understand their true wants and needs, it is impossible to have a true "customer focus." Quality planning integrates the voice of the customer with plans and action to ensure that the customer's needs are met and exceeded. The voice of the customer is the loudest voice you will hear. They may often expect the following quality:

- Prompt repair of systems
- Accuracy of answers, bills, estimates, and so on
- Reliability of real-time and on-line systems

- Availability of systems
- Information security
- Return on investment
- Visual appeal of their systems (e.g., terminals, windows, and icons)

QUALITY POLICY DEPLOYMENT

We all get caught up in the tyranny of the urgent—in the thick of things. Some call it firefighting. Since most software organizations are still stuck in the software tar pit, crisis management is the most common form of management. Software departments must begin to rise above this insanity and focus their energy on the important issues facing the department— issues that will enable the department to provide dramatic improvements in service and quality.

To start succeeding at quality planning, managers and employees must ask the questions:

- Where do we want to be five, ten, twenty years from now?
- How are we going to get there?
- Who are our customers?
- What are their needs and reasonable expectations?

To reach these objectives, we have to begin identifying the key areas for breakthrough improvements in quality and productivity. Then, we must initiate specific improvement projects to work on the many complex elements of each key area. The quality policy deployment process delivers these desired results.

First, we gather the customer's valid requirements (voice of the customer) for software creation and evolution. Regardless of how they state it, these requirements will often fall into the categories of reliability, timeliness, and cost (Figure 2.3). Using a prioritization matrix—one of the quality management and planning tools—we can identify the key strategies we can employ to deliver the customer's requirements. We can then relate the key strategies—reducing cost, cycle time, and defect rate—to the customer's objectives using a scale of high, medium, low, or none. Also, we can relate them to the corporate objectives and begin to develop what is called the "table of tables" or the "house of quality" (Figure 2.4). Working our way across the matrix, we can see that reducing application unavailability is strongly related to delighting customers and continuous improvement, but only weakly related to becoming a flexible and responsive information provider. The

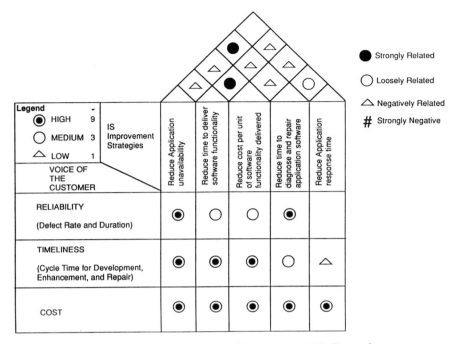

Figure 2.3   Voice of the Customer and IS Strategies

rate of importance for this strategy is five (high); our current ranking is a three (medium); competitor number one is currently a four (medium high); and we want to set an objective of becoming as good as competitor number one. The *ratio of improvement* is the objective divided by our current status (4/3 = 1.3). The *sales point* identifies how much of a selling point reliability would provide (1.2 is medium). The *absolute weight* is the product of the rate of importance, ratio of importance, and sales point (5*1.3*1.2 = 6). The *demanded weight* is the percent of total absolute weight (6/36 = 17%).

We develop these rows for each IS strategy. Our goal is always to be as good as if not better than our competition. Often, we will need to be better than our competition because they are not standing still either. As you can see from this chart, reducing the time to deliver new functionality has the highest demanded weight (33 percent) and reducing response time the lowest (12 percent).

Working down the columns, we total the relationship for each goal and strategy. Delighting customers has a total ranking of 39 (4*9 + 3), continuous improvement (33), and flexible provider (31). As a percentage of this total, delighting customers is 38% (39/103). The company

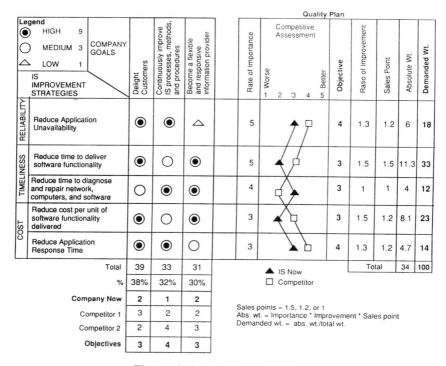

Figure 2.4   IS Table of Tables

ranking now is a two (low). Competitor number one is again higher at a three. Our objective is to meet or exceed their ability. Next we realize that we are currently pathetic at quality improvement and that we want to develop a leadership position in continuous improvement. Because of demands by our customers to get quality oriented and to apply for the Malcolm Baldrige award and ISO 9000 (European quality standard), we have to become vastly more quality-oriented or loose some of our major customers in the next five years. Competitor number two is already quality-oriented and major competition for our markets. We must dramatically improve in this area or suffer the consequences.

Once we've established these strategies and objectives, we have to figure out how to measure them and set targets and goals for improvement (Figure 2.5). We may already measure application unavailability. At two percent, it is acceptable, but just barely. The reason we measure unavailability is that 98 percent availability doesn't sound or look too bad on a control chart, but two percent unavailability focuses on what we need to improve. Our one year target is to reduce from 2 percent to 1.5

	IS Strategy	Quality Indicator	One Year Goal	Three Year Goal
RELIABILITY	Reduce Application Unavailability	Application Unavailability	1.5%	0.5%
TIMELINESS	Reduce time to deliver software functionality	Actual time per unit of function (KLOC, FP)	-10%	-60%
TIMELINESS	Reduce time to diagnose and repair application software	Mean Time To Repair for application software	97 min	55 min
COST	Reduce Application Response Time	Overall Application Response Time	4 sec	1 sec
COST	Reduce cost per unit of software functionality delivered	Cost per function delivered	-10%	-50%

Figure 2.5   IS Key Success Factors and Quality Indicators

percent—a 25 percent reduction in unavailability. Our three year goal is to reduce unavailability to 0.5 percent—a 75 percent reduction. We also want to reduce cycle time by 60 percent, repair time by 50 percent, response time by a factor of four, and cost per unit by 50 percent. These kinds of heroic goals are the drivers that get everyone focused on meeting or exceeding the customer's expectations. They link to the strengths of our competitors and the voice of our customers. From these targets and goals, IS top management plays ''catch ball'' with the rest of the organization to decide who is going to initiate the quality improvement projects that will ultimately lead to generating the desired improvement goal. Catch ball is a negotiation process that occurs from the top down in the organization to determine where and how IS will deploy quality improvement projects to achieve these quality objectives.

Quality function deployment, using prioritization matrices will begin to develop the linkage between what the customer wants and what IS can provide. From there, setting objectives for improvement will drive the improvement efforts of the IS staff.

Voice of the Business

The voice of the customer is not the only voice we hear. There is also the voice of the business which includes the voice of the employee. The voice of the business, for example, may demand that we grow the business by 15 percent per year, reduce costs, and increase shareholder value. IS employees may desire reduced overtime and more opportunity to learn and develop their skills toward mastery. These are other vital factors that must be woven into the quality planning process to ensure excellence. Often, by focusing mainly on the customer, many of these objectives can be achieved.

IS QUALITY OBJECTIVES

The wider you spread it, the thinner it gets.
— *Gerald M. Weinberg (1985)*

Top managers will spend long hours identifying and ranking the quality objectives for consideration during the coming year. Quality teams will focus their energies on these targets and goals for the next year, so it becomes crucial to pick the most important ones. It all boils down to doing the right things. To ensure a focused effort, there should be no more than seven items on this list of key quality objectives, preferably three to five.

Quality objectives must be measurable in ways that reflect the positive or negative impact on the customer. For information systems, these policies take the form of *increase* or *decrease* statements:

Objective	Measurement
• Increase customer satisfaction	Declining complaints or escalations
• Decrease application unavailability	Decreasing down time (hours)
• Improve software performance	Decreasing run time or response time
• Reduce software development costs	Decreasing cost per function point
• Improve software reliability	Declining faults or failures
	Cost of reruns

These measurements serve as a "dashboard" for IS leadership to monitor and improve the department. These indicators also serve as the basis for developing master quality improvement stories that drive the initiation of improvement teams. Without clear, focused measures of key indicators of customer satisfaction, initial quality improvements will lack focus. This often leads to IS management questioning the value of quality teams, when the root cause stems to their reluctance to learn about quality and make it their management system of choice.

Once we've identified these quality objectives, they need to be broken down into more tangible targets and goals that can be understood and applied by each software division or project. This requires negotiation— a game of catch ball. For example, if an IS department wanted to reduce application down time from 1000 hours to 800 hours, the 200 hours would need to be allocated across all of the applications. Some of these applications could easily supply 50 hours toward the goal, others only one to two. Within the larger applications, several quality improvement projects may be needed to realize the overall goal of 50 hours. In smaller projects, only one project may be needed.

While all this planning may seem like a lot of work, once completed, quality teams can do much more to meet the needs of the customer in a much shorter time. It is not uncommon to achieve a ten-fold improvement in on-time delivery of quality software in as little as two years.

The application of quality planning develops a common language for communication throughout the corporation that helps turn missions and visions into concrete details that people can focus on to realize the customer's objectives. Meeting or exceeding the customer's expectations is the key to achieving and sustaining competitive advantage.

ACCELERATING THE QUALITY IMPROVEMENT PROCESS

The critical success factor of high quality and productivity organizations is a method to introduce *improvements* continuously in their processes. This can be done through the use of a quality assessment and the use of a methodology to attain these goals.

This process or methodology has five iterative steps, which loosely follow the PDCA process:

1. Assessing the present software process maturity
2. Analyzing the results of the assessment to determine priorities
3. Setting goals for improvement
4. Implementing the improvements
5. Measuring the impact of the improvements (Chapter 9)

Assessment

Before a company embarks on quality planning, there is an even faster route to quality—benchmarking your company against others using an assessment. This brings us to the next law of quality: *Learn from the best.*

Benchmarking, vastly simplified, is the process of scouring the world for companies that are excellent at one or two processes that you need help in mastering; you study how they do it; and you bring it back and install it in your company. In essence, you can ''borrow with honor'' every good idea you find. Fortunately, some research institutes have already gone off and done a lot of this for you. You can use their research by conducting an assessment of your existing software process.

Software Process Assessment

By modeling and benchmarking against top software developers, the Software Engineering Institute (SEI) has identified 18 key processes and 343 key practices that contribute to software quality and productivity. One key process, for example, is project planning. Estimating software size (lines of code or function points) is a key practice within project planning. These processes and practices are arranged in what the SEI calls a maturity framework. The SEI has developed a 120 question assessment that can help you identify where your strengths are and where you could improve as an organization. The good news is that you can leverage their research; the bad news is that you probably won't like what you learn and it will take you several years to establish the improvements that lie ahead. Figures 2.6 and 2.7 show the results of 59 assessments on 27 sites and 296 projects. Over 88 percent of all sites and projects are still stuck in the initial level of process maturity—the software tar pit.

The SEI Process Maturity Framework is an evolutionary path of process improvement that has five levels: initial (chaos), repeatable, defined, managed, and optimized (Figure 2.8). At level 2—repeatable—software projects can be *repeatably* delivered on schedule with reason-

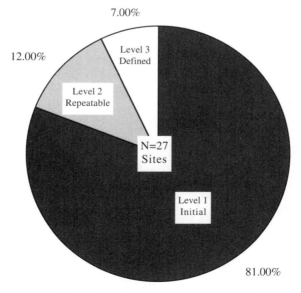

SEI Site Maturity Level

Figure 2.6   1991 SEI Site Maturity

SEI Project Maturity Status

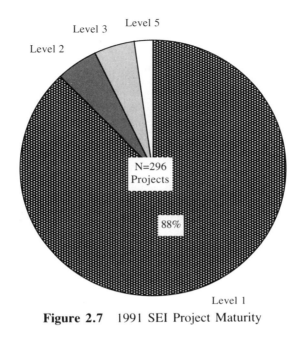

Level 5

Level 3

Level 2

N=296
Projects

88%

Level 1

Figure 2.7   1991 SEI Project Maturity

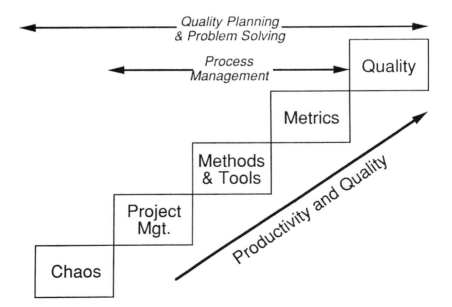

Quality Planning
& Problem Solving

Process
Management

Quality

Metrics

Methods
& Tools

Productivity and Quality

Project
Mgt.

Chaos

Figure 2.8   SEI Maturity Model

able quality. At level 3, the software process is defined, trained and followed by software engineers. *Process management* can be used at the repeatable level to define your software processes. Without a defined process for software creation and evolution, no further quality progress is possible. Once defined, IS can move to the next level, managed, where you begin to measure and analyze the process and its products. *Process management* can help identify the measurements necessary to determine the stability and capability of the software process. At the highest level, optimized, all software engineers apply the tools and principles of Total Quality Management (TQM) to continuously improving the software process and thereby the software products they produce. Quality *problem solving* can be used at all levels to identify and reduce the root causes of customer dissatisfaction. *Quality planning* links these tools and processes together to achieve breakthrough improvements in productivity and quality.

Assessing Software Process Maturity

The software assessment process uses the software process maturity framework questionnaires to determine the maturity of a development or maintenance process. As we learn more about our software processes, this questionnaire will evolve to support the refinements necessary to achieve software excellence. To get a yardstick analysis of where your organization lies now, take the quick assessment shown in Figure 2.9.

Critical Success Factors

There are three key leverage points for improving productivity and quality—people, process, and tools. The emphasis has been on technology—CASE—to provide the mythical silver bullet. Without a balanced focus on people and the process, we cannot attain the levels of quality and productivity desired. The key to quality is the process or methodology; yet people and technology play their parts. To maximize quality and productivity, we need to *begin* with a defined process and then establish the measurements and data collection required to move to the continuous quality improvement. Using the SEI Software Maturity Framework, we can identify the following critical success factors for each step on the stairway to software excellence and software quality:

Repeatable Process

1. Establish a Software Quality group to implement total quality management

2. Establish *software configuration control/management* for each project
3. Establish *formal procedures* for software engineers to:
   make estimates of software size
   produce software schedules
   estimate software costs
4. Measure and gather statistics of:
   software size for each software configuration item, over time
   defects, from requirements through production
5. Establish a *Change Management mechanism* for software engineers to control changes to the software—requirements, design, code, documentation, etc.
6. Establish a *formal procedure* for management to review software projects
7. Establish a *formal procedure* for software testing

Defined Process

1. Develop a *standardized* and *documented software* development/ maintenance *process* for each project
2. Establish a software engineering *process group* to evolve the development and maintenance processes
3. Develop a required software engineering training program for software professionals
4. Establish a formal training program required for *design and code inspections*
5. Conduct internal software design and code inspections
6. Track the action items resulting from design and code inspections
7. Establish a *mechanism* to ensure compliance with the software engineering *standards*
8. Establish a *mechanism* for assuring the adequacy of regression testing

Managed Process

1. Establish a *mechanism* used for the introduction of new technologies
2. Estimate design, code, and test defects and compare them to actuals

SOFTWARE EVOLUTION - QUICK ASSESSMENT

Repeatable

<u>Yes / No</u>

Y N   Do you have a Software Quality Assurance (SQA) function?

Y N   Do you use software configuration control?

Y N   Do you *formally review* each software project's contribution prior to making commitments?

Y N   Do you *formally estimate* software size, effort, and cost?

Y N   Do you *formally plan* software schedules?

Y N   Do you measure and track the size and complexity of each software module over time?

Y N   Do you measure and track errors/defects throughout the maintenance lifecycle?

Y N   Does management *formally review* the status of software projects?

Y N   Do you use a *mechanism* to control changes to the software requirements?

<u>Y N</u>   Do you use a *mechanism* to control who changes the code and when?

   If the number of yes answers exceeds seven, give yourself **REPEATABLE.**

Defined

Y N   Do you use a <u>standardized</u> and <u>documented</u> software maintenance *process* on each project?

Y N   Is there a software engineering *process group* that evolves the maintenance *process.*

Y N   Is there a required software engineering *training program* for software professionals?

Y N   Do you measure and track software design errors and defects?

Y N   Do you conduct internal software design reviews/inspections?

Y N   Are the action items resulting from design reviews tracked to closure?

Y N   Do you use a *mechanism* to control changes to the software design?

Y N   Do you conduct software code reviews/inspections?

Y N   Are the action items resulting from code reviews tracked to closure?

Y N   Is there a formal training program for *design and code review leaders*?

Y N   Do you use a *mechanism* used to ensure compliance with the software engineering *standards*?

<u>Y N</u>   Do you *formally verify* the adequacy of regression testing?

   If the number of yes answers exceeds nine, give yourself **DEFINED.**

Managed

Y N   Is a *formal mechanism* used to manage the introduction of new technologies?

Y N   Are requirements, design, and code review *standards* applied?

Y N   Are design, code, and test errors estimated and compared to actuals?

Y N   Are *design and code review coverages* measured and recorded?

Y N   Is the *design review data* analyzed to evaluate the product and reduce future defects?

Figure 2.9   SEI Quick Assessment

Managed (*continued*)

Y N Is *test coverage* measured and recorded for each phase of functional testing?

Y N Has a *metrics database* been established for *process measurement* across all projects?

Y N Is the *error data* from code reviews and tests analyzed to determine the likely distribution and characteristics of the errors remaining the product?

Y N Are analyses of errors conducted to determine their *process* related causes?

Y N Is *review efficiency* analyzed for each project?

<u>Y N</u> Is a *mechanism* used for periodically assessing the software engineering *process* and implementing indicated improvements?

If the number of yes answers exceeds eight, give yourself **MANAGED**.

Optimized

Y N Is a *mechanism* used for identifying and replacing obsolete technologies?

Y N Is a *mechanism* used for error cause analysis?

Y N Are the error causes reviewed to determine the *process* changes required to prevent them?

<u>Y N</u> Is a *mechanism* used for initiating error prevention actions?

If the number of yes answers exceeds two, give yourself **OPTIMIZED**.

Tools and Technology

Do the software development and maintenance personnel use:

Y N automated configuration control to manage software changes throughout the process?

Y N a high-order language?

Y N interactive source-level debuggers?

Y N interactive documentation facilities?

<u>Y N</u> computer tools for tracking and reporting the status of the software in the library?

If the number of yes answers exceeds three, give yourself **AUTOMATED**.

Figure 2.9 (*continued*)

3. Measure *software defects* and record them for each phase of testing and operation

4. Establish a *process database* for *process metrics* data across all projects

5. Analyze the defect data from inspections and tests to find where to improve the process. Conduct analyses of defects to figure out their *process* related causes

6. Establish a *mechanism* for periodically assessing the software engineering process and implementing suggested improvements

Optimized Process

1. Establish a *mechanism* for identifying and replacing obsolete technologies
2. Establish a *mechanism* for initiating defect prevention actions (TQM)
3. Establish a *mechanism* for rewarding continuous improvement and innovation

Tools and Technology

Tools and technology are used to support the creation and evolution processes, not as an end in themselves. As previously stated, an organization must have reached a level of having a defined process to be able to make proper use of CASE technology. The critical components of a successful, productive, high-quality software technology environment are:

1. Automated configuration and change management to control and track change activity throughout the software process
2. Reusable data, code, and documentation
3. High-order languages
4. Tools:

   Design and documentation facilities—25 percent of project costs are documentation

   Electronic communication facilities—E-mail, conferencing, voice, video etc.

   Change management

   Configuration management

   Editors

   Compilers

   Interactive testing tools

Analyzing the Assessment

Once the data has been collected and processed, a report will need to be issued that identifies key strengths and opportunities for improvement. Based on this report, the assessed project should do the following steps:

1. Form a team of technicians to analyze the report
2. Prioritize the critical success action items according to project needs

3. Identify:

What can be changed?

What must be changed by working through others?

4. Set objectives to institute a reasonable set of these items
5. Brainstorm solutions

Identify resources required (including other groups)

Identify the costs

Identify any roadblocks (and a plan to overcome them one at a time)

Identify the risks associated with each change

6. Create a plan for implementation of these goals during the coming year.

Format for an Assessment Response

Each assessment will need to identify the following:

1. The Level of Process Maturity
2. Strengths (key processes already in place that need to be reinforced)
3. Opportunities for Improvement (missing practices and processes required for the next level)
4. Goal for improvements in:
   - Critical Success Factors
   - Key Processes
   - Key Practices
   - Tools
   - Methods
   - Environment

Once the assessment is complete, the time has come for planning the changes and resources required, initiating the change, and using measurement to check the results. Software assessment is yet another form of PDCA that can be used to vault your company toward excellence.

BENCHMARKING

Benchmarking is a process for achieving superior performance in any critical area of work. By rigorously comparing ourselves to companies who are well known for their best practices in these areas, we can become more effective, often surpassing those benchmarked. We have to figure out how to improve and how much to improve. Benchmarking determines the reasons why a "best" company is the best, the processes they use, targets for improvement, and steps for implementing the change.

Benchmarking helps us learn the innovations and best practices of other groups or companies, set targets based on data, convince ourselves that we can do it better, measure performance, and be a more outer-world focused instead of inner-focused company. It leads to significant improvements in cost, quality, cycle time, and competitive ability. Benchmarking helps us learn how to compete. It is a key element of the Malcolm Baldrige award.

A benchmark can include any skill, behavior, or process that sets a standard of excellence against which our performance can be compared and judged. DeMarco and Lister (1987) found that there was a 10:1 difference in performance between companies. The *tens* are the companies you will want to find and benchmark against.

Competitive benchmarking involves finding work groups that are the best at what they do—inside the company, in other non-competing companies, or in competing companies—and then modeling that behavior. As the Japanese say: "To borrow with honor." Many companies that were at the brink of disaster have used competitive benchmarking to pull themselves back from the abyss. At Xerox, every group searched for ways to become more effective and efficient. Xerox studied companies as near and far as its partner Fuji Xerox, L.L. Bean, and Sears Roebuck & Co.

Benchmarking, whether personal, internal, or external, follows the PDCA recipe:

Plan	What:	Identify the capability, behavior, or skill to be benchmarked.
		Identify the key variables to measure.
	Who and where:	Identify the best groups or companies to benchmark.
	How and when:	decide how to collect the information required.
Do	Collect the information.	
	· How do we do it?	
	· How do they do it?	
	Compare these two sets of information.	

Determine the gap between your company and theirs.
Set heroic goals for establishing and improving the
benchmarks.
Establish and initiate an action plan.

Check   Monitor the progress and improvement.

Act   Improve the established benchmark using the quality improvement process.

First, you begin by identifying the benchmarking topic. Benchmarking (Figure 2.10) can focus in the area of reducing costs or increasing
revenues. Increasing revenues invariably come from differentiation in
the areas of product reliability and features, customer sales and service,
and our image with customers, suppliers, and competitors. Decreasing
costs come from improvements in labor, materials, and overhead.
Benchmarking could evaluate any process, product, or service that affects these variables—requirements gathering, configuration management, help desk management, or response time. Ask yourself: ''Where
are we less than the best? Where is the gap the greatest between our
present state and our desired state? What has the highest cost? What is

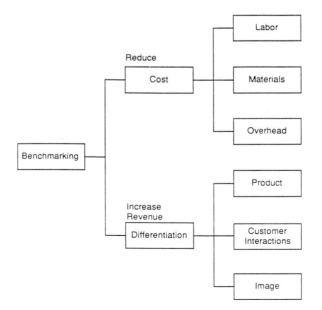

Figure 2.10   Benchmarking Arenas

the most significant area? Where do we have the greatest room for improvement?'' Prioritization Matrices (Chapter 3) can help. The indicators for benchmarking must be available, objective, collected reliably, and easily compared.

Once you've identified what to benchmark, you will need to identify the best people or companies to benchmark. These could include direct or potential competitors, non-competitors, and groups inside your company. Ask yourself and your customer: "Is there a proven model for this process or behavior? Who uses it now? Where are they located?'' Surprisingly, there are often groups or individuals within your company who do this already. Benchmark at home first and then, if you don't find satisfactory methods, move out into the field. Ultimately, you will need to select five to seven diverse companies that have the best or most creative strategies for doing what you need to do. Are they gaining market share? Do they provide better customer service? Are they generally known as well run? Are they superior in some activity—shipping, billing, R&D, new product development, sales, human resources, and so on?

Once you've decided where to benchmark, you need to decide how and when to benchmark. There are many sources of benchmarking information: government, trade, industry, or company publications; technical conferences and seminars; interviews with customers, suppliers, distributors, competitors, industry experts, and ex-employees; market research; and reverse engineering of customer products. Ultimately, to identify each company's level of performance and understand how that performance is achieved, you will need to develop a formal survey to ferret out the key ingredients of the benchmark's success. Then you will need to apply the survey systematically in face-to-face interviews. Benchmarking involves comparing both results and processes. We not only want to know how good the competition is, but how do they do that consistently?

The next step is to collect the information both in the benchmarking companies and within our work group. How different are we? What do they do that makes the difference? By contrastive analysis, we can figure out the gap between our present and desired state. Using the gap, we can set heroic goals (Figure 2.11) for establishing breakthrough improvements and then continuously improving on those breakthroughs. We may want to emulate the best, leapfrog the competition, or realize dramatic reversals by changing the rules of the game. There may be several targets for improvement en route to the goal. To reach each target, we will need a detailed action plan to transform the existing environment to one that allows productivity and quality to happen more naturally.

Once we have begun moving toward our goals and targets, we will

Costs

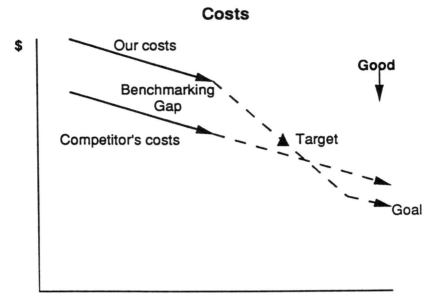

Figure 2.11 Benchmarking Gap and Heroic Goals

need to monitor our progress and observable improvements with quality indicators that demonstrate our motion toward the desired state of excellence. Rarely can an organization just adopt someone else's business practices. Through PDCA we can adapt the benchmark findings to align with our company. The indicators we use to measure our progress will focus on the characteristics of our inputs, outputs and processes—specifications like response time, accuracy, timeliness—and other keys to excellence such as cycle time, defects, and reliability.

Finally, once we establish a benchmark, it will tend to fade through everyday entropy unless we constantly improve the established benchmark using the quality improvement process. Industries are always changing. New competitors appear. Existing competitors aren't standing still. Competitors are moving targets. What are they doing to improve? Are we moving as fast as we can?

To identify and select benchmarking topics successfully, you need to do more than just brainstorm problems in your area. This process will often lead you to topics that are "solutions" or vaguely defined problems. The following process will help you refine the topic:

1. Brainstorm a list of your key customers. If the list includes more than $7 + 2$, multivote down to five main customers:

- Market Unit mechanization group—who define the system
- Computer operations—who run the system

The service representatives who actually use the system would not be considered key customers, because we don't provide them anything directly. They are the next process customers of the mechanization group and computer operations.

2. For each customer, brainstorm a list of products (e.g., requirements, design, code, executable programs, JCL, etc.) or services (e.g., system operation, trouble diagnosis, etc.) that your group provides:
   - Market Unit mechanization group—enhancements and repair work
   - Computer operations—run books, programs, and data
3. For each of these products or services, list the processes used to deliver them (e.g., for code, processes might include coding, inspecting, and unit testing).
   - Market Unit mechanization group
   —enhancement process
   —corrective maintenance process
   - Computer operations
   —documentation process
   —software release process
4. With this complete list of customers, products, and processes, brainstorm a list of potential benchmarking topics:
   - software maintenance process
   - software evolution process
   - documentation process
   - software release process
5. Make your brainstormed topics more specific by challenging the words used in the theme and improve them by asking: Who, What, Where, When, or How specifically?
   - correcting software defects after program failures
   - enhancing and expanding system capabilities
   - writing, publishing, and distributing operational documentation
   - managing the configuration and delivery of software releases
6. Use the term definition matrix shown below to define each of the words in the benchmarking topic:

Term	Definition
Customer	Market unit automation group
Defect	Any software failure or inaccurate output
Document	Run books, operator manuals, training guides

7. Identify measurements to be used in evaluating the benchmark:
   - Is the information available in our company?
   - Is it common enough that we can compare across companies?
   - Is it collected in the benchmarking companies?

Is the benchmarking topic an input, output, process, or effect? We measure the inputs and outputs by specifications and characteristics. We measure processes by cycle time, defect rate, or other similar measure. We measure the effect of successfully producing a product or service by cost, profit, market share, or customer satisfaction.

Who Is the Best?

Once you know the benchmarking topic, you need to decide who to benchmark against. The three main candidates, in order of preference are:

- other groups within your company
- other groups in non-competing companies
- groups in competing companies

Within your company is a rich resource. Very often, there are pockets of excellence that can be easily tapped to establish benchmarks. The major information systems with the *fewest* problems, lowest overtime, and highest customer satisfaction are often a key place to begin your search. These groups are obviously doing something right. What is it? In a software environment where continuous firefighting is the norm, we come to think of the main firefighters as our heros, but it is in the quiet systems where there are few fires that there is the most to learn about excellence. These groups know how to prevent fires. The advantage of internal benchmarking is that it is inexpensive and you have easy access to resources to help you establish the benchmark.

Non-competing companies are another rich resource. Since we have no common customer, we can share openly our key abilities and benefit from each other's experience. The only problem is that there are so few companies that are excellent at software creation and evolution, they could easily be swamped by benchmarking requests. External benchmarking with non-competing companies gives a broader slice of knowledge, but costs more and takes longer to do.

Competitors are moving targets. Competing companies are the ones least likely to share information, but we can often glean a tremendous amount of information about them from industry periodicals, publicly available documentation, or from reverse engineering of their products. The look and feel of a competitor's product, for example, will often give you clear information about the benchmark for yours. Competitive benchmarking is a skill. Use internal and external non-competing partners first, and then if you still don't have the information you need, switch to competitive benchmarking.

External companies that meet the mark of excellence can be found by doing a literature search of recent articles about excellence or by contacting key consultants in the field for referrals. Benchmarking is always looking for the best in any field. What constitutes "best," however, may vary. The most productive software organization may not have the "best" customer satisfaction. The most reliable of products, if you can't figure out how to use it, may not be the "best" either. Get clear about what the "best" means and then go for it.

In Xerox, they then calculate the gap between where they are and where they want to be as a percentage that normalizes the difference:

gap = 1 − (Xerox/Benchmark)
gap = 1 − (Benchmark/Xerox)

If, for example, the Space Shuttle software has a defect rate of 0.11 per KLOC and you have a defect rate of 3 per KLOC, we could calculate the benchmark (Figure 2.12) as follows:

$$gap = 1 - \left(\frac{0.11}{3} \right) = 96.3 \text{ percent}$$

If we had a defect rate of only 2 defects per KLOC, the gap would still be high (94.5 percent). Similarly, if we had a productivity rate of 6,000 KLOC/year and someone else had a productivity rate of 11,000 KLOC/year, then assuming the measurements are the same we would have a gap of 45 percent.

How Do We Do It?

To successfully benchmark, we have to know how we do things now. A flowchart of the process with a description of the inputs and outputs

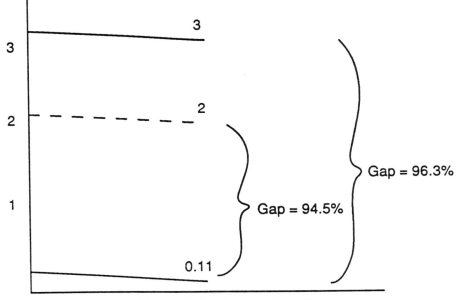

Figure 2.12 Benchmarking Gap

provide a starting point (process management). Then we need to know the customers and their valid requirements for our product or service. We also need to know who owns the process within our company. A billing system, for example, is only part of a billing process which is often owned by a business or market unit, not the IS unit.

How Do They Do It?

With all this other information in hand, we are now ready to visit with our benchmarking partners. The key is to be honest and open about the information you are requesting; then if it is out-of-bounds, your partner can decline to answer. You also should be prepared to tell the person about anything that you do in this area. Openness goes both ways.

You will need to:

1. Select a method for collecting the data: phone, mail survey, personal interview, direct observation, evaluating company publications, reverse engineering, or by attending public seminars.
2. Identify your benchmarking partners and get their permission to work together.
3. Establish dates and times for gathering the data.

4. Develop the questionnaire and pilot it with an internal group to make sure you get the information you want.
5. Initiate data collection and set a date for analysis.
6. Set a date for sharing your analysis with your benchmarking partners.
7. Begin implementing key findings of the benchmarking study.

Again, nothing happens unless someone does something. In a typical benchmarking study, there will be no "silver bullet" solution, only a cluster of activities that form a system that allows productivity and quality to occur. You will need to implement all the discovered activities.

Benchmarking requires top management support to focus on improvement opportunities that will be critical to reaching corporate goals. Top management must not punish the staff for the gap between where we are and where we want to be, because ultimately, top management is responsible and accountable for the gap. Top management must sponsor and endorse the benchmarking activities, whether it is an SEI assessment or an actual benchmarking effort. Then resources must be allocated to acquire the expertise and skills to identify and establish the benchmark. There must be time, money, and people allocated, full time, to the effort. We also must remain open minded, because what we discover will often seem foreign to the way we do business today. We must be open to embracing the changes required to attain our goals. Finally, we must have an ongoing process for integrating these changes into the way we do business.

Benchmarking can be a powerful tool for making major strides in productivity and quality. Once your baseline process is as good as the best in the industry, then you can begin to improve the process continuously so that you always stay one step ahead of the competition.

SUMMARY

Quality planning or policy deployment is a key element of a successful TQM implementation. Following the PDCA process, planning involves understanding the voice of the customer, relating their needs to IS strategies and indicators, and setting targets and goals for improvement. Like a rifle, quality planning focuses the quality improvement efforts on the few key objectives required to begin to meet or exceed the customer's expectations. Without quality planning, the quality efforts will be more like a shotgun—scattered and somewhat ineffective.

IS top management must develop the quality plan. By setting goals and objectives, they align the organization with the customer's needs. By then playing "catch ball" with the middle management team, they can identify where the improvements will come from to reach their goals. Together, management deploys process management, problem solving, and benchmarking projects to improve many areas at the same time to ensure that IS will reach the goals established. The more management gets in front of the quality change, the more smoothly the change will flow through the organization. By planning what we want to accomplish with our quality efforts and the key areas for improvement, we can maximize the effectiveness of our initial teams and the returns they produce. Quality planning focuses the organization to deliver customer satisfaction in ways that exceed all expectations. Planning is one of the keys to the successful implementation of TQM.

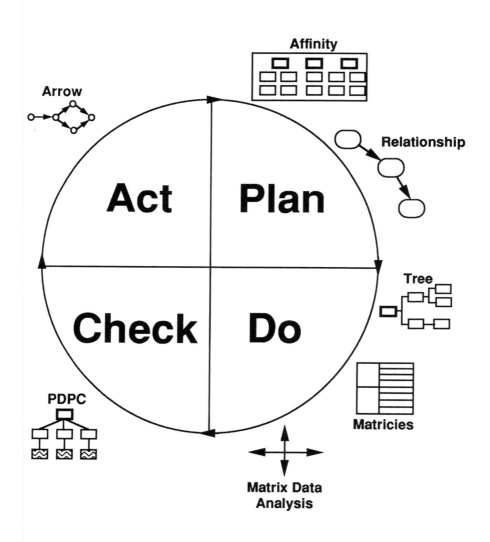

CHAPTER 3

The Management and Planning Tools

Make no little plans; they have no magic to stir men's blood.
—Daniel Hudson Burnham

The seven management and planning tools are more qualitative than quantitative. Unlike the problem-solving tools described in later chapters, these tools help us plan for quality and design new processes or reengineer existing ones. I call them tools for dreamers, because they help break us out of our old ways of thinking and lay out a plan with enough critical thinking to ensure success. Walt Disney called this "imagineering." There were three key elements to his success: the *dreamer* who imagined what could be done, the *realist* who developed the plan and took action to make the dreams real, and the *critic* who carefully analyzed and offered improvements on both the dream and the plan *before* implementation. As you will see, the seven management and planning tools embody these three elements for product and service creation.

These tools also help us plan IS activities in ways that will focus the quality improvement effort and prevent problems from ever occurring. As we'll see later, the original seven quality improvement tools can help quality improvement teams solve most quality improvement *problems*. The original seven tools are quantitative tools for analysis. They are a diagnostic tool kit. The original seven quality improvement tools focus on *data* and the analysis of data. Essentially, the patient already has the disease and we are trying to diagnose and fix it. The seven management and planning tools, on the other hand, seek to prevent the patient from ever developing the disease of poor quality.

These tools assist in planning and deploying all aspects of software. They can also be used to gather requirements for software. They can be used to gather the voice of the customer and translate it into IS products and services. The affinity diagram and interrelationship digraph offer general planning tools. Intermediate planning includes the tree diagram, matrix diagram, and matrix data analysis. Detailed planning involves an arrow diagram, which is similar to a PERT (program evaluation and review technique) chart, and a process decision program chart (PDPC). They are designed to be used in sequence and they can be used individually.

GENERAL PLANNING

The affinity diagram and interrelationship digraph offer interesting tools for gathering and organizing the information gathered from your customer. These can be used to gather, correlate, and relate huge quantities of information (especially written or verbal comments). The affinity diagram (Figure 3.1) helps you group your customer's valid requirements into natural groups which show the relationships between items and groups. The affinity diagram helps you gather and group large amounts of "language" (e.g., needs, wants, wishes, ideas, and opinions) into natural relationships. This more organic and creative approach to understanding the user's needs is also a useful tool for object-oriented analysis.

The affinity diagraming method helps break old patterns of thought and reveal new patterns and more creative ways of thinking about a problem or opportunity. The affinity diagram helps organize the team's thoughts most effectively when:

- The issues seem too large and complex to grasp, not simple or immediate
- You need some way to break out of old, traditional ways of thinking
- Facts or thoughts are chaotic
- You need to quickly uncover your customer's requirements

The affinity diagram helps you map out the "solution space" or "geography" of your problem or opportunity. Parts of the overall problem will naturally cluster into components that can be investigated independently, in sequence or in parallel. A team can use its gut feel to organize hundreds of individual items in under an hour. Team members

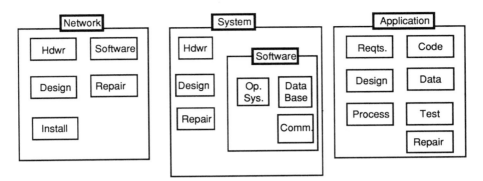

Figure 3.1 Affinity Diagram

should include the ones that have the most knowledge required to explore the issue. The process is simple:

1. State the issue to be examined in broad terms: "What are the issues surrounding or involving . . .
   - the delivery of very low defect software
   - reducing software life cycle time and costs
   - increasing the flexibility and maintainability of software

2. Using customer feedback, surveys, complaints, or your experience begin generating and recording ideas. Using yellow sticky notes for each item identified and a large wall or white board, record each idea exactly as stated and begin sticking them on the wall where everyone can see them. To ensure that everyone is included, go around the participants in a clockwise fashion asking each in turn for a "headline" to describe their thought. Put the contributor's initials on the note so that you can come back to them easily for clarification.

3. Begin to arrange the cards in related groupings. As these thoughts emerge about the subject, the person at the board may begin to see various groupings. Begin grouping the available notes as they are offered and keep the intensity of note generation going as long as possible.

4. Complete the relationship groupings. Involve the group in clustering the notes into related groupings. It is often best to have everyone stand and do this silently to prevent talking the issues to death. Be prepared for some "loners" among the notes that don't seem to belong anywhere. Avoid forcing them into a group; they often belong in their own individual group. Some notes may need to be duplicated for different groupings.

5. Once the groups have been formed, look for a note that captures the intent of each group and place it at the top as a header card. If there isn't one, create one with a word or phrase that does capture the intent.

6. Once completed, this round of the diagram (Figure 3.1) can be transferred to paper for further evolution. New ideas and relationships often come up later. Related groupings should be located next to each other.

The affinity diagram effectively combines brainstorming and story-boarding to bring out the creative juices in the team and encourage breakthoughs in thought and ideas. It is a powerful tool for problem solving as well as requirements and design.

Interrelationship Digraph

The interrelationship digraph, in contrast to the affinity diagram which only shows logical groupings, helps map the *logical* relationships between the related items uncovered in the affinity diagram. More complex problems require more sophisticated tools to represent the complexity. The interrelationship digraph can be used when there are overly complex interrelationships among the parts or components of the problem, when proper sequencing of issues is required, and there is enough time to fully analyze the problem at hand. Unlike the flowchart, which is linear, the interrelationship digraph encourages nonlinear or multidirectional thinking.

The digraph shows the cause and effect relationships among many key elements. It can be used to identify the causes of problems or to work backward from a desired outcome to identify all of the causal factors that would need to exist to ensure the achievement of an outcome. The process to create the digraph is as follows:

1. Have the *right* 7 ± 2 people come together to work on the problem or opportunity.

2. Spend time to clearly state the problem or issue under discussion—software defects, customer retention, whatever. Write this on a sticky note.

3. Take the key issue and place it either in the center of a white board (Software Defects in Figure 3.2) or on one side or the other (Software Reliability in Figure 3.3).

4. Generate related issues by brainstorming or by using the notes generated for the affinity diagram (except the header notes). As a

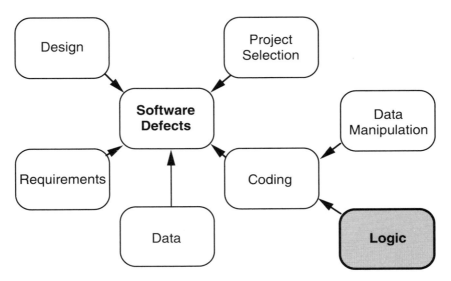

Figure 3.2 Interrelationship Digraph (central)

rule of thumb, there should be more than nine and less than fifty notes when completed, otherwise the problem is either too simple or too complex for this method.

5. Once the notes have all been created and arranged with respect to the key issue, draw one-way arrows to indicate the cause-and-effect relationship among all of the components of the diagram. Avoid two-way arrows; decide which component has the most influence and draw the arrow in one direction only. For example, in Figure 3.2, logic errors *cause* coding errors which *cause* software defects. In Figure 3.3, database software *affects* system reliability which *affects* software reliability.

6. Identify the key issues with darker lines or other shading—logic errors and human entry errors.

7. Revise the diagram as necessary.

The key factors affecting the main problem or opportunity can now be examined using the tree diagram. As interrelationships and interactions are explored, the diagram can be enhanced to show additional learnings as they become clear.

The interrelationship digraph can also provide a clear picture of how objects interact in an object-oriented system. Each bubble serves as an object and the cause-effect arrow describes a message initiated by a given object that affects another. Most bubbles can be described using nouns

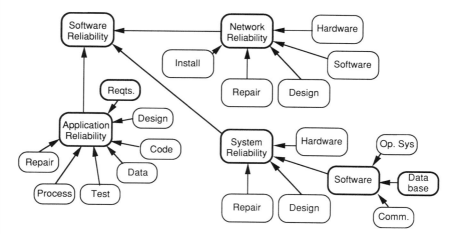

Figure 3.3 Interrelationship Digraph (directional)

and the arrows as verbs (e.g., man *turns* handle; handle *opens* latch; man *opens* door).

INTERMEDIATE PLANNING

The tree diagram, matrix diagram, and matrix data analysis provide the next level of planning for quality. The tree diagram maps specific tasks to primary and secondary goals. It maps the methods required to achieve corporate goals. The matrix diagram shows the interrelationship of large groups of characteristics, functions, tasks. It is the most widely used diagram. The matrix data analysis chart can be used to more graphically display the relationship of key attributes in the matrix diagram.

Tree Diagram

In America, we have an unfortunate ability to leap from the concept to the details without considering all of the issues required for implementation. These come back to bite us later, causing significant delays. The tree diagram helps identify all of the activities required. The tree diagram (Figure 3.4) shows the key goals, their sub-goals, and key tasks. It is similar in design and function to the cause-and-effect (Ishikawa) diagram. The affinity diagram and interrelationship digraph will usually surface the key issues for breakthrough improvement in quality. The tree diagram helps identify the sequence of tasks or functions required to

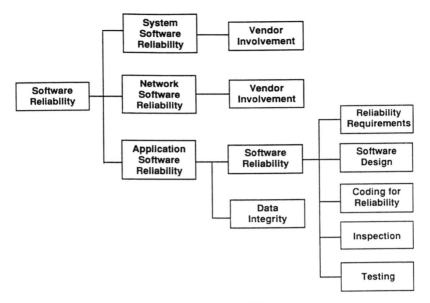

Figure 3.4 Tree Diagram

accomplish the resolution of each issue. It forces us to think about all of the interim tasks required to accomplish an objective. The tree diagram helps identify what needs to be done, how to do it, and the relationship between goals and activities. The tree diagram can be used any time an implementation process is considered complex, or there are significant consequences for completing only part of the tasks, or there are significant roadblocks to successful implementation.

The tree diagram can help translate customer desires into product characteristics for Quality Function Deployment (Figure 3.5). It can also be used like an Ishikawa diagram to uncover the causes of a particular problem (Figure 3.6). The process for constructing the tree diagram is similar to the Ishikawa diagram in many respects:

1. Develop a clear and specific statement of the problem, issue, or objective to be addressed. In many cases, this statement can come from the affinity diagram or interrelationship digraph, or it can just come from a specific instance of a problem.

2. Starting with this on a card or sticky note at the left of a wall or white board, brainstorm all of the tasks and sub-goals necessary to accomplish or resolve the issue. Ask the question: "What do we need to do to accomplish this goal or resolve this problem? In

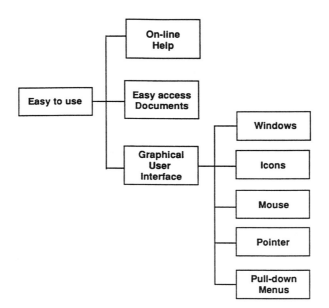

Figure 3.5 Customer Desires into Product Characteristics

the case of cause-and-effect analysis, ask: ''Why did this occur?'' As you brainstorm, begin ordering the sequence of notes to show the logical flow of what has to happen to accomplish the objective.

3. Once you've completed the first round, continue to ask the question about each of the generated tasks until they are chunked down to an actionable level.

4. Check the logic of the diagram in the same way as the Ishikawa: Start at the right and work your way back to the left by asking: ''If we do this, will it lead to the accomplishment of the previous task?'' If the answer is no, then the logic is flawed and you will need to clear it up before proceeding.

Matrix Diagrams

Where the tree diagram helps us identify the logic and flow required to accomplish a given task, the matrix diagram helps prioritize tasks or issues in ways that aid decision making. Matrix diagrams can also identify the connecting points between large groups of characteristics, functions, and tasks. It can also show the ranking or priority of each

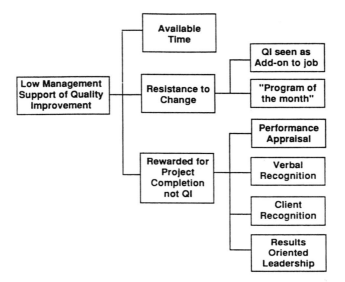

Figure 3.6   Cause-effect Tree

connection in relationship to the others. Matrices are a key element of QFD and a powerful tool to demonstrate the rich interconnections that exist in a software environment.

Prioritization matrices (Figure 3.7) can help narrow the field of key issues and options. Often combined with tree diagrams, prioritization matrices can rank various choices in terms of impact on the customer, reduction in cycle time, defects, costs, and so on. Prioritization matrices give us a way to represent all of the subjective knowledge a team has about various aspects of the problem or improvement.

Matrices can be used in many ways to show relationships. Matrices match a horizontal row of characteristics with a vertical column of other characteristics (Figure 3.8). They can be shaped like an L, a T, or a three-dimensional, inverted Y. The L-shaped matrix helps display relationships among any two different groups of people, processes, materials, machines, or environmental factors. The T-shaped diagram is simply two L-shaped diagrams connected together showing the relationships of two different factors to a common third one. The Y-shaped matrix helps identify interactions among three different factors. The X-shaped matrix (two T's back to back) is occasionally useful.

Figure 3.9 combines matrices with tree diagrams to show the relationship between the trees or other characteristics. Two trees can be used or more commonly, one tree, on the left, is used to map the tasks developed

Improvement Opportunity	Impact on			
	Customer	Cycle Time	Defect Rate	Costs

1 = Low, 3 = Medium, 9 = High

Figure 3.7 Prioritization Matrix

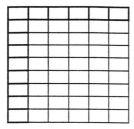
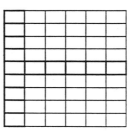
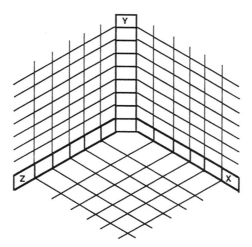

Figure 3.8 L, T, and Y Matrices

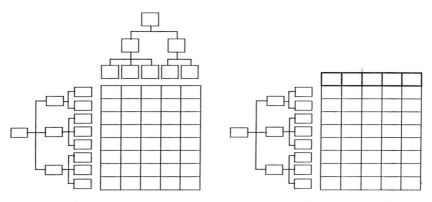

Figure 3.9 Matrices Using Tree Diagrams and Other Characteristics

with tree diagramming to the departments and organizations that will use them.

The processes for developing a matrix are relatively simple:

1. Using tree diagrams or brainstorming, generate two to four sets of characteristics to be compared.
2. Choose the proper matrix to represent the interactions.
3. Put the characteristics on the axes of the matrix.
4. Rank the interactions as 9–highest, 3–medium, 1–low, or blank (none).

Matrices are invaluable tools for determining interactions and therefore widely used. The matrix diagram helps patterns of relationships emerge and evolve. In the complex information systems of today, even in the most logical of systems develops unforeseen interactions. The process has been related to a plate of spaghetti: pull on one strand and many other strands will move. Matrix diagrams can help predict which ones will move.

Matrix data analysis (Figure 3.10) helps present the information contained on the matrix diagram into a more graphical format for easier use. It can more easily show the relationship between two customer-oriented characteristics; in this case, speed and ease of use of various operating systems. Although more often used for market research, planning, and developing new products, the matrix data analysis diagram can be used in many ways to help customers understand the trade-offs in their requirements.

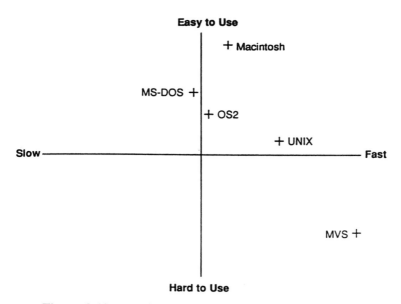

Figure 3.10 Matrix Data Analysis of Operating Systems

DETAILED PLANNING

The two remaining tools for detailed planning are the process decision program chart and arrow diagram. The PDPC helps identify the possible exceptions that might occur when attempting to implement solutions to problems. The PDPC also helps cast a critical eye on the implementation plan. The PDPC assumes that the path from where you are to any goal will be uncertain and imperfect. Otherwise, all we would have to do is plan a product and create it, and then we would be done. Unfortunately, there are many things to learn along the way. This is why the Shewhart cycle includes checking and acting to improve. The PDPC chart helps check our underlying assumptions, prevent problems from occurring, and plan a course of action if problems occur.

PDPC Chart

The PDPC is like the tree diagram in structure (Figure 3.11), except that it seeks to identify all of the things that can go wrong and specify countermeasures to prevent or correct them. The PDPC chart lets our natural critic run wild and offers our realist a chance to put activities in place to prevent problems before they occur. Development of the PDPC can begin with the tree diagram of a process or product. Start with the

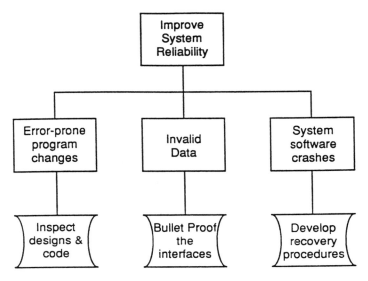

Figure 3.11   PDPC Chart of Reliability Countermeasures

first step and begin asking ''What could go wrong at this step?'' ''What other paths might this take?'' The PDPC diagram lets the critic in all of us find a natural expression that supports rather than defeats the activities necessary to accomplish change.

The PDPC chart lends itself to new or unusual tasks or processes that may be complex. It can help prevent problems any time the risk of failure is high. The PDPC chart asks: ''What would happen if the worst possible thing happens?''

Arrow Diagram

The arrow diagram (Figure 3.12) is closely related to a critical path method (CPM) or PERT diagram. It is also known as an activity network diagram. It can be used to plan the schedule for any series of tasks and to control their completion. The arrow diagram removes most of the exotic complexity of CPM and PERT methods, and retains the flow from task to task and the timing required for each task. It does, however, require that you know what each task is and how long it takes. Without such knowledge, it's difficult to develop the arrow diagram. To develop the diagram:

1. Brainstorm all of the tasks required to complete a given project, including the estimated time required for each task. Again, note cards are useful for this process.

The Seven Management and Planning Tools

Charting your course
to new adventures
and safe harbors.

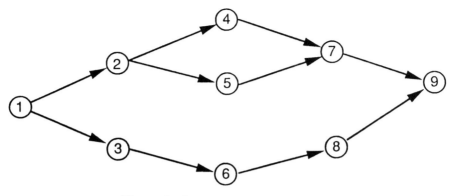

Figure 3.12   Arrow (PERT) Diagram

2. Sequence all of the cards from the start to finish, removing duplications, adding new ones as additional tasks are identified, and placing parallel activities where they belong.
3. Reevaluate the shortest, longest, and average estimated times for each task and identify the longest path through the diagram.
4. Use the diagram to track progress of each activity throughout the project life cycle. Any time an element gets in jeopardy, it may need to be examined and necessary resources shifted to complete it.

SUMMARY

The seven management and planning tools help plan quality improvements, identify valid customer requirements (affinity diagram, interrelationship digraph, tree diagram, matricies, matrix data analysis), potential roadblocks to providing them (PDPC), and processes for delivering them on time and on budget (arrow diagram). These tools help plan and manage complex issues in a business environment. These tools will also help quality improvement teams hone and refine their efforts to more effectively meet the needs of their customers. Although teams need to master the original seven quality improvement tools, they may also receive great benefit from starting to use these tools to focus their efforts.

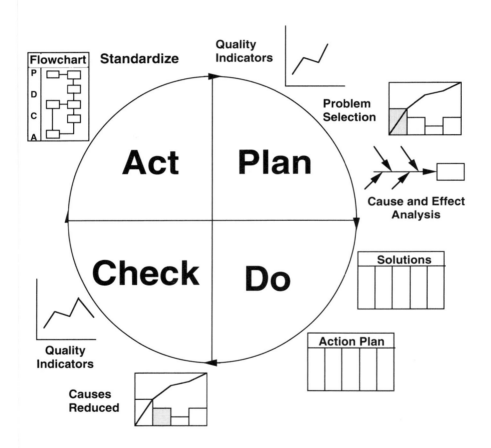

CHAPTER 4

The Software Quality Problem-Solving Process

Deal with the difficult,
While it is still easy.
Solve large problems
When they are still small.
Preventing large problems
By taking small steps
Is easier than solving them.
By small actions
Great things are accomplished

—Lao Tzu

The software process, like any process, is like gardening: we plan what we want to grow, plant the grain we want to harvest, and then we wait for the plants to grow and bear fruit. Unfortunately, in any freshly turned garden, weeds will grow, insects will infest, and birds will gorge. Without patiently checking the growing plants and taking action to weed the garden, our crop will never survive or thrive. Weeds, like defects, have a visible part (the symptom) and the invisible part (the root cause). All too often, reactive programmers, analysts, and managers fix the symptom and fail to fix the root cause of their problems. Software quality improvement pulls up the weeds, root cause and all. This process of pulling weeds prevents them from sowing more seeds and, over time, fewer and fewer weeds grow in the garden. No garden may ever be completely defect free, but it can approach perfection.

One of the more elegant ways of looking at these symptoms and causes, corrections and their effects uses the SCORE model.

THE SCORE MODEL

The SCORE Model is borrowed from Robert Dilts (Dilts 1991) because it is so effective at describing the quality improvement process. The SCORE model (Figure 4.1) consists of symptoms, causes, outcomes, resources, and effects. It shows the relationship in time of each of these key elements of the improvement process. In most software, defects are a symptom of a problem in both the product *and* the process that produced it. Defects, however, are not the root cause; they are only the top of the weed—the part we can see. Behind the symptom, something done by someone during the creation or evolution of the software *caused* the defect. By analyzing the root cause of these defects and bringing resources to bear on the software process, we can change the software process to prevent defects. Fewer defects will effect our competitive ability by:

- delighting customers
- reducing costs and rework
- increasing market share and profits
- and expanding the company's market and employment

One of the confusions that sometimes occurs with the problem-solving process comes from a certain human desire to use the same ointment for every injury. Problem-solving processes are invaluable for identifying and fixing the root cause of problems *in the process*. If the system is down, however, it is much better to dig in and fix the symptom *in the product* as quickly and efficiently as possible. Then, later, go back and determine what caused the problem using the problem-solving process.

The resources we bring to bear on evaluating and improving the software process include:

- the people who perform each step of the software life cycle
- the quality improvement process: PDCA—Plan, Do, Check, and Act

Some people hope that PDCA will stand for "please don't change anything," but in the revolutionary global market, this is not the case.

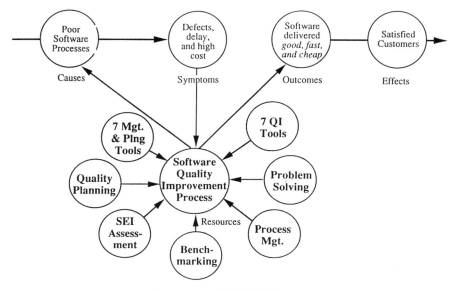

Figure 4.1 SCORE Model

Just as fixing a software defect takes time, fixing the originating process defect takes time. Fixing the process defect requires that we get back into the logic of the software process and the requirements and designs used to identify the root cause of the problem and potential solutions that will help achieve our outcomes. To be successful, quality improvement processes need well-formed outcomes.

WELL-FORMED OUTCOMES

Well-formed outcomes are: positive, specific, self-initiated, and controlled by the software staff in the appropriate contexts. Well-formed outcomes need to take into account the ecology of the entire software process and preserve the original intent of the process or behavior being improved. Some questions to ask and answers you might generate include:

- What do you want, specifically?
  —Zero defects
  —Reduced cycle time
  —Reduced response time
  —Increased transaction rate

- How will you know when you have it?
  - —Extremely low defect rates in delivered software 3/million
  - —50 percent reduction in software life cycle
  - —0.5 second response time
  - —Double the previous transaction rate
- Where, when, and with whom do you want this?
  - —New software products and ongoing software releases
  - —All new software creation projects
  - —On-line systems
  - —Airline reservation systems, etc.
- When you achieve this, what else will improve or be at risk?
  - —Overtime will decline
  - —Employee morale will improve
  - —Transaction error rates will decline
  - —Timing problems may occur because of increased transaction rate
- Which of the resources that you already have can be used to achieve this outcome?
  - —Quality improvement process
  - —Existing software process
- What is the first step?
  - —Use PDCA to begin to analyze the root cause of defects and prevent them

PDCA

No problem can stand the assault of sustained thinking.

—Voltaire

The PDCA—Plan, Do, Check, and Act—problem-solving process originated with Dr. Shewhart at Bell Labs in the early 1920s. It was here, in America, that today's quality gurus learned about quality improvement from one of its pioneers. All processes, including the problem-solving process (Figure 4.2), use some form of the PDCA process. To succeed at achieving our outcomes, we must:

- Plan how we are going to achieve them
- Do the work required to put them in place
- Check whether they are working or not
- Act to improve based on what we've learned

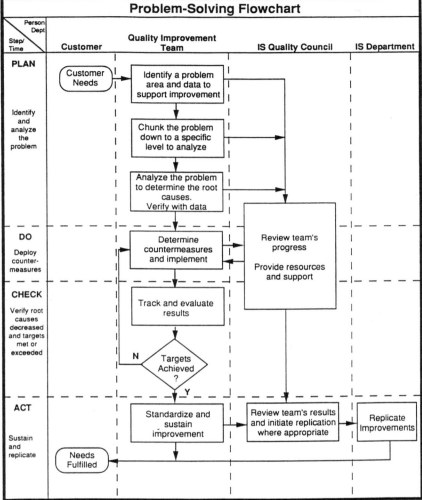

Figure 4.2   Quality Problem-Solving Process

PDCA uses a few main tools (Figure 4.3) to solve quality problems: checksheets, graphs, pareto charts, Ishikawa (or fishbone) diagrams, and flow charts. Checksheets (Figure 4.4) help a problem solver gather data about the software creation and evolution process. Graphs help identify trends in key indicators. Pareto charts (Figure 4.5) help identify the *vital few* problems as opposed to the *trivial many*. Then the Ishikawa diagram helps identify the *root causes* of problems. Flow charts help document processes so that they can be improved. From these tools, the quality

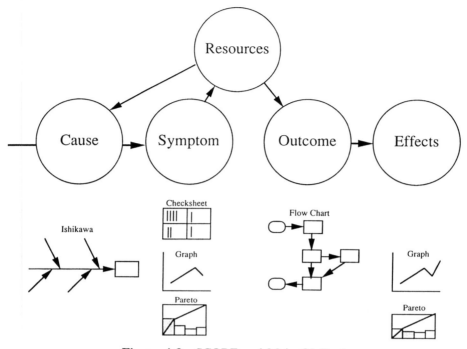

Figure 4.3   SCORE and Main QI Tools

Defects by Module Checksheet

	Module 1	Module 2	Module 3	Total
Total Defects	||	ЦЖ ЦЖ ЦЖ ЦЖ ||||	|	27
	2	24	1	27

Figure 4.4   Defects Checksheet

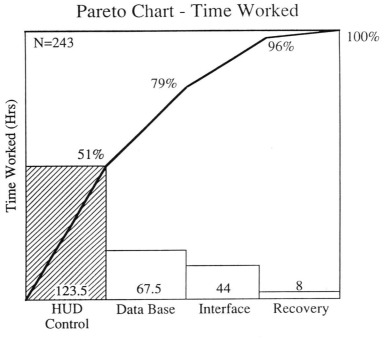

Figure 4.5 Pareto Chart by Sub-system

team can begin to identify how to evolve the product or process to eliminate quality problems.

PDCA—Plan, Do, Check, Act
  Plan—   Investigate the problem
                Define the process and measurements
                Chunk the problem down to an actionable level
                Hit enough singles and the runs will come in
  Do—   Identify and implement proposed solutions
  Check—   Track results
  Act—   Integrate, standardize, and sustain the improvements
                Enhance the process and measurements
                Duplicate the process and measurements where appropriate

Understanding quality improvement is not a one-chapter experience. There are more quality improvement techniques and tools out there than you can possibly imagine, but learning to use these three will benefit every aspect of your software process.

THE SEVEN QUALITY IMPROVEMENT TOOLS

The seven basic quality improvement tools include checksheets, Pareto charts, Ishikawa diagrams, scatter diagrams, histograms, graphs, and control charts. Using the first three, we can solve 85 percent of all quality problems. The remaining four help solve most of the remaining problems. The next seven tools, described in Chapter 3, help solve the more complex problems that begin to appear as we eliminate the simpler, obvious ones.

Most of us have experience driving a car. We use the speedometer to gauge our rate of travel. We use the odometer to track how far we've gone. We use the gas gauge to tell how much gas we have left and to estimate how far we can go. We use engine temperature gauges or warning lights to know how the electrical and mechanical portions of the car are performing. None of us would think of operating our cars without this information, yet most of us work in an information systems organization that has no such instrumentation. All we care about is whether the project crosses the finish line, regardless of how long it takes.

The seven quality improvement tools offer the essential ways to instrument the software life cycle so that we can begin to understand what's working and what's not. They are the key to massive improvements in quality and productivity.

Checksheets

Since software life cycles are often a data-free environment, checksheets (Figure 4.4) give us a way to begin collecting the kind of information we need to understand the software process. This is also a fairly inexpensive way to begin gathering data to determine if it will tell you anything. A useful sample can be taken in a week or two. Then, if it makes sense, we can begin to automate the collection of the information or simply continue to manually collect it as often as required to develop a useful trend of information.

Pareto Charts

Vilfredo Pareto, the Italian mathematician, postulated at the end of the last century that 20 percent of the people had 80 percent of the money, and that even if redistributed to the masses, in a short time they would have it all back. Pareto's rule—the 80/20 rule—is the key to much of the quality improvement process. In any IS environment, there are unlimited problems to be solved. The problem is that we cannot afford to solve all of them because 20 percent of the problems cause 80 percent of the waste and rework. The Pareto chart (Figure 4.5) gives us a graphical way of showing the "vital few" problems that need to be worked on.

The main bar of a Pareto chart, if it is under control of the people solving the problem, will be the key area to investigate. The other contributors may be important, but they can wait. We need to focus on solving the most important contributor to our problem first.

The main bar of a Pareto chart can often be chunked down into a more detailed Pareto. This allows us to focus on an even more specific problem and resolve it more quickly. Most initial teams struggle to solve their first problems because they try to work on too broad of a problem. By taking the main contributor, HUD Control (Figure 4.5), and chunking it down into its component parts (Figure 4.6) the team can focus its energies and quickly resolve the most important piece of the problem (icongen). Then, with the energy they've gained from solving that piece, they can go back and solve the rest, one at a time. Just remember that inch by inch, it's a cinch; yard by yard, it's going to be hard.

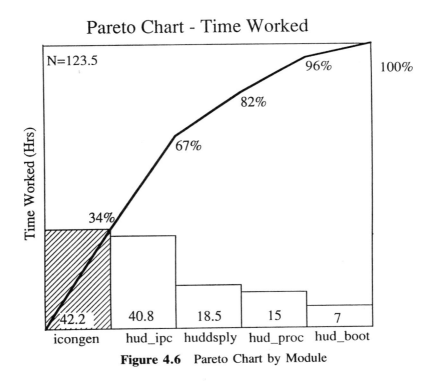

Figure 4.6 Pareto Chart by Module

Ishikawa Diagrams

Once the problem has been chunked down to a workable size, the team needs a visual way of working their way back to the root cause of the problem. No more fixing of just the symptoms, we want the root cause. We want a productive garden, not a weed patch.

The Ishikawa diagram is a key tool for identifying the causes of the problem and helping the team identify the root causes. There are several different kinds of Ishikawa (or fishbone) diagrams: standard, process, and Pareto to name a few.

The standard diagram (Figure 4.7) identifies the most common contributors to quality problems—people, processes, machines, materials, measurement, and environment. When you don't know what else to do, this is an excellent starting place. One of the most common ways of starting to construct this diagram is to brainstorm various causes of the problem. To maximize your productivity and minimize any relationship problems, start with the process bone and avoid the people bone until last. Another way to do this is to create an affinity diagram (Chapter 3) and then use the groupings as major bones.

The process Ishikawa is an exploded view of the process. The process diagram shows each step of a software process in order from left to right (Figure 4.8). This is often useful for analyzing the process more fully. The steps of a software project, for example, might include initiation, requirements, design, code, test, release, installation, and operation. Initiation ensures that we do the right work, so it might be more important than all of the other steps. Requirements and design are the breeding ground of as much as 60 percent of all software defects, so it

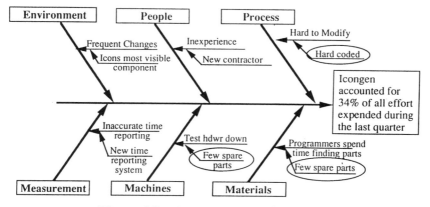

Figure 4.7 Generic Ishikawa Diagram

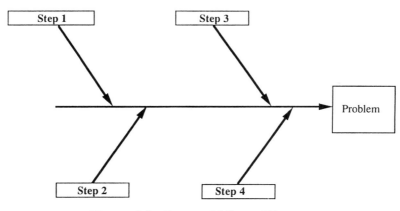

Figure 4.8   Process Ishikawa Diagram

pays to examine them thoroughly. Code, release, installation, and operation account for the rest of the problems.

A Pareto Ishikawa uses data from a Pareto chart to determine the
major bones of the diagram (Figure 4.9). From gathered data, we know
that the most common cause of defects is logic. Working from right to
left, we make major bones for each of the contributing categories. Using
data is always preferable to using gut feel, but most IS organizations will
have trouble finding the data to support this type of Ishikawa diagram
initially.

Graphs

Most people are familiar with the most common types of graphs—pie,
line, and bar, and it is surprising how few people can read them accurately. The pie chart shows the relative contribution of many things to the
whole. Like the Pareto, the slices of the pie should be arranged in
descending order starting from 12 o'clock and going clockwise around
the circle (Figure 4.10). The pie chart is a fairly static representation;
there is no concept of time attached to it. The line chart is best used to
indicate trends in data over time (Figure 4.11). It needs a ''good'' arrow
to help orient the reader's mind since the predominant metaphor in our
society is that ''up'' is good and ''down'' is bad. The bar chart can be
used to show more discreet differences (Figure 4.12).

These simple graphs are powerful tools for directing an organization's
thoughts. If we set up an indicator of bills or paychecks in error (Figure
4.13), then the organization will seek to drive it down to zero, because
what gets measured gets done. If we measure *only* lines of code produced

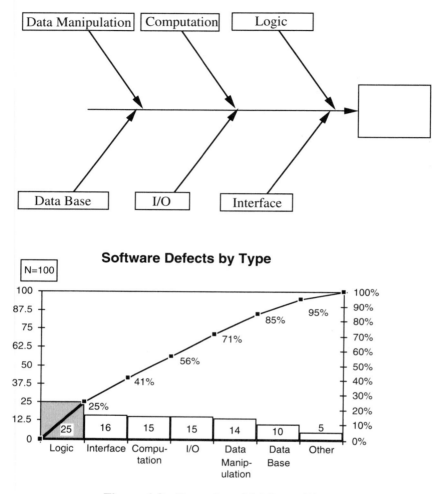

Figure 4.9   Pareto-based Ishikawa Diagram

per month, then the staff will try to optimize that indicator, often creating serious problems. If we focus on the customer, however, and their pain surrounding our product, the indicators we choose can drive dramatic improvements in quality as perceived by the customer. For example, with an on-line system, a line-graph indicator of hours lost due to application unavailability will drive dramatic improvements in our response to system problems. The system may still have bugs, but our ability to respond to them may slash unavailability by 50–75 percent.

Software Defects by Type

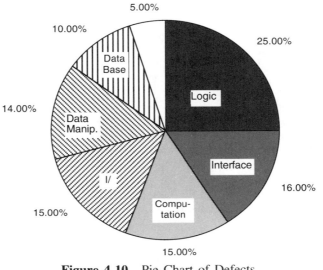

Figure 4.10   Pie Chart of Defects

Software Defects by Week

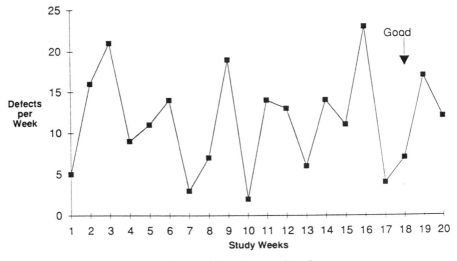

Figure 4.11   Line Graph of Defects

Software Defects by Week

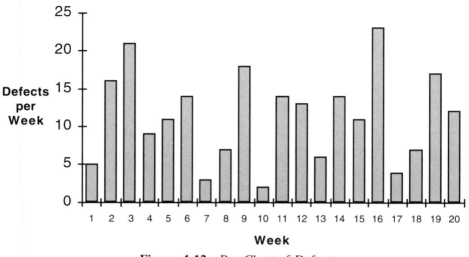

Figure 4.12 Bar Chart of Defects

Percent of Bills in Error

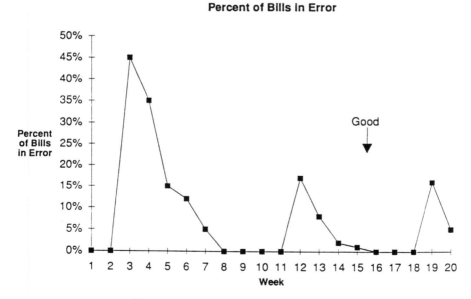

Figure 4.13 Billing Quality Indicator

Histograms

Histograms help show the distribution of data. It groups information into buckets. Figure 4.14 and Figure 4.15 show the number of modules of a given size in two different applications. Would it surprise you to learn that the second system is much easier to maintain?

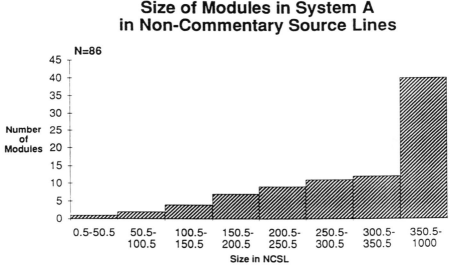

Figure 4.14 Histogram of Complex System

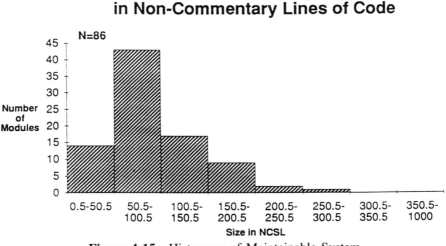

Figure 4.15 Histogram of Maintainable System

Control Charts

Control charts (Figure 4.16) help determine whether a process is "statistically" in control or wildly gyrating. Using at least 20 data points from different data sources—system down time per day, defects per KLOC, overtime worked—we can begin to determine if our systems and processes are within control or not. Since most IS organizations have barely repeatable processes, these are often out of control.

Causal analysis using the Ishikawa diagram can then identify the root cause of each out of control point. Over time, IS teams can eliminate these *special causes* and stabilize the process. Then they can begin to use PDCA to ensure that the process is capable of meeting the customer's needs.

Scatter Diagrams

Scatter diagrams (Figure 4.17) help identify the relationships between two variables. Could there be a correlation between the size of a program in lines of code and how long it runs? A scatter diagram would give you

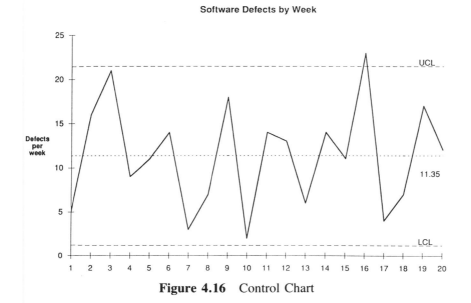

Figure 4.16 Control Chart

the answer. Scatter diagrams help verify the cause and effect between two variables. They are often helpful in verifying the root cause of a problem.

Flow Charts

Flowcharts (Figure 4.18) are a vital tool for visualizing a process. Although they have largely been abandoned by information systems organizations as a design tool, they are still highly effective ways to look at existing processes and fine tune them, *before* automating them. One group, for example, examined the process for getting a project approved and funded. At the time, the process was taking 45 days, longer than many of the small projects took to complete. The flowchart showed that there were 17 processes; almost a half a dozen sign-offs were required. Although many of these steps were necessary for larger, more expensive projects, they were a waste of resources for smaller projects. A revised process was developed for smaller projects that had seven steps, one approval, and took only six days. Flowcharting processes is the founda-

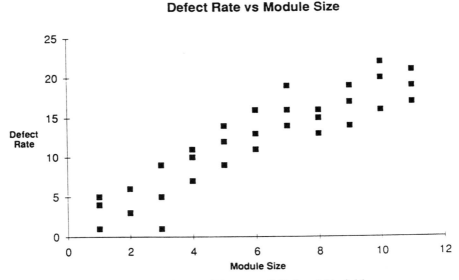

Figure 4.17   Scatter Diagram of Related Variables

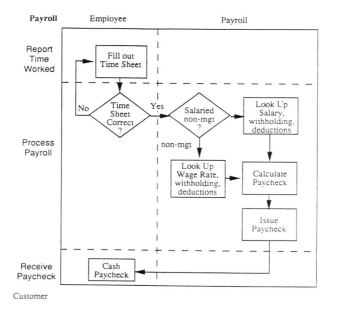

Figure 4.18 Simplified Payroll Flowchart

tion for *process management*—the definition and measurement of all processes so that they can be managed and improved. IS managers and analysts point to their wall of three-ring binders holding their methodology and say "there's our process," but it is rarely what they actually follow. Process management, using flowcharts, will define the process *as is*, identify where to measure the process to insure that the customer gets what they are asking for, and then seek ways to improve the process and its many components. We'll discuss process management in more detail in Chapter 10.

To construct a flowchart, you will need representatives from your suppliers, customers, and your group, including the supervisor, and a facilitator. These must be the people who actually do the work and everyone must participate in the development of the process. The people who work in the process understand it more completely than anyone else. Use a white board and sticky notes that can be moved around easily. Depending on the size of the process, multiple sessions may be required to fully define the process.

Use questions to illuminate activities and products of the process. "Where do the machines and materials come from? How is it transformed into a product or service? Who makes the decisions? How is it tested? Where do the outputs go? Who uses them?'' The only question to avoid at this point is ''Why?''

Once the flowchart is complete, improvements can be easily identified. Loops, for example, may mean rework. Why are we doing this over again? Some steps may be done in parallel instead of serially to reduce the time. Some steps may be combined; others may be given to the right group to do the work. Once the flow is streamlined, the process can be automated to more effectively serve the customer.

Process flowcharts help suppliers, customers, and employees figure out where they fit in the creation and delivery of service and products. They serve as useful training tools for new employees, suppliers, and customers. They promote a common understanding of what must be done to deliver a quality product or service. Communication opens up and work begins to flow instead of becoming logjammed as it once did.

SUMMARY

All of the quality improvement tools are useful in analyzing and solving problems in the software process. Simple graphs, checksheets, Pareto charts, and Ishikawa diagrams will typically solve 85 percent of all quality problems. Control charts, histograms, and scatter diagrams can help solve most of the remaining problems. The more advanced tools (Chapter 3) will help identify and resolve more complex problems as they arise. For most programmers, analysts, and managers, however, the simple basic tools are all you need for the moment. Refer to Appendix B for a complete example.

The quality improvement tools help us identify the problem during the *planning* phase of the quality improvement process, and then help us measure the results of our countermeasures during the *checking* phase of PDCA. Based on what we've *done* to improve and the results we've obtained, we can then *act* to improve. Teams and individuals continuously cycle through the problem-solving process, eliminating problems, and developing more skill at problem solving. Eventually, the problem-solving process becomes almost an unconscious way of thinking about problems and opportunities. This is the ultimate goal of quality improvement, to install an excellent strategy for problem-solving in every member of the organization, so that every day, in every activity, processes and products are continuously improved.

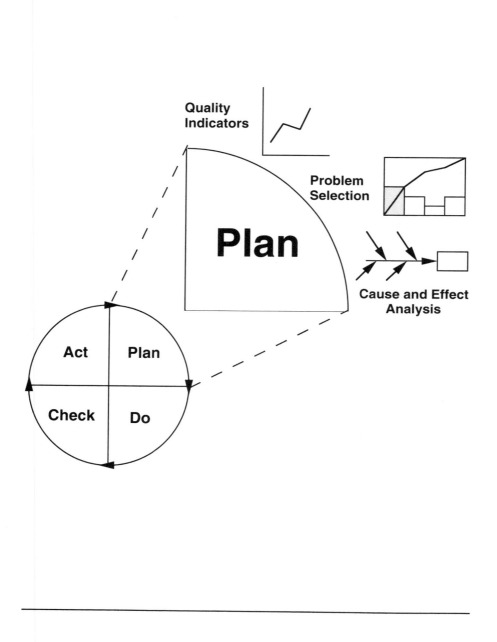

CHAPTER 5

Plan—Investigate the Problem

In most American businesses, employees and managers alike have been trained since birth to be reactive, to leap to solutions, to fix the symptom of the problem rather than its root cause. As Deming would suggest, 85 percent of all problems have their root in the processes used, not the people involved. A process is an interrelated collection of tasks that use specific inputs to create and deliver specific outputs. The software process, for example, uses specific customer requirements, software, hardware, and people to deliver a software system that is part of a larger process—billing, payroll, production control, etc. Where the software process may be owned by the IS organization, the larger process (e.g., billing) belongs to a different and often higher element in the corporation; often a business or market unit (Figure 5.1).

WHO'S THE CUSTOMER?

- **The first law of quality:** Know your customers.

For most quality improvement needs, the customer is the person who receives your output—the *next process* customer. This could be your supervisor when you give them a status report. This could be your employees when you give them guidance and leadership. This could be the *internal* customer who uses your software to serve a paying *external* customer.

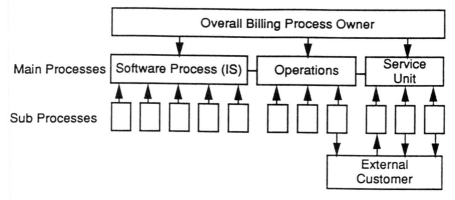

Figure 5.1   Process Ownership

• **The second law of quality:** Know your suppliers.

Just as you have next process customers, you are the next process customer of someone else. To some extent, your software can be of no higher quality than the computer resources, administrative staff, or data that you use to create the software. Your management chain may supply you with resources and support, and you may supply them with information of progress and potential risks.

There are people who service your local workstations and LAN, and others who operate the test computer. Your customer supplies you with requirements, test data, and subject matter experts. The government may supply you with regulations (e.g., tax tables for payroll).

To succeed in creating high-quality software, you have to clearly understand who your customers are and who your suppliers are. You will need to conduct at least an overview customer-supplier analysis.

Customer-Supplier Analysis

In every organization there is a customer-supplier chain (Figure 5.2), everyone serves someone else, who serves someone else, who ultimately serves the external paying customer.

One of the best ways to begin to understand your software process is to conduct what is called a customer-supplier analysis. For most people, this in itself is a revelation. Suddenly the number and complexity of customers and suppliers involved in producing a software product becomes glaringly obvious. For others, whole software groups become painfully aware that they don't know who their customer is at all. In some cases, support groups discover that they have been creating 60–80

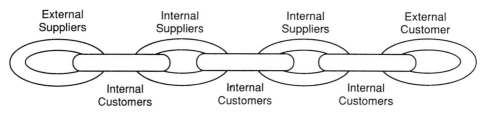

Figure 5.2   Customer-supplier Chain

hour weeks of work which has *no customer*. This is occasionally a painful but useful process of self-discovery.

Everyone in an IS organization has *next-process* customers—people who directly receive their requirements, designs, code, data, tests, documents, training, and so on—and *external* customers—*direct* customers who call in to request a product or service, and indirect customers like government agencies that dictate certain rules within the system. Next process customers can include other departments, work groups, or employees. If you are a designer, for example, coders and supervisors could both be your next-process customer.

Every customer-supplier analysis has five key ingredients (Figure 5.3):

- Upstream suppliers who provide the inputs to your process
- Inputs that your organizations use to produce its products
- Value adding processes that your group performs
- Outputs (Goods or services)
- Downstream customers who receive your outputs

Customer-supplier analysis investigates the entire food chain required to create and evolve a software application. A software application group, for example, might turn the application over to an operations center to run it. Along with the application goes a variety of supporting documentation and training to enable the operations center to run it. Your internal customer may also need status reports, documentation, and training to use the system. Together with the computer operations group, your customer will be able to serve the end customer.

To begin to analyze your customers and suppliers, ask the following questions:

1. What is the purpose of your work group? (Software creation, evolution, support, etc.)

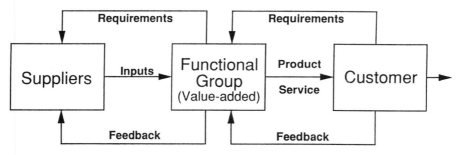

Figure 5.3   Customer-supplier Model

2. What do you produce? (Use nouns—programs, documentation, status reports, etc.)
3. Who uses your products or services?
4. What are your customer's requirements? How do you know? What are the characteristics that they look for in your product or service?
5. What are your main value-adding processes? (Use verbs)
6. What are the primary inputs to your value-adding process?
7. Who are your suppliers?
8. What are your requirements of your suppliers?
9. What is your feedback system?
   - What are your indicators of failure, inspection, and prevention costs?
   - How do you measure that you are meeting your customer's requirements?
   - How do you measure that your suppliers are meeting yours?

WHAT'S THE PROCESS?

Software Processes

The software and evolution processes consist of gathering requirements, designing systems or enhancements, coding, and testing. Using process management (Chapter 10), we can identify how these are being done today at a high level. Then we will need to develop lower level processes to describe how we do each of these major components. Requirements, for example, may be gathered by joint application design (JAD) or by more rapid techniques (Chapter 13). If, as the SEI suggests, our processes really aren't defined or measured, then we will need to define them as part of this first step toward quality improvement.

User Process

Our customer's processes are no more clearly defined than ours are. Automation is very effective in helping us do the things we already know how to do well. It is not effective, however, in helping us do things in the most effective and efficient manner unless we are already doing them well. Effective user processes must precede the automation of systems. Otherwise, creating an application will only trap the user in unproductive methods of behavior for years to come. Most processes, especially white-collar ones, evolve *away* from their original business intent over time.

According to Phillip Thomas (Anderson 1991), people waste about one third of their time working inefficiently, but *delays* in their business processes waste 90 percent. The time is taken up with steps and procedures that add no value or benefit to your customer or yourself. Inspections and testing add little value to a product; all they do is remove defects that early processes inserted into the software. When you prevent the defects from entering the software, you no longer need to inspect or test them out. There is only one reason to inspect or test a product—to gather data about where the process isn't working to serve as a guide about how to improve the process to prevent defects in the first place. You might think that removing these steps and procedures would increase errors, but it reduces them. By building a PDCA loop into each cycle, you:

- Inspect to identify the defects created in this cycle
- Use the data to identify the root causes of defects from each cycle
- And improve the process *each time* you go through.

Instead of one cycle a year for a typical software project, you can get many times as many improvements each year. The faster you or your customer cycle through a process, the more you can improve the quality of the product or service.

If you just automate the existing process, you are doing a disservice to your customer. The best way to help your customer is to begin by to drawing a picture of their process using a structured flowchart, identifying measurement points, and then eliminating any steps that fail to add value. Building a process management system is essential to understanding, simplifying, and automating a customer's process.

As you read this, some of you may be as skeptical as I was when I was originally exposed to this concept. After all, we abandoned flowcharts as a design tool years ago. They've long since been replaced by data flow and entity relationship diagrams. What's all this stuff about flowcharts?

Well, flowcharts are not the best program design tool, but they can easily diagram a user's process in such a way that:

1. You can understand it
2. You can identify how to simplify it *before* you automate it.

Begin by involving the user, their customers and suppliers. All members must contribute to the development of the flowchart. Keep the evolving flowchart visible to everyone at all times. Encourage questions; they are the life blood of getting a well-defined process. Use questions to illuminate issues like:

- Who makes the decision?
- Who supplies what to whom?
- When does each process occur?
- What would happen if . . . (we did something else)?
- What stops us from doing it a different way?
- Where does the product go?

The only question to avoid is the "why" question, which invariably throws people into an endless loop of telling war stories and taking unproductive side trips.

By involving the people who actually perform the process, they gain a sense of control over it. Once this feeling is established, they often feel open to making change in the process. Once they have described the process, they can also begin to identify useful improvements.

You can evaluate each step or series of steps in a process by asking the following questions:

- Is it making me (or my customer) more responsive?
- Is it reducing costs, cycle time, or defects?
- Does it free any resources I have tied up or save me money?

If the answer to these three questions is *no*, cut the step out of the process *before* you hard wire it into the software. Your customer will love you for it.

A well-diagrammed process assists users and their customers and suppliers in knowing their roles. It also improves communication among all parties and gets you, the system creator, an inside track on understanding their real needs. The resulting flowchart often serves as useful documentation for requirements and training.

WHAT'S THE PROBLEM AREA?

Most problems that teams want to solve are at too high a level. Rather than nibble away at the elephant, they try to swallow the whole thing in one gulp. To begin to identify the *right things* to work on, we need to identify problem areas. What is a problem area? A problem exists anywhere there is a *gap* between where we are and where we want to be. So, a software team could have a problem with defects in the production system—more defects than they would like. Or the IS management team might want to provide more value at lower cost and higher reliability. In other words, we're doing okay now, but we could be two to five times better, faster, and cheaper—a gap between where we are and where we want to be. Masaaki Imai (1986) calls these problem areas *themes*

Problem Evaluation Matrix

Problem Area (Theme)	Customer	Product or Service	Process	Measurement
Increase Application Reliability	End User	Application Availability	Software Life Cycle	System Interruptions and downtime
Reduce Cycle Time	Business Unit	Application	Software Life Cycle	Mean time to implement changes
Improve Customer Perceptions of Information Systems	Information Systems	?	?	Survey
Reduce Application Response Time	End User	Application Response Time	Hardware, Software, Network Design	End-to-End System Response Time

Figure 5.4   Evaluating Themes and Problem Areas

because they are broad areas where we are motivated to find improvements to satisfy and delight the customer.

To help teams focus on problems that can be solved by the quality improvement process, you will need to know their customers, products, services, processes, and measurements (Figure 5.4).

To help you identify and select themes successfully, you need to do more than just brainstorm problems in your area. Brainstorming alone will often lead you to topics that are "solutions" or vaguely defined problems. The following process will help turn your focus on your group, your customers, your products, your processes, and the measurements you will need to successfully complete your Quality Improvement (QI) story.

To allow for rapid and accurate creation and evaluation of themes, please use the following process, the problem analysis matrix (Figure 5.4), and the term definition matrix below.

Theme Selection Process

Step	Process
1.	Brainstorm a list of your next-process customers. If the list includes more than 7 ± 2, multivote down to five main customers.
2.	For each next-process customer, brainstorm a list of products (e.g., requirements, design, code, executable programs, JCL, etc.) or services (e.g., system operation, trouble diagnosis, etc.) that your group provides.
3.	For each of these products or services, list the processes used to deliver them (e.g., for code, processes might include coding, inspecting, and unit testing).
4.	For all of these customers, products, and processes, identify the data and measurements available to complete a QI story (e.g., code defects, response time, program failures, system unavailability, etc.).
5.	With this complete list of next process customers, products, and processes, brainstorm a list of potential themes that could be solved using the QI process and *the available data*. Multivote to 3-5.
6.	Make your brainstormed themes more specific by challenging the words used in the theme and improve them by asking: Who, What, Where, When, or How specifically?
7.	Use consensus to select your theme. Define the words in the selected theme using the term definition matrix:

Term	Definition
Customer	Customer service representatives using the XYZ system

Specifying Themes

Step six of the process requires more discussion because it directly impacts the success of the team. There are only two types of themes: *increase* and *decrease*. These are often two sides of the same coin: an increase in reliability is the same as a decrease in number of defects or the defect rate. An increase in timeliness is the same as a decrease in cycle time—the time to develop or deliver a product or service. An increase in availability is the same as a decrease in unavailability or down time.

It is usually easiest to measure and graph either time, defects, or cost. So most themes can be easily expressed as a decrease in one of these indicators:

- **time**   (cycle time, time/unit)
  - —availability   (application system availability or unavailability)
  - —efficiency   (response time, run time, percent tape used)
  - —reliability   (time between system failures or defects)
- **defects**   (# of defects, defects/time)
  - —accuracy   (e.g., percent of bills, reports, checks in error)
  - —complaints
- **cost**   (cost/unit, cost/time)

Themes based on specific measurements like these have a strong chance of success. Themes based on subjective data, like surveys, have a limited initial chance of success. A theme like "improve customer perceptions," for example, is too general, vague, and difficult to measure. It only serves the IS organization. It seems to ask the question "Do I look good?" rather than "How can I help my customer?"

QI teams create world hunger themes by over *generalizing*. To understand a theme or problem area clearly, we must investigate, investigate, investigate, until a clear map of the problem can be drawn. The way we explore these confusing themes is through language:

I keep six honest serving men
(They taught me all I knew)
Their names are What and Why and When
And How and Where and Who.

—*Rudyard Kipling*

Generalizations are a form of fog and these are perhaps the most insidious of flaws. When the team fails to describe something clearly, it's often overlooked until much later in the QI process. Time drags on, tempers flare, and credibility flies out the window. Teams don't go out of their way to over generalize. They do so by using vague nouns and verbs. Vague words allow each team member to draw their own pictures, sounds, and feelings about the team's problem.

To get a theme that can be solved in 52-80 hours of meetings, teams need to:

- Challenge all nouns with the following:
  —Who, specifically?
  —What, specifically?
  —When, specifically?
  —Where, specifically?
- Challenge all verbs with:
  —How, specifically?

Example:
Problem: Improve system response time
—What system, specifically? (Billing)
—What kind of response time, specifically? (Terminal)
—When? Day? Night? Evenings? Weekends? (Business Hours)
—Where, specifically? (Customer Service Center)
—How specifically, would you want to improve response time? (Reduce it).
New Theme: Reduce billing system response time at the Customer Service Center terminals during regular business hours.

Processes Disguised as Nouns

Another form of generalization involves *processes* that have been turned into *objects*—verbs that have been turned into nouns. Words that end with -ment, -ion, -ance, -ence, -bility, usually fall into this category— manage*ment* (manage), informat*ion* (inform), mainten*ance* (maintain), availa*bility* (to make available). These vague words often obscure the specific understanding a team needs to successfully complete a QI story.

For an example, take the word *perception*. The verb is *perceive*. To begin to clarify the team's direction, the team needs to transform the noun back into a verb: "*Who* perceives *what?*" (The internal customer perceives our product's quality.) "*How* do they perceive it, specifically?" (By using the product.) "*What* do they perceive?" (Response time, bills in error, etc.) These forms of generalizations are so common that we often overlook them, and then the theme remains too general to be chunked down to the next lower level.

Use "who, what, when, where, and how" to challenge these generalizations. Make them more specific before evaluating the themes using the problem evaluation matrix.

WHAT ARE THE CUSTOMER'S REQUIREMENTS?

Once you've clarified the customer's requirements, you then need to ask "Are they valid?" The customer may always be right, but what they ask for may not be possible. There can be invalid requirements. For example, producing a software system without any defects and at no cost is an invalid requirement. To help you determine if a requirement is valid, you can use the acronyms SMART and RUMBA.

SMART stands for:
- Specific
- Measurable
- Achievable
- Reasonable
- Time constrained

RUMBA stands for:
- Reasonable
- Understandable
- Measurable
- Believable
- Achievable

If you consider your relationship with the customer to be more of a dance, then you might prefer to use RUMBA to test requirements. The intellectual approach is to be SMART about defining requirements. So, just suppose the customer asks for a minor enhancement when the system is already in the middle of system test and due to go out on Friday. Because of the way most software processes work, the request may not be reasonable. Opening up code to make last minute enhancements during system test is an invitation to disaster. Similarly, the vague request for "ongoing support" is neither specific or time constrained. Remember, your concept of "ongoing support" and your customer's are often light years apart. When your customer tells you to "jump," ask "how high?, how far?, and where?" before you leap into action. We are used to reacting to requests without making sure they make sense. Use questions to clarify. Negotiate until you reach a win-win solution. Otherwise, neither you nor your customer will be satisfied.

Tools for Customer Satisfaction

In every business, there are "moments of truth" where you have an opportunity to build your relationship with your customer or to destroy it.

The old saying goes "You never get a second chance to make a first impression." And I would add that you have to keep enhancing that impression every time you meet with your customer, even the most surly ones. Your toughest customers will bring you more business than you can imagine if you satisfy their needs.

Every time you pick up the phone to make a call or answer one, you are at a moment of truth. Every meeting with your customer, even if it's only for a moment in the hallway, is a moment of truth. Software projects are lost in the relationship arena rather than the technical arena in most instances. Relationships are a prize worth achieving. Develop them.

WHERE'S THE DATA?

Quality improvement teams stumble if they try to evaluate a problem when there is no data. The first time a team goes through the process, they should select problems where data is readily available. Good data comes from:

- knowing what to measure and how to measure it
- having a consistent unit of measurement created by those being measured
- having a regular frequency for measuring it
- having goals and targets for improvement in the measurement
- having people committed to collecting the information

So before choosing a problem, the questions to ask are: Is data already collected? Is it collected at least quarterly? Who collects it? What measurement would indicate that we had achieved the desired level of quality? For most organizations, data exists in some format. Most of it, unfortunately, is only indirectly customer focused. Some common examples include:

- Change Management System—change requests and trouble reports
- Operational Logs—software completion codes
- Defects per KLOC (1,000 lines of code)

To begin to get at the heart of customer satisfaction, however, we will need to begin collecting, tracking and evaluating indicators of their dissatisfaction. Some "customer-oriented" indicators of dissatisfaction could include:

- Number of customer complaints and escalations
- Percent of customer bills in error
- Hours of system down time per month

More experienced teams can begin to identify and collect this kind of data where it doesn't exist. In most cases, this means everywhere in the IS organization. Most indicators in an IS organization focus on internal indicators of efficiency rather than external, customer-oriented indicators of effectiveness. To collect data within a process, measure the inputs, outputs, and key hand-offs within the process (e.g., from requirements to design). Input indicators measure supplier quality. Output indicators measure customer satisfaction and dissatisfaction. In-process metrics measure conformance to the customer's valid requirements. Other useful indicators include trends in key customer-oriented metrics like cycle time, defect rate, and cost/function.

The key quality improvement tool for collecting data is the checksheet (Figure 5.5). This simple example collects information about customer complaints and categorizes them. From the checksheet alone it is fairly easy to see that complaints are fairly evenly distributed throughout the year, but that almost half concern the category of support. Of course, you wouldn't need to collect a whole year's worth of data to know that customer support needed improvement. The first twenty complaints would

Customer Complaints
Monthly Checksheet   Year 1992

	Jan	Feb	Mar	Apr	May	Jun	Jul	Aug	Sep	Oct	Nov	Dec	Total
Relationship	III	II	I	II	I		II		III	II	IIII		20
Support	卌	IIII	II	卌	II	卌 II	III	卌 III	III	卌	III	卌 IIII	56
Software	II	I	卌	I	II	II	III	III	I	II	I	III	26
Documentation		II			I	II		II		I			8
Training	I						II			I	II		6
Other		II		II		I	II		II	I			10
Total	11	9	10	10	6	12	12	13	9	12	10	12	126

Figure 5.5 Checksheet

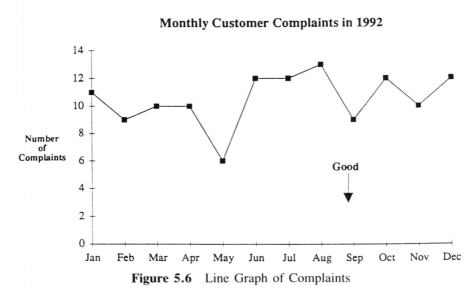

Monthly Customer Complaints in 1992

Figure 5.6   Line Graph of Complaints

give you enough data to initiate immediate action to improve the support process. Even from the first two months of data it is fairly obvious that the problem area is support and the theme to work on is "Reduce customer complaints about support."

Then you can use the data to draw the line graph shown in Figure 5.6. Customer complaints are higher than we would like and they need to be decreased.

Once you have begun to collect indicators that represent the customer's dissatisfaction with your product or service, you can then begin to focus on improving it. The first step is to further evaluate the problem and to write a problem statement.

WHAT PROBLEM, SPECIFICALLY?

The old saying asks: "How do you eat an elephant?" Answer: "One bite at a time." The biggest challenge facing a quality improvement team or individual is choosing which bite to take first, which problem to solve. Often, there are problems that have been lying around for years—world-hunger sized problems. Teams often forget that quality improvement is *kaizen*—small, incremental improvements to dozens of components of the overall problem. The countermeasure to this scoping problem is to narrow the team's focus to a problem that can be solved with 20–100 hours worth of effort. Narrowing the focus is known by many names— stratification, chunking down, or decomposition.

Chunking down helps the team focus on one specific problem within the overall theme or problem area that can be solved with a selected group of countermeasures. Many teams fail by trying to eat too much of the elephant at one time. If you've ever stuffed too much food in your mouth, you know what happens. You chew and chew and chew because you don't want to look silly by spitting part of it out. So you keep chewing, trying to maneuver the food into a position that you can swallow it. Even then, it goes down with effort and often causes indigestion because you didn't chew it enough before swallowing.

The same thing happens to a team that doesn't get specific enough about what it's going to solve. The main tool to assist in chunking down to a specific problem is the Pareto chart (Figure 5.7) although pie charts, bar charts, and histograms can also be used.

Pareto Charts

The Pareto chart helps the quality team focus on the *vital few* components that contribute the majority of the problem. In this way, the team's effort is both effective and efficient. How many times have teams worked out

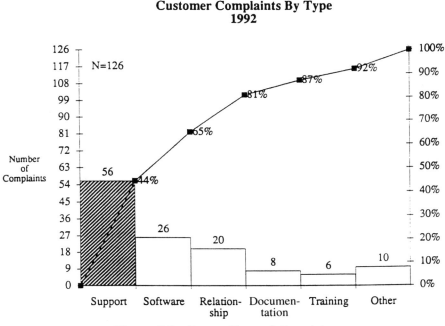

Figure 5.7 Pareto Chart of Complaints

detailed solutions to the *many other trivial* problems associated only to discover that they've wasted their time?

The Pareto chart combines a bar graph with a cumulative line graph. The bars are placed from left to right in descending order. The cumulative line graph shows the percent contribution of all preceding bars. This graph shows where the effort can be focused for maximum benefit.

Looking at Figure 5.7, the support category is twice as high as its nearest neighbor and accounts for 44 percent of the total number of complaints. Using this information, the team would focus on improving support before spending any effort on any other category. Unfortunately, any team attempting to begin work on "support" issues would quickly discover that this is too broad of a topic. Most teams can benefit from chunking down another level (Figure 5.8) or two. Only when it seems to be ridiculous to chunk down any farther does it make sense to stop.

Figure 5.8 reveals that response to emergency problems is a key customer complaint. Forty-one percent of complaints about support revolved around responsiveness. With this information in hand, the team can move forward to solve the customer's specific problem.

Problem Definition

The old adage states that "A problem well stated is a problem half solved." This is doubly true of quality problems. Problems must be

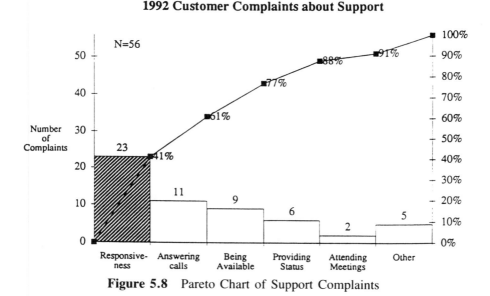

1992 Customer Complaints about Support

Figure 5.8 Pareto Chart of Support Complaints

specific, measurable, and focus on the pain caused by the gap between where we are and where we want to be. To be specific, a problem must tell as much as possible about who, what, when, where, and how the problem occurred.

There are three key types of problems: *increase* (e.g., sales), *decrease* (e.g., expenses), and ideally *zero* (e.g., defects). The problems shown in Figures 5.7 and 5.8 are a *zero* problem. Ideally, we never want a customer to have to complain. Now, we can write a problem statement that describes the problem:

> During 1992 in the IS department, responsiveness to emergency problems accounted for 41 percent of all customer complaints about support and one-fifth of all complaints. Ideally, no customers should have to complain about responsiveness.

This problem statement is specific, measurable, and focuses on the pain between our desired and actual level of support.

Goals and Targets

Now that we have the problem defined, we can set a target for improvement. The goal, we know, is zero customer complaints about responsiveness. Like other elephants, however, we can't eat the whole problem in one gulp. We have to set targets to get there.

Here the team uses the best knowledge available to set a target. Half the distance to the goal is one commonly used target. With data from other IS organizations, we could say that we want to be ''as good as the best,'' which is another common target. Or we can identify how much we think we can improve (e.g., 75 percent reduction in complaints).

Given this specific problem statement and a target for improvement, the team can then begin to analyze what went wrong.

WHY DID THE PROBLEM OCCUR?

> *For every thousand hacking at the leaves of evil, there is one striking at the root.*
>
> *—Thoreau*

So far, we've only examined what happened, where it happened, who was involved, when it happened, and how it happened. Now, we want to begin to evaluate *why* it happened. By analyzing why the problem or defect occurred, we can identify the *root causes* of the problem. Rather than fixing the symptom in the software, we can eliminate the defects in the process or materials that caused the problem in the first place.

Software engineers are notoriously good at fixing the symptoms in their software, but are then usually so consumed with the next release or the next problem that they never go back to examine why the problem occurred. The symptom observed is not only a symptom of a problem in the product, but also in the process that created it. If the symptoms are observable in the present, then the root cause must have occurred somewhere in the past. The root cause could include the process, materials, machines, environment, or people involved. What is required is a little bit more effort to go back and determine how the problem was injected in the first place. This requires extra resources in the present, but prevents future problems of a similar nature.

Using the SCORE model (Chapter 4, Figure 4.1), we can generalize the quality problem solving process to include:

1. Observing *symptoms* in the present
2. Adding *resources*, in the present, to analyze the problem, identify the root *causes* that occurred in the past, and propose solutions to prevent the root causes from occurring in the future
3. Identifying a target, an *outcome*, for improvement
4. Observing the results of implementing the proposed solutions to determine if the desired *effects* are achieved

The quality improvement tool that helps us identify the root causes of the problem is called a cause-effect, Ishikawa, or fishbone diagram.

Ishikawa Diagrams

Take away the cause and the effect ceases.

—Miguel De Cervantes

The Ishikawa diagram (Figure 5.9) is named after Kaoru Ishikawa. It's also called the cause-effect diagram because it shows the relationship between the effect—the symptoms observed—and the causes. It's also called the fishbone diagram because of its resemblance to a fish's skeleton, with the head at the right and the bones back to the left.

Development of the Ishikawa diagram follows the PDCA cycle. First you have to figure out what kind of diagram to draw, then develop it by asking *why*, and then check the logic, and then act to improve it until all causes are identified.

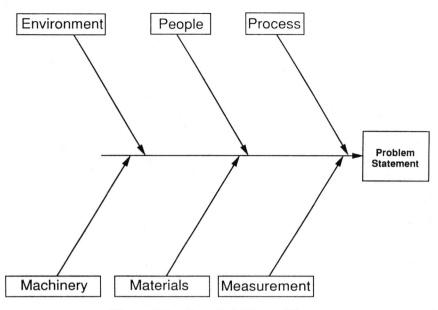

Figure 5.9 Generic Ishikawa Diagram

Plan—What Kind of Ishikawa Diagram?

There are a number of different types of Ishikawa diagrams. Fortunately they all begin the same way, by putting the problem statement (the symptom) in the head of the fish. Next you have to determine the major causes of the problem. These form the major bones off the spine of the diagram. Some common types include:

- Generic—M^3P^2E (Figure 5.9)
- Software specific (Figure 5.10)
- Process (Figure 4.8)
- Pareto chart (Figure 4.9)

The generic Ishikawa identifies six major categories of causes—people, process, machines, materials, measurements, and the environment. Since Deming says that 85 percent or more of problems stem from variation in the process, it is usually the best place to start looking for causes. In some cases, software engineers inspect designs and code irregularly, causing unwanted defects to remain unidentified in the software. Similarly, people might not be trained. Management brings in an

Ishikawa Diagram for Software Process

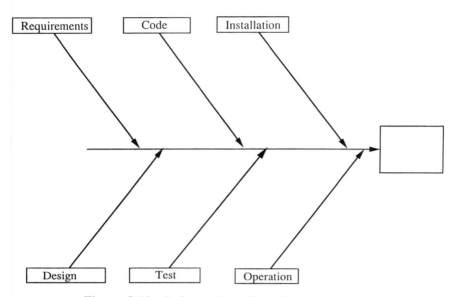

Figure 5.10   Software Specific Ishikawa Diagram

expensive CASE tool, but fails to train the people in its use. In the trial-and-error process of learning the tool, people make mistakes. Machines (i.e., computers) might not be properly maintained and therefore dysfunctional. If you've worked around computers for very long, you've experienced a day where your terminal, network, or computer are flaky, going up and down every few minutes. In this kind of situation, the chances of injecting a defect rise dramatically. The materials (i.e., software and documentation) may not work properly, causing further errors to be injected into the product. And finally the environment (your office) may contribute to defects as well. DeMarco and Lister (1988) found that an open office contributes to interruptions that decrease productivity and quality, whereas an enclosed office with a door will put you in the top quartile of software performers.

The software-specific Ishikawa (Figure 5.10) simply takes the generic categories and applies more common software terms to each major category of cause. It focuses on software process, people, computers, software, data, and the environment.

Ishikawa diagrams can also be generated by brainstorming and using the affinity diagram (Chapter 3) to identify the "major bones" of the Ishikawa diagram.

The process-specific Ishikawa (Figure 4.8) focuses on the software life cycle—requirements, design, code, test, installation, and operation. It offers an exploded view of the process leg of the software-specific Ishikawa.

The software-code Ishikawa (Figure 4.9) focuses on the application software itself—the logic, computation, interface, data manipulation, data base, and input/output (I/O) that make up the system. It can be used to evaluate specific process problems regarding any of these categories or it can be a useful debugging tool when you've reached your wits end trying to locate a particularly nasty defect.

The Pareto chart-driven Ishikawa uses data that you've collected to identify the most common contributors to the problem. If, for example, you've identified that computer down time is 48 percent of your problem, bad data is 26 percent, operational processes another 20 percent, and user error is 6 percent of the problem, then use the major categories of down time, bad data, operational processes, and user error.

Any of these Ishikawa diagrams can be changed to reflect more accurately the nature of your software environment. For example, development processes may be somewhat different from maintenance or evolution processes. Real-time software may require changes from business-oriented software. The only thing that matters is that you have a common starting point for analyzing the root causes of the observable symptoms in your software products. Consistency breeds an absence of variation, which will help you converge on a solution more quickly.

How do you choose where to start? First, if you have useful data or indicators of where the problem occurred, then use the data to direct your analysis using the Pareto-based Ishikawa. Data is always preferable to gut feel. Otherwise, choose one of the diagrams and get started. Indecision is nearly always the worst mistake you can make. Try one and you'll quickly discover if you are on the right track. If not, PDCA! Change course. Change the categories and start again. Converge on a solution. Over time, with experience, you'll get better at using this tool, but it takes a willingness to get in and try it on. And how do we "try it on?" Well, we start by asking *why?*

Do—The Five Whys

Developing the Ishikawa requires that you first pick the most likely major cause that will yield a root cause. If you have data, this choice is obvious from the Pareto chart. If you don't have data, use gut feel to direct your initial voyage of discovery. If nothing else, start with the process or the first step of the process and ask "why?" (Figure 5.11):

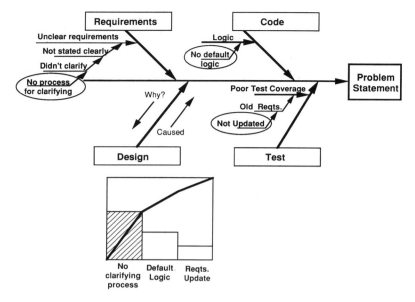

Figure 5.11 Validating Root Causes

Ask why:	Why did the software process cause this symptom?
Answer:	Didn't get clear requirements.
Ask again:	Why didn't we get clear requirements?
Answer:	Customer didn't state them clearly.
Ask again:	Why didn't the customer state them clearly?
Answer:	We didn't ask enough questions about the customer's requirements.
Ask again:	Why didn't we ask enough questions?
Answer:	No process for evaluating clarity of customer requirements.

You may have to ask "why?" up to five times to get to an actionable level. In this case, we can begin to contrive a process for evaluating the clarity of customer's requirements. Once you've gotten to an actionable level, stop and move back up the ladder and ask "Are there any *other* reasons why we didn't ask enough questions?" If not, keep moving back up and asking for other causes until you get back up to the major category.

Don't be surprised along the way if the team notices dozens of other unrelated issues. Simply capture them on a separate sheet of paper so that you'll have them when it comes time to analyze another leg of the diagram.

As you ask why, it's a good idea to check the logic of the diagram as you are constructing it. Otherwise, it's easy to get off track.

Check—The Logic

If we ask ''why?'' to work our way *down* the diagram, we use the word ''causes'' to check the logic *up* the diagram. So, using the previous example, not having a process for evaluating the clarity of customer requirements *caused* us to not ask enough questions about the customer's requirements which *caused* the customer to not state them clearly which caused the requirements to be unclear, which *caused* the observed symptom.

Rather than wait until you've gotten to an actionable level, it is more useful to check after each new bone is added to the diagram. Otherwise, until you are familiar with the construction of this diagram, it is easy to get into circular logic. Somewhere in development of the diagram you ask why and the answer is some previous bone on this leg of the diagram. So, for example, if you began with ''unclear requirements'' and asked why a few more times and then got the answer ''unclear requirements,'' you will know that your logic went haywire somewhere along the way. If you ever get into circular logic, check the logic using *causes* until you discover where you went awry.

Act—To Improve Logic and Diagram

As you ask why and check the logic, continue to improve the wording and redraw the diagram to increase its clarity. You may have to take some of the major bones and draw them as separate diagrams when they get too crowded.

You may also want to check the scope of your diagram. If, for example, the diagram grows from a trout into a whale with bones going everywhere, there are a couple of possibilities:

1. You didn't chunk down far enough in the previous step
2. You chose too broad of an Ishikawa

More often than not, you didn't chunk down far enough in the previous step. So, go back, gather more data, and take the Pareto chart down another level. Rewrite your problem statement, set a new target, and step back into Ishikawa diagramming. The generic Ishikawa is often too broad. The software process Ishikawa may require that you identify the step in the software life cycle that contributes the most to the problem (possibly requirements or design), and do a cause-effect analysis of just that one step. The more specifically you focus on the analysis, the more quickly you will converge on a solution. You will want to solve everything at once, and you will be much better off to keep narrowing your focus until you find one root cause you can eliminate. Then you can look for the next one and the next one.

Select Root Causes

Once you've completely developed the Ishikawa diagram, you need to identify what you think are the *root* causes of the problem. Root causes are always actionable causes at the foot of any leg of the diagram (Figure 5.11). There are a couple of ways to identify them:

1. Look for actionable causes that occur multiple times on the diagram. These are usually root causes.
2. Use the subjective feelings of the group to identify the potential root causes.

Once you've identified the potential root causes, circle them to identify them from the rest. There will typically be three to nine root causes. Again, any more than this and you can suspect that the previous step didn't chunk down far enough.

Verify with Data

Now, before we leap into fixing these potential root causes, it pays to spend a little more time to verify that these are actually root causes. Remember, gut feel is one thing; data is another. You may need to go back and analyze your existing data or create a checksheet and collect a small sample to verify your root causes. Invariably, some of the identified root causes cannot be verified with data. These drop off your list and you establish some pecking order for solving the others. Again, a Pareto chart can help identify the most prominent root cause and establish a declining ranking for the rest (Figure 5.11).

At this point, revise the Ishikawa diagram one more time to:

- remove circles around the invalid root causes
- place the major bones with the most prominent root causes closest to the head of the diagram (Figure 5.12). This will help your reader identify the most important root causes just from looking at the diagram.

Once you have completed the Ishikawa diagram, identified the root causes, verified them with data, it's time to figure out what to do about

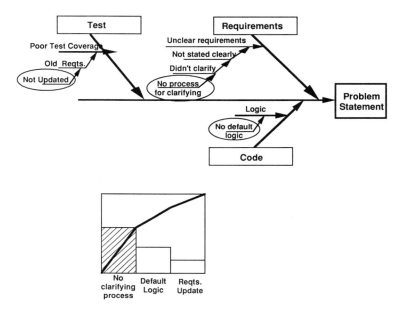

Figure 5.12 Prioritized Ishikawa Diagram

them. In the next chapter, we'll look at how to develop proposed solutions that will eliminate or reduce the root causes.

SUMMARY

Congratulations! You've just completed the planning step of the problem-solving process. You've learned how to identify a problem area, measure, and graph it with an increasing or decreasing indicator involving time, defects, or cost. You've learned how to scope this problem down to a clear problem statement using one or more Pareto charts. Next, you discovered how to use cause-and-effect analysis to identify potential root causes and then to verify them with data.

This is the most unfamiliar and perhaps uncomfortable part of the problem-solving process because we are so used to using gut feel to fix symptoms in the process. To truly succeed at improving software quality, we must take the time to find measurable indicators of the problem, chunk it down into bite-sized chunks, and identify the root causes of problem. Otherwise we are just propagating our current system of ineffectiveness. Having identified and verified the root causes of the problem, we can now begin to figure out what to *do* to ensure that we pull up the weeds *and* the root causes of the problem.

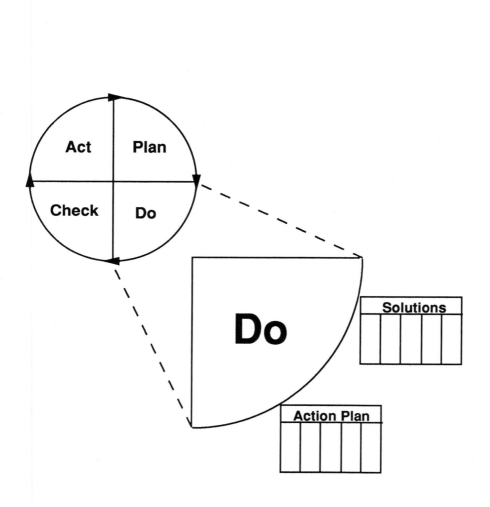

CHAPTER 6

DO—Identify and Implement Proposed Solutions

Wise people seek solutions
The ignorant only cast blame

—Lao Tzu

In the planning stage, we identified the customer, a broad problem area, the specific problem to be solved, and the root causes of the problem. If you have done this well, the proposed solutions, or *countermeasures* (Imai 1986), will just jump out at you. They probably appeared magically as you did the analysis. Now you need to dream up the best potential solutions to try first, build a plan to implement them, evaluate the effectiveness of the solutions to ensure their successful implementation, and then implement them.

Walt Disney was renowned for creating imaginative solutions to seemingly unsolvable problems. He called it *imagineering*. To succeed at improving software quality, software engineers need to become *imagineers*. We can use Walt's own strategy to help us create innovative solutions to quality problems.

Using Walt Disney's *dreamer, realist*, and *critic* (Dilts 1990), we can have fun doing each part of this step of continuous improvement. The dreamer can look at each root cause and dream up a wide variety of possible solutions. The realist takes the solutions and begins chunking them down into the specific steps required. The realist prepares an action plan to implement each one. The critic evaluates the proposed solutions and the action plan to identify potential problems with each. All changes have forces acting to inhibit or encourage their implementation. The critic ferrets these problems out *before* implementing the change. The critic knows that an ounce of prevention is worth a pound of cure.

The Dreamer asks: "What would be the most elegant, effective, and efficient solution to this root cause?"

The Realist asks: "What would be the most effective way to implement this solution?"

The Critic asks: "What are the potential problems with this solution? What could go wrong with this plan of action?"

PROPOSED SOLUTIONS

The critic realizes immediately that any solution is only a *proposed* solution until we've had a chance to test it and evaluate the results. Many an idea has looked good on paper only to be less than adequate when tested in the "real" world. Some people might view these discoveries as failures. Columbus, for example, failed to discover a shorter route to the East Indies, but he made a very different discovery; he found a new continent. Thomas Edison, after thousands of experiments to develop a light bulb, observed that he hadn't failed, but rather found thousand of ways not to invent the light bulb.

Great inventors share the belief that "there is no failure, only feedback." This is a very useful belief for quality improvement imagineers as well. Quality is continuously improving; it is a journey, not a destination. Quality improvement is a voyage of discovery. If something doesn't work, try something else. Disney's dreamer, realist, and critic help us focus our energy in the areas of most likelihood. Without the critic, the dreamer and realist can create bizarre solutions that won't work in the real world. Without the realist, the dreamer's ideas remain in the netherworld of the imagination. And without the dreamer, the realist and the critic are doomed to rely on what has worked in the past. The global economy prohibits relying on the past. Where the past may offer solutions that can help solve 80 percent of the problems, the other 20 percent require innovative solutions.

To help link the dreamer, realist, and critic, we can use a matrix (Figure 6.1) and an action plan (Figure 6.2) to organize their contributions. In the PDCA cycle, the dreamer is a *planner*—a visionary; the realist is both a *planner* and a *doer*; the critic is the *checker*; and both the

Proposed Solution

Root Cause	What? *(dreamer)*	How? *(realist)*	Effectiveness *(critic)*	Barriers *(critic)*

High = 9
Medium = 3
Low = 1

Figure 6.1 Proposed Solutions Matrix

Action Plan

What? *(dreamer)*	How? *(realist)*	Who?	When?	Indicator?

Figure 6.2 Action Plan

dreamer and the realist *act* to improve their existing visions and directions based on the critic's input. It often takes several iterations of dreaming, planning, and checking to identify the best possible countermeasures and action plans. Using PDCA at this step prevents future problems and disappointments because all changes have enemies and all plans have problems when first conceived.

Dreamer

Since we've already identified the root causes of our problem and verified them with data, the dreamer's job is to visualize possible solutions that will most effectively reduce or eliminate the root cause. In many instances there can be more than one countermeasure for a root cause. This is good because choice is always better than no choice. Sometimes complex, expensive technological countermeasures are less effective than simple, straightforward people-oriented changes.

To begin to complete the matrix (Figure 6.1), we put the identified root causes in the left-hand column and let the dreamer create the list of possible countermeasures. The possible solutions are *what* we are going to do, not all of the specifics of *how* we are going to do it. *How* we implement the countermeasures enters the domain of the realist.

Realist

If the dreamer asks: "What are we going to do, specifically?" then the realist asks "How are we going to do it, specifically? What are the specific steps?" The realist takes the high level vision of the dreamer and reduces it to the specific steps that are needed to make the dream a reality.

The action plan (Figure 6.2) is the realist's tool of choice. Put the dreamer's proposed solution in the left-hand column. Then let the realist identify the various practical ways to transfer this vision into reality. There may be several approaches to implementing this one countermeasure and the realist maps out each of them. Usually, there are no more than 7 ± 2 steps in each approach. Using this more detailed information, the realist completes the next column: "How?" Then, the realist knows that nothing happens without people assigned and a due date, so the realist sketches in the people and milestones for implementing each countermeasure. The realist also knows that implementing too many countermeasures at once makes it difficult to evaluate the impact of each one, so the realist spreads the countermeasures over enough time that the results can be measured more accurately.

The realist also asks the question: "How will we measure the effect of this improvement?" The final column of Figure 6.2 tells us how the proposed solution will be measured and evaluated.

Now, given the dreamer's vision and the realist's plan, the critic gets involved to look for deficiencies in both.

Critic

The critic's job is to identify the tar pits and jackals and problems that always surround improvements and change. The critic asks the tough questions:

What's wrong with these proposed countermeasures and plans?
Who and what are the barriers to its implementation?
Will this easily fit into our existing culture?

Any time a quality team meets to critique the vision and plan, they should pick a different place than their normal meeting room. Disney had a screening room that his animators called the "sweat box" because of the intense evaluations conducted there. Meeting rooms can become an "anchor" for what kind of work you will do in them. A wise choice will move the critical meetings to a different room so that creativity and pleasure remain untouched by the sharp nature of the critical evaluation.

Once in a different meeting room, the team can start to use the questions above to evaluate their thoughts and ideas. Remember to focus on the idea, not the person who dreamed it up. How often do we shoot down our best ideas and people by criticizing the person, not their dream or plan? Get some distance from the idea; see it as something outside of yourself and then you can begin to evaluate it respectfully.

One of the tools for evaluating proposed solutions is *Force Field Analysis* (Figure 6.3). This technique evaluates the forces in the organization that are acting to prevent the improvement (the barriers) and the forces that are acting to support the improvement. To develop this tool:

1. Brainstorm the forces acting to prevent this improvement.
2. Brainstorm the forces acting to encourage this improvement.
3. Identify the *barriers* that will not be automatically overcome by the positive forces acting for the change. Add these barriers to the matrix, Figure 6.1.
4. Let the dreamer and realist offer ways to enhance the proposed solution and the action plan to counteract these opposing forces.

Forces acting for the change

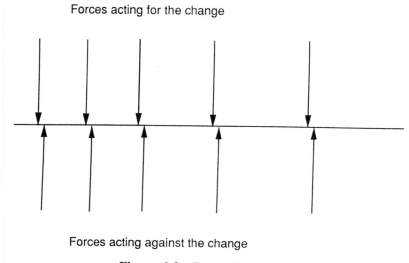

Forces acting against the change

Figure 6.3   Force Field Analysis

The PDPC diagram (Chapter 3) can also help diagnose the potential problems that lie in the path of the proposed countermeasures. Another tool for critically evaluating the proposed solution is cost-benefit analysis. The critic can ask: "How much will this cost to implement and how much value will it return?" Regardless of the business climate, an inexpensive solution is preferable to an expensive solution as long as the results are equivalent. A more effective, but expensive, solution is always preferable to an inexpensive, yet ineffective, one. There are occasions where the cost-benefit of an improvement, when evaluated over the short term, makes little or no sense. When evaluated over a long term, however, based on retaining customers and enhancing their satisfaction, the improvement makes perfect sense.

Once the proposed solutions have been evaluated from all of the team's perspectives, it is time for the team to review its work with the quality leadership—a manager or the quality council—to get approval and buy-in. The team often benefits from inviting an executive trained in quality improvement to their meeting to review their plan. An outside perspective gives the team one more viewpoint from which to improve their planned improvement. The team should also present their improvement story to the IS quality council to get the buy-in and resources necessary to implement the countermeasures. With their support, the realist can begin to implement the action plan.

IMPLEMENT THE CHANGE

With a well-prepared action plan, the realist will have no problem implementing the improvement and measuring the results. The act of implementing improvements, however, will reveal information that was previously unavailable to the team. The dreamer, realist, and critic may be called upon to PDCA the plan as they move forward, gathering more knowledge and understanding.

SUMMARY

The "do" stage of PDCA is a critical stepping stone to success. Not only do we have to engage our creative abilities to determine countermeasures to the root causes of our problems, but we must also engage our realist to create an action plan and cost/benefit analysis to ensure that we can accomplish the improvement. We must also engage our internal critic to identify the forces in the organization that will oppose the change and create countermeasures to deal with them.

Initiating change is one of the most challenging parts of the quality improvement process. When done well, it can carry the organization to new heights of quality and productivity; done poorly, it will create frustration, anxiety, and antagonism. In the next step of the PDCA process we will discover how to check the results of implementing our countermeasures and determine what needs to be done next.

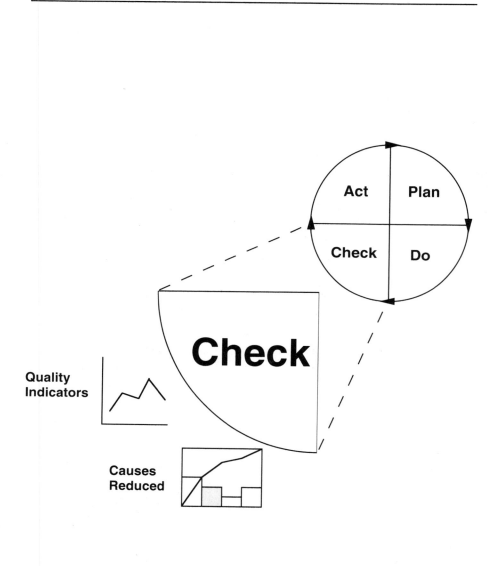

CHAPTER 7

Check Results

Measures of productivity do not lead to improvement in productivity.
—W. Edwards Deming (1986, pg. 15)

You have to keep score.

—Jack Fooks, VP Westinghouse

An old adage says: "Plan the flight and fly the plan." Unfortunately, software projects and quality improvements, like airline flights, are off course 90 percent of the time. If you only plan the flight and fly the plan, you're likely to end up in some unusual places. To ensure that they arrive at their destination, pilots constantly check their position and adjust course. Quality improvement projects must do the same to ensure that the countermeasures implemented actually do reduce or eliminate the root causes of the problem. Otherwise, you're more likely to build a bureacracy than eliminate root causes. Many of today's problems are a by-product of previous "improvements" that did little more than add another layer of waste to an already cumbersome process.

To this point, the quality team has used line graphs, bar charts, Pareto charts, histograms, control charts or some other kind of graph to demonstrate that a problem exists. They have analyzed the root causes of the problem, developed and begun implementing proposed solutions. Now the team goes back to those earlier graphs and collects the data required to develop new ones that give them a picture of the impacts of their changes. These *comparative* graphs tell the team whether their counter-measure is working or not.

Figure 7.1 shows a line graph with its target for improvement and the various points at which countermeasures were implemented. It allows us a straightforward look at how the proposed solutions actually reduced the root causes. In the marketplace, we'd like an increasing percentage of a larger pie. Figure 7.2 shows how the marketshare has increased both in size and percent. Figure 7.3 shows a comparison of two Pareto charts, demonstrating that the main problem has been reduced by 40 complaints since 1992. Figure 7.4 uses histograms to demonstrate how the complexity of an entire system has been reduced by repeated applications of reengineering and perfective maintenance.

Being able to determine the results of applying improvements requires that teams learn how to measure data. Measurement is another whole topic in and of itself (Arthur 1985), and let's spend a little time looking at it now.

MEASUREMENT

The ability to measure has fueled virtually all past technological advances. Each new measurement has given us ways to extend our crude natural abilities to better measure height, width, depth, weight, texture,

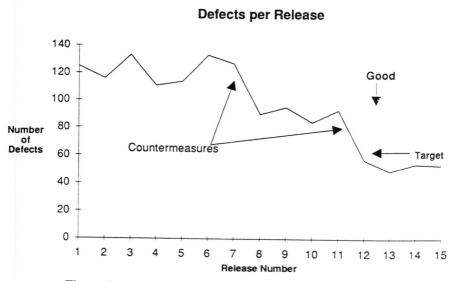

Figure 7.1 Line Graph of Defects and Countermeasures

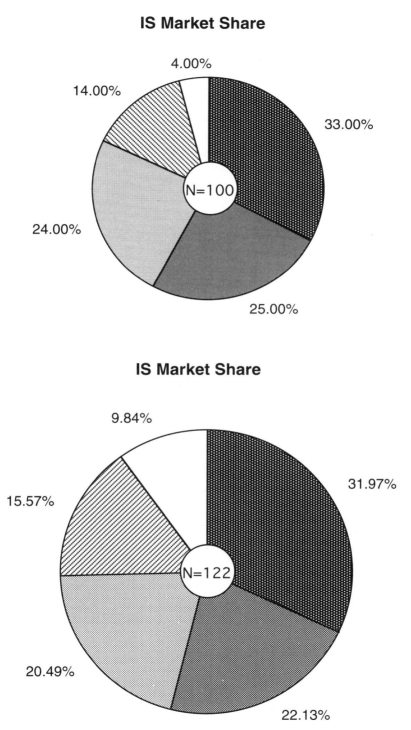

Figure 7.2 Comparative Pie Charts

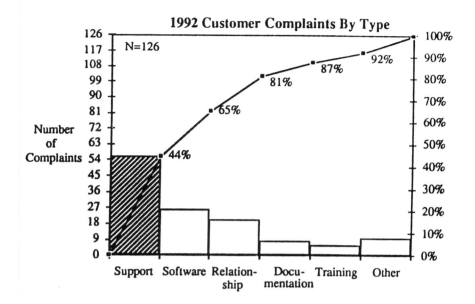

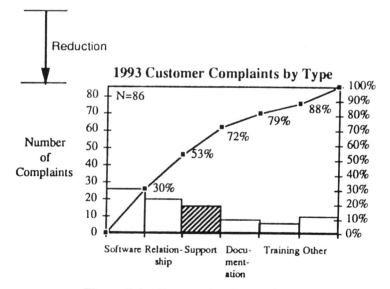

Figure 7.3 Comparative Pareto Charts

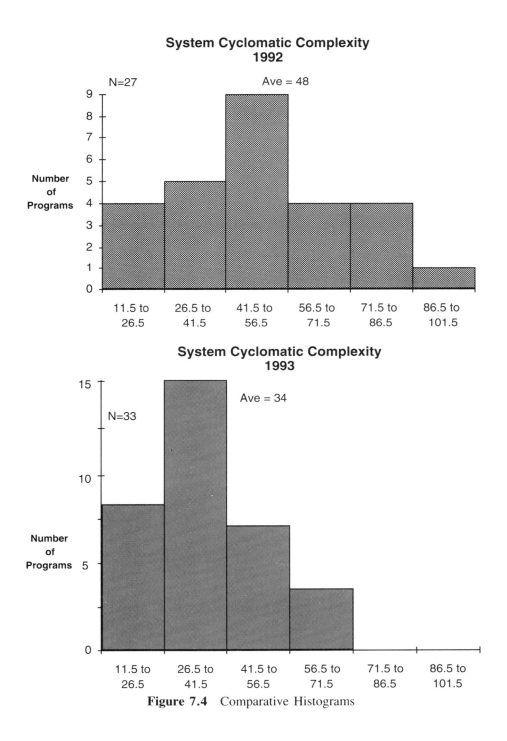

Figure 7.4 Comparative Histograms

smell, temperature, and a myriad of other things in the realm of our senses. This is the major advantage of measurement—it enhances our ability to sense things not accessible to our native abilities and intelligence. Unaided, our brain takes in all of the data from the senses— sight, sound, smell, taste, and touch—transforming these crude impulses into measurements, which it then uses to estimate distances, dimensions, clarity, flavor, and so on.

> *Count what is countable, measure what is measurable, and what is not measurable, make measurable.*
>
> *—Galileo Galilei (1564-1642)*

> *In physical science a first essential step in the direction of learning any subject is to find principles of numerical reckoning and methods for practicably measuring some quality connected with it.*
>
> *—Lord Kelvin*

The industrial revolution spawned the construction and manufacturing paradigms. Using these as models from which to base our search for software measurements, researchers have driven themselves (myself included) crazy. We've looked for ways to establish estimating handbooks like the ones builders have. We've focused measurement on ancient thoughts of production per worker hour. We've tried to find ways to make these other paradigms fit, but they just won't.

When we measure software using the "construction" paradigm, we end up focusing on due dates missed and little else. We punish programmers for doing the best they know how to do within the limits of the process they are using. When we measure software using the "evolution" paradigm, we end up with something else all together—an emphasis on quality and process improvement—because measurement is only a means to an end, not an end in itself.

So how do we measure software in such a way that it begins to help us rather than hinder us? When I was growing up, there was the door jamb of my room where I would stand and my mother would mark my height. Beside each mark, she would put the date, many of which were my birthday. Every year I could "see" how much I'd grown and the progress I was making towards adulthood. At the same time, my knowledge and skills were measured by progress through various grades of schooling.

I measured the growth and development of this book in the same way. Writing a book would be difficult if I had no measurement of progress toward completion. To keep myself sane, I measured its growth in words, pages, and chapters.

Measurement of growing things looks for increase in both size and ability. Measurement of growing things looks forward to birthdays, not to the day when the building can be torn down and replaced with a more gleaming, modern edifice, or an old car can be sold and another purchased to replace it. Measurement of software should celebrate the life and growth of the system, not a headlong rush toward obsolescence.

In its early years, we should expect rapid growth in size and ability in a given system. In the prototyping creation stage, similar to pregnancy, the software should grow rapidly from a concept into an initial working system. Then, once delivered, it can be nurtured and grown both mentally and physically. The human brain is full sized in early childhood. The brain is what allows the child to learn. In a software system, the data bases and repositories of the system should be fully formed early in the system's life (3–5 years). Next, structural growth of most humans and systems will continue for several years and usually ceases in the late teens. From here on, systems may add more size and muscle, but the structure remains the same. Occasionally, systems will grow fat and require special assistance to regain their earlier trim. The true measure of human growth beyond the physical plane is the mental growth. Systems grow mentally through the evolution and addition of data. At some point, the physical development of a system will slow and the growth of its abilities will continue through the growth and evolution of its data, information, knowledge, and wisdom.

Measurement of growing systems also helps us detect and correct deficiencies *before* they become life threatening. There is an old story about a company that was having problems with the boilers in its plants. A special engineer was brought in to check the boilers. After listening to the groans and creaks for a little while, the engineer pulled out a small hammer and tapped a valve. Miraculously, the system began to hum again. The management was delighted and then they asked for the bill. The engineer asked for $300. ''$300,'' they exclaimed, ''but all you did was tap on a valve.'' The engineer nodded and told them that it was only a dollar for tapping on the valve, but $299 for knowing where to tap.

Measurements and indicators tell you where to tap. Measurement only serves to extend our abilities to understand the software process in ways *invisible* to the naked eye. Measurement is the *check* that precedes the identification and elimination of problems in the quality process. To reach the highest level in the SEI maturity framework—the highest step on the stairway to software excellence—you must be able to measure how your software grows and when it begins to diverge from the evolutionary tree.

Hitachi has been tracking productivity and defect rates for 25 years (Gross 1991). This massive data base helps them determine how to improve their software process and how many people will be needed for a given project. Can you say the same?

ESTABLISHING MEASUREMENTS

As Tom DeMarco has said, "What gets measured, gets done." Establishing measurements will take time and dedicated resources to design and develop the key metrics needed to track improvements in your process and results. As you might expect, there are four phases of establishing data collection and measurement: planning, doing, checking, and acting to improve.

Plan   1. Setting the goals for measurement
       (Why are we collecting data?)
       2. Modeling the process and data
       (What do we need to collect and when?)
       3. Creating the measurement process, training, and tools
Do   4. Implementing the entire measurement process
Check   5. Evaluate the results of instigating measurements
Act   6. Continuously improve the measurement process, tools, and training

Once you have a measurement process in place, you can begin to improve the software process. Another strategy for successful application of software measurement continues the use of PDCA:

1. Evolutionary Planning
   - Collect data about the environment—resource usage, change and defect history, product dimensions, and other similar projects.
   - Define quality relative to the customer, project, organization—percent of customer bills in error, customer complaints, customer requests for clarification of bills, employee turnover, morale, and so on.
2. Do
   - Tailor the software process, methods, measurements, and tools to satisfy the project goals.

3. Check
   - Analyze the data from other projects *before* starting the project
   - Analyze data from the project as it proceeds
   - Analyze the results after the project is finished
4. Act to improve
   - Process
   - Tools
   - Materials
   - Work environment
   - People

Continuous quality improvement relies on the PDCA cycle to continuously evaluate every step of the software life cycle and make improvements. Without the data to do so, only minimal progress can be made because we can only use the subjective experience of the team to analyze the problems and devise solutions. We begin by setting goals for measurement.

SETTING GOALS FOR MEASUREMENT

To establish goals for measurement, you will need to establish corporate goals first and then general IS objectives (Chapter 2). Once these goals are chosen, you will need to set priorities for accomplishing each of these objectives. Once the goals, objectives, and priorities are known, it becomes much easier to select measurement methods and tools that will lead to the desired result.

Establish corporate goals. At Motorola, for example, the corporate-wide direction is to achieve six-sigma level defects per unit (fewer than 3.4 in a million). This includes lines of code.

Develop general objectives. For each of the quality criteria like usability, maintainability, flexibility, and reliability, you will need specific, measurable objectives. For example, would your customer appreciate a four-fold increase in reliability? Probably. When it comes time to enhance the software, would you appreciate a ten-fold increase in flexibility? Absolutely. Would you want to cut the software development cycle by 50 percent? You bet, and it can be done through PDCA.

Set priorities. Which of the general objectives are the most important to long-term success and survival? Make these your top priority. I would choose reliability, flexibility, maintainability, and cycle time. Seeking to optimize all of these at once will drive you to revolutionary ways of developing software—Rapid Evolutionary Development (Arthur 1992).

Match measurements to the prioritized objectives. Select measurement methods and tools to carry them out with the minimal amount of effort. An automated measurement is better than a manual one, and a manual measurement is better than none at all.

MODELING THE PROCESS

Using the methodology or structured flowcharts, identify the flow of the process. Then begin to identify how you intend to measure growth in size, complexity, and defects of the evolving system. Identify where you can begin to get clarity about the customer's satisfaction or dissatisfaction with the evolving system. If you can identify what causes them the most pain, then you'll know what to work on. In one maintenance environment, for example, the initial estimates *were* slipped once with a little problem, but then slipped again to almost twice the second estimate. In between, the customer had made commitments based on the second estimate. When the project manager discovered the need to slip the schedule the first time, they let the customer know immediately, but then they rushed the second estimate, which resulted in the customer's dissatisfaction. So an indicator of the number of times an estimate is slipped and the percent of the original estimate slipped would help identify reasons for customer dissatisfaction early in the process. If 40 percent of estimates are being missed and taking up to twice as long to complete, you'll need some fancy footwork to manage the customer's expectations. Which brings us to creating measurements that will keep you ahead of your customer.

CREATING MEASUREMENTS

To actively manage productivity and quality, we need to know if they are improving or degrading. This implies the need for software metrics that track trends in software development. The rules for successful measurement are:

- Make measurement beneficial for the person collecting the data.
- Make measurement flexible to respond to custom requirements.
- Define the process first, then the measurements.

- Measure processes and verify them through feedback.
- Define recognition, reward, and advice procedures for people who measure.

The most common metrics of software *size* are Function Points (FP) and non-commentary lines of code (NLOC). From these two metrics, it should come as no surprise that the two most common metrics for measuring productivity are Function Points per staff month and non-commentary lines of code per staff month. Function point measurement relies on the ''big picture'' of the system's behavior. Function point measurement has been largely a manual process, while NLOC has been automated for many of the leading languages. Productivity measurement in a software evolution or maintenance environment uses added, changed, and deleted functions or lines to indicate productivity.

Reuse of software data, documentation, and code dramatically affect productivity and quality. To factor reuse into your productivity equation, count:

1. How many times an object—data, design, documentation, code, or whatever—is reused.
2. How many NLOC are in the module or data, and the number of times reused.
3. How many function points are reused.

Productivity metrics can help you understand how the proposed changes are affecting the process, but productivity metrics are also inherently dangerous *because* they will drive programmer behavior, even if it is counter-productive. You are much better off if you measure quality and let productivity take care of itself, because it will.

The most common metric of software quality is defects per thousand lines of code (KLOC). Current (1990) overall defect rates are 20–60 defects per 1,000 lines of code. Delivered error rates are 1–10 errors per 1,000 lines of code (Mills 1987). This is a good metric for determining the capability of your coding and testing processes, but it misses the requirements and design stages where 60 percent of all defects enter the process.

Defects per KLOC is a useful internal measure, but less useful for measuring how customers feel about the system. You can have a very low defect rate and also have very unhappy customers. To better understand customer dissatisfaction, you can measure system *un*availability, mean time between failures (MTBF), or mean time to repair (MTTR) or some other measure of the customer's direct experience of the system.

The next most common software metric is complexity, measured using McCabe's Cyclomatic Complexity (CC). It has been widely established that modules with a CC of 10 or less have *zero* defects and are flexible, maintainable, and reusable, while modules of complexity greater than 50 are unmaintainable (Figure 7.4). This implies an inescapable cost as the module's complexity rises above 10.

To maximize the quality of each module, you should attempt to build modules with a Cyclomatic Complexity of 7 ± 2 (5–9). This "target value" will reduce variation and minimize the cost of software development *and* maintenance.

The Top Ten

Barry Boehm is widely respected in the measurement community for his work at TRW. Barry Boehm's top ten metrics (IEEE Software, Sept. 1987):

1. 100 times more expensive to fix a delivered error than one caught early
2. Software schedules can only compress by 25 percent (using existing methods and tools)
3. Every dollar of development will cost you two for maintenance.
4. Software development and maintenance costs are a function of the number of executable instructions in the product: Cost $= f(ELOC)$
5. Variations between people account for the biggest differences in software productivity: Moral: Get the best people working on your project or train everyone to the level of the best.
6. Ratio of software to hardware cost is 85:15 and growing.
7. Only 15 percent of software development effort is programming (i.e., coding). Best practices now spend 60 percent of their time on requirements and design, and only 25 percent testing.
8. Software systems and products cost three times as much per instruction as an individual program. System software products (i.e., compilers and operating systems) cost nine times as much.
9. Walkthroughs (and inspections) are the most cost-effective technique for eliminating existing software errors, catching 60 percent of all errors.

10. Software phenomena follow a Pareto distribution (Figure 7.3):

20 percent of the modules consume 80 percent of the resources

20 percent of the modules contribute 80 percent of the errors

20 percent of the errors consume 80 percent of repair costs

20 percent of the enhancements consume 80 percent of the adaptive maintenance costs

20 percent of the modules consume 80 percent of the execution time

20 percent of the tools experience 80 percent of the tool usage

Rule 10 reiterates one of the primary reasons for using the quality improvement process—focus on the worst first. There is never time to fix everything, but there is always enough time to fix the worst modules. If you knew which 20 percent incurred the most defects or enhancements, you could initiate work to reengineer them. Eliminating defects will please your customer, and improving the flexibility of the most commonly enhanced programs will reduce your customer's cost per enhancement, pleasing them even more. If you knew which modules took 80 percent of the execution time, you could reengineer those as well to reduce the customer's costs for execution time or reduce the response time to make their people more productive or your system more responsive. Whether the system is an on-line monster serving thousands of customers or a fire-control system in a jet fighter, finding and improving reliability, flexibility, and efficiency problems will serve your customer well. Once you've figured out how to measure these things, then you have to implement them.

IMPLEMENTING MEASUREMENTS

Measurements must be implemented very carefully unless you want to stimulate the IS immune system and kill the whole project. First, you can and should involve the people who will be using the measurements in the process of developing them. Use the Rapid Evolutionary Development process (Arthur 1992) to create the initial set of measurements. Pilot these measurements in one of your projects and improve them based on what you learn. Your first indicators of quality and productivity won't be the best, so plan on using PDCA to continuously improve them, especially after the first pilot. Once these improved indicators are in place, spend the money and time to train everyone in how to interpret and use the indicators so that everyone knows what the measurements are and how they can be used to *help improve the process*. Otherwise, two mid-level managers will go head-to-head trying to prove that their organization is better than the other. This kind of competition can only hurt—if not kill—your measurement and quality improvement processes. Measurements that target, compare, and punish workers will kill productivity and quality. Make sure that groups use the indicators to measure their own growth, not to compare themselves to others. This brings us to evaluating the measurements themselves.

EVALUATING MEASUREMENTS

Use the PDCA process to evaluate the effectiveness of the measurements you do implement. Don't be afraid to toss some out and create new ones. Measurement, like every other process you follow, must grow and evolve if it is to be effective in your environment. Static measurement processes, like any other unchanging activity, are a sure sign of decay.

Too many measurements are another sign of decay. There should be a measure of supplier quality (e.g., development system availability), internal measures of productivity and quality (e.g., function points per staff month, defects found at each phase of development), and external measures of productivity quality (e.g., efficiency, MTBF, MTTR, customer complaints) and customer satisfaction. Again, shoot for 7 ± 2 indicators of how you are doing. Each group may have a few more detailed measurements, but the goal of measurement is to keep track of how you are doing, not to employ more people. The people doing the work should be collecting the measurements. Then they can focus on improving the process.

CONTINUOUS IMPROVEMENT

Measurements have no value and will only burden a company unless you use the seven basic quality improvement tools to continuously improve all of your processes, products, and people. Attempting to improve processes without measurements is a painful process. You need data about the process to be able to improve it. So measurements must precede quality improvement activities to enable you to develop a useful base of information. Since most defects originate in the requirements and design phases, inspections are a key point in the software life cycle to begin collecting measurements.

Inspections

Appraisal (or checking) software quality usually involves inspection, auditing, testing, and tracking and resolving errors. Most IS departments squander their budget on testing the code, completely ignoring the other more important aspects of the process. Prevention and appraisal activities are *most effective early in the software life cycle*. "By increasing prevention activities significantly and by doing appraisal activities more efficiently, total quality costs can be cut in half within two to three years" (Zultner 1988). No organization can afford to pay its IS staff to create and then correct software defects.

> *A defect is an instance in which a requirement is not satisfied.*
> —*Michael Fagan (1986)*

Once an analyst or a programmer has planned and created a product, inspections serve as a way to check for defects and act to improve the product. Inspections can save 9–25 percent of development expense (Fagan 1986) because defects are found before they multiply and spread. Inspections also minimize the number of defects that escape the testing process, thereby minimizing costly down time and rework with delivered systems.

> *Cease dependence on inspection to achieve quality.*
> —*W. Edwards Deming*

You don't inspect code to find defects in the code, but rather to find defects in the *software process*. The software process produces two products—code and defects. If you eliminate the root causes, the *origin*, of the defects, then you eliminate the defects *forever*.

Routine inspection to improve quality is equivalent to planning for defects. By the time you inspect a product, it is too late to create quality, you can only remedy poor quality. Even an hour spent inspecting a program is wasteful if the knowledge gained isn't put to further use. Measurements are the key output of the inspection process. They give us the data on how to improve the process to prevent defects from occurring.

The goal of inspection is to gather data that will help determine the common causes of defects, improve software processes, and reduce costs—not just to remove defects from requirements, designs, and code. The common causes could be the requirements, design, or coding processes. Then we act to change the process to eliminate the cause. An

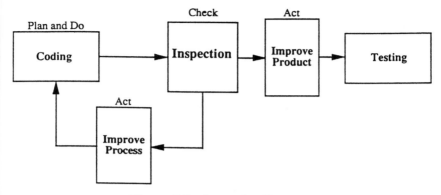

Figure 7.5 Inspection Process

inspection yields vital information about how the *process* is defective (Figure 7.5). Then, using a cause-and-effect diagram we can begin to figure out the root cause of the defect and prevent it in *all* future programs.

The inspection process uses the PDCA cycle to improve both the product and the process.

The Inspection Process

Plan	Select materials, participants, and roles
	Learn the material under review
Do	Find defects
	Classify and record the type of defects found
	Discourage solving the defects, just find them
	Having checked the product, the author acts to correct the identified defects
Check	Follow up to ensure all corrections and to prevent the injection of new defects
	Evaluate the types and numbers of defects found
Act	Improve the process using data derived from the inspection process
	Improve the inspection process to catch more of the common defect types

Inspections and walkthroughs are powerful tools for checking the quality of software products—requirements, designs, and code—and also for checking the quality of the software process that created them.

Using them only to find defects in the product, however, misses a key opportunity to improve the capability of your software life cycle and your own competitiveness.

Testing

Testing helps *detect* defects that have escaped detection in the preceding phases of development. Here again, the key byproduct of testing is useful information about the number of and types of defects found in testing. Armed with this data, teams can begin to identify the root causes of these defects and eliminate them from earlier phases of the software life cycle.

PEOPLE ISSUES

In a typical software organization, the key to successful measurement is successful use and handling of the people who will use the measurements. Usually, everyone will want to know what's in it for them. This is the voice of the employee. For programmers and analysts the answers are:

1. Feel great about your job
2. Develop a sense of professionalism and pride
3. Achieve a sense of satisfaction from teamwork
4. Receive recognition from peers and management
5. Become self-actualized
6. Have more leisure time, because of overtime not spent in rework (defects)
7. Have more time for professional development
8. Give you the ability to know where you are, why, and how to improve
9. Achieve prestige
10. Be the best

For managers, the answers are:

1. Improved competitive position
2. Increased revenue through competitive position and products
3. Company expansion through increased revenue

4. Increasing stock price and decreasing cost to borrow capital to finance expansion
5. Improved reputation
6. Increased respect from clients
7. More opportunity through more effective use of resources
8. Loyal, committed work force

SUMMARY

Software measurement is a vital key on the stairway to software excellence. Without them, evaluating and improving software processes would be impossible. Software measurements can also be dangerous. If used to measure people instead of processes or tools, they will create havoc in your IS department.

The steps to successful measurement include:

1. Define company/project objectives
2. Assign responsibility for collection
3. Do research
4. Define initial metrics to collect
5. Sell the initial collection of these metrics
6. Get tools for automatic data collection and analysis
7. Establish a training class in software measurement
8. Publicize success stories and encourage the exchange of ideas
9. Create a metrics database
10. Establish a mechanism for changing measurements in an orderly way

To adequately begin to measure productivity and quality, we can begin collecting the following measurements and using them to continuously improve the software process:

1. Function Points per staff month (increasing trend)
2. Non-commentary lines of code/staff month (increasing trend)
3. Defects per KLOC (decreasing trend)
4. Cyclomatic Complexity (histogram with a target of 5–9/module)

5. Customer complaints
6. Response time
7. System availability
8. Accuracy of outputs (percent of bills in error)
9. Cycle Time

For more information on software measurement, see (Arthur 1985) and (Grady 1987).

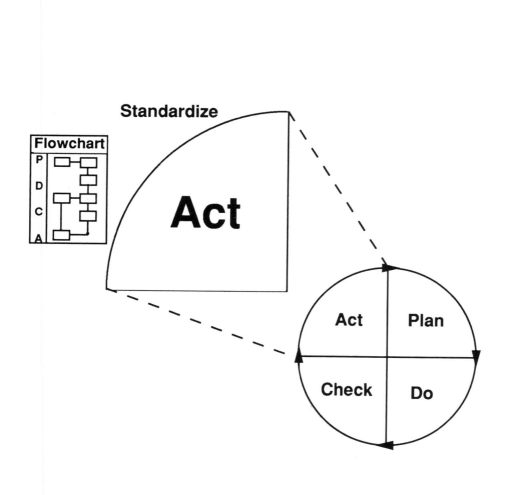

CHAPTER 8

Act to Integrate and Sustain Solutions

Most people hate to do their taxes. I always hated sorting my receipts at the end of the year and then I hit on the idea of a small filing box with folders for each major category of expense—home, car, donations, and so on. When I'm ready to put a receipt away, I put it in the appropriate folder in the box. That way, when it comes time to do my taxes, my receipts are already sorted for me. This, for me, eliminated the worst and most time consuming part of doing my taxes, usually about four hours of tedious sorting. Now, all I have to do is add up all the expenditures, put them in the right places in my tax software, and by January 31, I know where I stand.

This simple solution, sorting receipts when I get them instead of at the end of the year or a month, simplifies my tax preparation process. It also provides me easy access to receipts during the year, if I need them, because they are already filed in some standard place and usually in chronological order. When the government or I develop a new category of expense, I create a new folder for it. The filing box costs about $10 and I keep it in the same place that I used to store receipts. I have used it for the last five years and it shows no signs of wearing out.

I use this simple example to illustrate that improvements need to be integrated into the normal way that people do business. Over time, it can be improved, based on what is learned about using the improvement and ultimately, it needs to be shared with others so that they can benefit from the improvement.

If planning, doing, and checking brought us the resolution of our problem, then this, the final act, is perhaps more important than the preceding three steps. In the chaotic and barely repeatable world of software creation and evolution, when an engineer or group of engineers solved a problem—a process problem—they usually carried the knowledge away in their minds, often to be forgotten for the next project or rediscovered by another group of engineers only a few rooms away. To prevent this loss of wisdom, this fourth step of the quality improvement process acts to:

- Integrate this newly discovered way of doing business into the existing methods
- Encourage other similar groups or individuals to adopt, adapt, or replace it

Why in the world would we want to take these discoveries and make them, dare I say the word, *standard*? The main reason is that businesses, like organisms, exist to survive, thrive and perpetuate the species. To do so, businesses and their information system organizations have to be better and faster than their competitors. The Juran Institute has identified that there is a 10:1 return on investment for quality teams (Juran 1986). Much of this benefit comes from integrating the validated solutions into the group's existing processes so that they will be there for future generations. Much of the rest of the benefit comes from distributing the findings in such a way that all employees may benefit by applying, revising, or replacing the improvement. The application of these solutions across the IS organization begins to create the consistency required to sustain high quality software creation and evolution.

Some people would call this final act *standardization*. Unfortunately, software engineers seem to have a revulsion about this word. A standard is "something established by authority, custom, or general consent as a model or example." An authority, by the way, is always someone who doesn't know anything about *my* job. With quality improvement, however, problems are solved by the people who have the job and the problem. Another problem with the word *standard* is that it also means "sound and usable but not of top quality." A standard is often the lowest common denominator that everyone can agree to use. The phrase "try to please every one, and you will please no one" comes to mind. What we really want is a *consistent*, but not necessarily identical, way of applying improvements across the IS organization.

To prevent these misunderstandings, let's call this process of weaving solutions into work processes *integration*. This word also means different things to different people. What I mean by integration is that:

- The group that solves the problem will integrate the entire solution into their daily work
- Other groups will be required to do one of three things:
  1. Adopt the improvement completely
  2. Adapt it to fit their environment, customizing it to fit
  3. Demonstrate how what they do is better

The first task required of the improvement team is to integrate the improvement into their process. To succeed at integrating improvements into the group's existing process, we must:

- Define the revised process
- Establish ways of tracking consistency through measurement
- Make plans for improving the improvement (evolution)

To succeed at weaving the improvement into the fabric of the IS organization, we will need a way to *plan* to distribute the improvement, *do*—distribute the improvement, *check*—the application of the improvement, and *act* to improve based on the additional discoveries made by other teams.

In the world of quality improvement, the much abused phrase "that won't work here" must be backed up by data proving how you do things better. It's not enough to say, "I'm a real-time software engineer. *That* won't work here." The question that must be asked and keep being asked is "How do you know? Prove to me that you do something better." A sign at the entrance to Motorola says "In God We Trust, all others must bring data." This is an excellent motto to live by when acting to improve processes across the IS organization.

PROCESS CONSISTENCY

Achieving consistent application of each improvement is vital to sustaining productivity and quality. One of the most elementary forces of nature is entropy. Without taking action to ensure that the improvements are applied systematically, they are often lost. Entropy slowly erodes the gains made by an improvement (Figure 8.1) unless we add enough

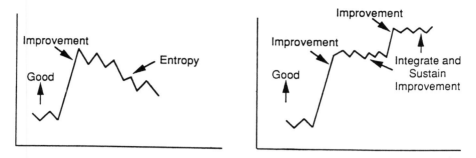

Figure 8.1 Entropy and *Kaizen* After Improvement

energy to hold onto it. A process improvement is like a car: once you accelerate to get up to highway speed, you have to keep your foot on the gas to sustain your speed. Let your foot off the gas, even slightly, and the car slows down. An integrated process solution is like a cruise control in a car or an autopilot in a plane—it consistently tracks the improvement's speed and direction, increasing energy and changing direction as required to keep the improvement on course and moving at a constant rate of speed.

To achieve this level of consistency, the team needs to define the improved process, machines, and materials involved, and weave them into the existing process. For example, rapid prototyping may find a niche in the previous requirements process. Walkthroughs and inspections may find their way into key windows in the software life cycle. Multi-tasking workstations may find their way into the hands of programmers and analysts. If you've got the data to show why and where you need to improve, few things can stand in your way.

Besides existing process improvements, a process may be completely replaced by the new process in a few circumstances. There was a time, for example, when cars had no cruise control and aircraft had no autopilot. There was a time when carriages had no engine, only a horse. Revolutionary processes accompany revolutionary changes. Most of the time, however, incremental revisions of the existing process are all you need to pull ahead of your competition. One of the most useful tools to illustrate the change is the process management system.

Process Management Systems

Process management systems (Chapter 10) use structured flowcharts to identify the customers, value-added processors, and process steps required to deliver a product or service. By defining the process flow and measurements the improved process can be 1) integrated and 2) duplicated or replicated by other groups using a similar process. Structured process flowcharts (Figures 1.3, 2.1, and 4.2) document the improved process for future generations. They are also essential to the successful replication of the solution in other work groups. They need not be elaborate. Each method is part of a larger process and every method can be broken down into smaller steps. Ideally, process flowcharts can be drawn at any of these levels and should contain no more than 7 ± 2 steps, methods, or processes per level. This will simplify understanding for all potential users.

As programmers, analysts, and managers develop and implement quality improvements, these processes tend to get a little more complex at first and then simpler as more and more steps are reduced to their essential functions. As the bureaucratic veneer is stripped away from the process, the elegance of the process begins to shine through. Simplicity, not complexity, is the goal. Once we have the process defined, we can identify the key points to begin measuring the customer's satisfaction or dissatisfaction.

Measurement Systems

Back in the planning stage of the improvement process, we determined key indicators of the customer's dissatisfaction. To ensure that we can integrate, sustain, and improve the process even further, we need a measurement system that periodically, or continually, checks to see that the improvement is integrated into the way we do business. Otherwise, entropy will take its toll (Figure 8.1). Most of these measurements will be customer focused: are they satisfied or aren't they?

In the requirements process, for example, we might track the percent of requirements actually discovered in comparison to the total over the entire life cycle. If we're only getting 66 percent of the requirements identified in that phase, what process improvements can we put in place to increase that percentage? In the estimating process, for another example, we could track the accuracy of the estimate using DeMarco's *Estimating Quality Factor* (1982). The estimating group can track the difference between the estimate and the actual *over time*. The goal would be to reduce the total area and the number of times the estimate is changed.

Once an improvement is implemented in either of these two processes, we wouldn't need to track their indicators all of the time; perhaps only quarterly to ensure that the results are retained. Then, once we've acted to integrate and measure the process improvement, we can look toward the next evolutionary enhancement of the process.

Software Process Evolution

Once integrated into the existing process, the entire process is available for further improvement, further evolution. No process is perfect. Assume that it can always be improved, that it can always evolve. Otherwise, eventually some other process will displace it. Darwin's "survival of the fittest" applies to processes as well as organisms.

Some processes, however, outlive their usefulness. Be willing to embrace revolutionary new processes when they arrive. Clinging to an outdated process because you have so much time invested in it is not a useful choice. The goal is always the same: for you and your company to survive and thrive in a world of change and uncertainty.

Spreading the Religion

Once an improvement has been planned, done, and checked, it can begin to be distributed among the other tribes of the company who would benefit from its use. Since the improvement was documented with nice, neutral facts, it is hard to argue that "it won't work here" without other nice, neutral facts.

Distributing the improvements to the appropriate points of the compass is the quality council's job. The rest of the organization should be allowed no more than six months to integrate the improvement into their work processes. We need to allow for existing work loads, but not let anyone off the hook for being part of the continuous improvement process.

IS managers should be recognized and rewarded for adapting or adopting improvements in their span of control. IS management or leadership become the missionaries of improvement, helping their people implement the improvements . . . scheduling the changes in appropriate windows of opportunity. IS managers have three ways to respond to the quality council, all of which involve data:

1. *Adopt* the improvement as described and use data to show their improvement
2. *Adapt* the improvement to their environment and use data to prove its merit
3. *Provide* the data and processes to prove that they do it better

Initially, this will require encouragement from the quality council and maybe even a hard-line stand against the old guard, and it will be worth it. When Cortez arrived in the new world, he burned his ships. There was no turning back. Every organization that adopts quality improvement will reach a point where it will have to "burn its ships," because there is no going back. Let the cowboys and buckaroos of software abandon ship and move on to other less efficient companies that will tolerate their antics. Quality improvement is an adventure, a journey toward excellence.

Team Future

Once the team has integrated the improvement into their process, they can choose where they want to go from here. They may choose to:

- Do more in the area they've investigated
- Investigate other components of the Pareto chart
- Implement more countermeasures
- Turn to an entirely different problem
- Change team members
- Disband entirely and start different teams in other areas of interest

These are all reasonable choices. Quality improvement empowers the team to act in the best interest of the company. Trust them. They know what to do next.

USING THE QI TOOLS IN DAILY WORK

The quality problem-solving process works for any kind of fact-based problem analysis. Programmers, analysts, and mangers can use the PDCA process to examine and improve any software process, product, or service. To succeed at solving any problem, it must be within your scope of control (Figure 8.2). Individuals can use the QI tools and problem-solving process on any problem within their control. A programmer, for instance, can use the Ishikawa diagram to evaluate the root causes of a particularly complex program bug. Or they might find an interrelationship digraph helpful. An analyst will find the management and planning tools helpful in all aspects of software design and analysis. People have even used these tools to improve their golf game (60 percent of their strokes are on the green, so putting is a key area for improvement).

Any meeting can benefit from the use of the QI tools. Supervisors will find these tools helpful in staff and planning meetings to quickly organize

and direct the energies of the group. In one instance, use of the affinity diagram and action planning reduced a two-day meeting to just three hours.

The seven problem-solving tools and the seven management and planning tools are a powerful tool kit for structuring your thinking. They also provide a common language for sharing your understanding of a problem or opportunity. They offer a simple way for programmers to talk

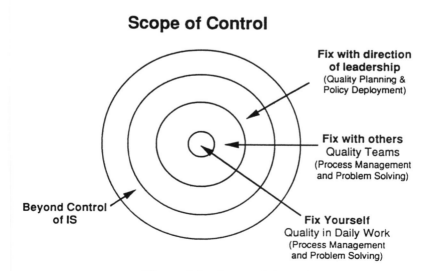

Figure 8.2   Scope of Control

to top management and vice versa. This simplifies communication of ideas from one mind to another.

The quality improvement tools used in their appropriate place in the PDCA process provide a powerful method for identifying and eliminating the root causes of problems. As the problems go away, defects decrease, productivity increases, and the customers become more satisfied.

The preceding chapters have focused on the process and technical legs of quality improvement. The next chapter deals with the complex people issues involved in quality improvement. In a society that rewards individual heroics, we have to learn how to engage people to work as a team.

CHAPTER 9

Quality Improvement Teams

Consider the next law of quality: People solve problems. Continuous quality improvement comes from the active participation of the people in your organization. The quality movement requires that we begin to see everyone, from janitor to manager, as an important person in the scheme of software creation. What would happen if each of us decided that everyone does everything they do for a positive reason? Much of the mystery would fall away and each of us would gain a personal respect for the other person's point of view. The person that is the most annoying or different from us is the person that offers us the broadest potential shift in ways to view things. By learning to respect each person and their beliefs and values, we can create a solid starting point for quality improvement. The knowledge required to change the company's future lies not with just a select few leaders, but with each person who does a job in the company. Working together in teams, these individuals can create meaningful ways to improve the software life cycle, ways that might have been overlooked using just a plain, vanilla task force or management directive.

The only way to accomplish the total quality culture change is to involve every employee—top to bottom. The employee team is the main mechanism for total quality management. These teams focus on identifying customer needs and perfecting processes that will deliver goods and services to fill those needs, thereby delighting the customer. The customer is another person for whom we want to have the highest respect, because they know what they want, even if they often find it difficult to articulate. It is our job, as software specialists, to extract their desires and knowledge in such a way that we can meet and exceed their expectations. Aside from gathering their valid requirements as described in Chapter 4, there are more advanced skills for gathering user requirements (Arthur 1992). Whether the process involves customers, suppliers, or software specialists, we can maximize the power of quality improvement by respecting their ideas and knowledge and bringing it to bear on existing problems and future opportunities.

In many companies, teamwork is not the way that software actually gets done. More likely, each programmer or analyst are viewed as a lone cowboy or cowgirl who singlehandedly rescue various portions of the project. At the SEI process maturity level 2—repeatable, such heroics are common. Software managers rely on software gurus and heroes to pull the project through. To achieve a quality environment, however, the emphasis will have to change to one of quality teams continuously improving their own processes. There will be fewer heroes and more of a sense of community. And with community comes a sense of responsibility to everyone else.

The next law of quality: The employees who will have to change as a result of the quality improvement have to be involved in planning, doing, checking and acting to create and improve the change. The improvement teams are composed of *functional* team members who are familiar with the task, method, or process under investigation. They must be trained in the quality improvement process and group dynamics, so that they can apply the techniques to achieve their goals. Together, they build a story that shows the SCORE (symptoms, causes, outcomes, resources, and effects) required to improve their process.

TQM is not a simple change in the way IS departments conduct business. It is a revolutionary change—from chaos and cowboys to consistency and community. The components of TQM include:

- Team dynamics—communication, consensus, brainstorming, etc.
- Quality council, management, and reward structures to support quality improvement
- Ongoing training in all aspects of TQM
- The quality improvement process or methodology (e.g., PDCA, process management, policy deployment, quality function deployment)

First, we must begin to recognize that quality improvement succeeds through relationship mastery. Suppliers and customers are a family that grows and succeeds together, not lone outposts on the new frontier. To succeed at quality improvement, we must master the art of establishing and maintaining relationships with customers, employees, peers, and suppliers.

FORMING TEAMS

As trivial as it may initially appear, there is a process for forming successful quality improvement teams. There should be three types of teams formed:

- *Task teams* whose problems and indicators are identified by IS leadership based on the quality policies being deployed throughout the organization.
- *Functional teams* of co-workers who share a common customer, process, product, and service. These teams have voluntary participation from their functional work group. These teams should not have cross-functional members from other groups. This only leads to difficulty in completing the process. Cross-functional teams often fail to complete the process. At Florida Power and Light, cross-functional teams were abandoned for this reason. In the early going of TQM, cross-functional teams do not receive the leadership support required to help them along. Cross-functional problem-solving should be initiated by IS leadership.
- *Leadership teams* to support, monitor, and review the quality team's progress. Leadership teams focus on laying the groundwork for TQM, PDCAing the TQM implementation, initiating task teams, and developing policies, goals, and targets for improvement. At Florida Power and Light, lead teams were formed in 1985 to direct quality improvement activities in their work site or department (Hudiburg 1991).

All quality teams should have trained team leaders, who handle the problem solving process, and trained facilitators, who handle the group dynamics and serve as experts in the problem solving process. The selection of the initial quality improvement staff, team leaders, and facilitators will influence the success of TQM. These people need to be "early adopters" of new methods, technologies, and so on. They need to be well-respected in the technical community. They need to be skilled in handling people issues as well as technical issues. They must be deeply interested in the whole quality paradigm. Choosing the right people to begin the TQM transformation will help ensure the success of the initial quality teams and improvement efforts.

In the beginning phases of TQM, it will be easier to start functional teams than task teams because IS leadership won't know any more about identifying problems and indicators than their employees do. TQM is work and traditional IS leadership will attempt to delegate the work required to start task teams. Unfortunately, this results in team failures as well. If IS leadership can't figure out how to measure the problem area and specify a problem to be solved, then neither can the team. Either that or the team will solve something other than what the leadership team wanted. So in the early going, expect a ratio of 20 percent leadership-directed and 80 percent functional teams. Once policy deployment swings into high gear, the teams will shift to more of a 50–50 balance, because more teams will be focused on high-priority, business-related problem solving activities.

Nothing is more crucial to quality team success than getting the right members on the team (either functional or leadership-assigned members). Without the right players, no team can play well together. Who would you want on your "dream team?" The next crucial element is selecting problems for improvement. Functional teams must pick problems within the scope of their control: their customer, processes, products, and services. The initial products they pick must have readily available data or the team will flounder trying to create poorly-constructed surveys or other means of gathering information. The data must be hard data—counted or measured on a frequent basis. It could be time spent, dollars, number of defects, number of milestones met or missed, and so on, but it does have to be objective, not subjective. Using subjective data for the team's first problem-solving adventure is a tar pit from which few teams return. Once a team has more experience with the problem solving process, they will find a need to gather more subjective customer data, but they shouldn't try it in their first attempt.

Once formed, teams need to meet regularly and consistently. Meeting times should fall during the work day; this tells the team that quality is part of their work, not just an add-on. If possible, the team should meet in the same room at the same time every week. This way, the room and time become an anchor for the team's problem solving activities. It reduces startup time in each meeting because the room is familiar, everyone has their preferred seat, and people feel like they are picking up where they left off.

As the team moves along, it will need to present its findings to gather leadership support along the way. The most common points to present to a leadership team are:

- After an indicator and a problem are selected
- Following the identification of root causes and countermeasures, but before implementation
- After results and during integration of the improvements

The presentation should take 15 to 30 minutes and no more. Teams should send out their quality improvement story before the presentation for review. Then in the meeting, they discuss their graphs, charts, diagrams, and findings. The problem-solving process is told with pictures and a few words, not with tomes of black print on white paper. They should also identify the intangible benefits derived from working on the problem and any useful byproducts. Teams often discover "no brainers" that can be implemented immediately to begin to alleviate the problem. More than one team has achieved incredible results along the way and only used the countermeasures step to standardize how to maintain the gains.

GROUP DYNAMICS

Quality teams succeed through working together. In the early going, members are coming together and seeking their niche in the team. To secure their position, there will be some squabbling or storming during team meetings. To the untrained eye, this might appear to be a problem, but it is actually one of the key stages a team must experience if it is to achieve a high-performance mode. Once the storming is over, there is a period of calm and finally the team gets down to conquering the task.

During the early phases of team formation, the team leader and facilitator lean heavily on verbal skills to help the team come together. Icebreaker exercises help the team members learn about each other and, although seemingly non-productive in relationship to the task, correctly forming the team will ensure that it performs at peak efficiency and effectiveness. If the team forms poorly, it will constantly drop back into the storming stage and progress will be impeded.

Once the team arrives at the performance stage, the team leader and facilitator shift to focusing on the problem to be solved. They keep a three-month plan in front of them so that they know where they are going so that they can keep the team focused and moving. The behavioral issues move to the back burner.

Once a team has reached the performance stage, addition or loss of team members can devastate the team's performance. Addition of a new member almost always throws the team back into the early stages of team formation. Avoid changes in membership if at all possible. It can be useful, however, to occasionally bring in different facilitators to provide new viewpoints to the team. This helps avoid what is called "group think" where everyone agrees, but they are headed down the path to failure. It's easy, for example, to get caught up in solving someone else's problem. Quality teams can only solve problems in their own work area.

Having teams led by one person and facilitated by another ensures that both the task and the people issues will be observed and managed during the team meeting. Without both, teams can become dysfunctional and cease to make progress. Group dynamics play a key role in the success of quality improvement teams.

SUSTAINING MOMENTUM

It does not matter how slowly you go as long as you do not stop.
—Confucius

As teams move through the process, leadership and the quality staff should monitor the teams and their progress. If a team gets stuck or bogged down, it should call on the internal staff to help it get going again. Without a sense of accomplishment, attendance at team meetings will fall off and progress will slow even farther. Teams should feel free to call on a supervisor to visit the team and offer encouragement or direction. Most IS managers are "interrupt-driven." If you call and get on their calendar, they'll show up. If you wait for them to call to visit the team, it will rarely happen. Most teams will need frequent coaching to chart their way through their first problem-solving process. As they get into more difficult problems, they will need further help in advanced statistical and quality tools. Be willing to ask for help. Quality is about learning and sharing and growing together as an organization.

Indecision is nearly always the worst mistake you can make.

Because the process is unfamiliar, teams often hesitate to move forward. The best teams are often thinking ahead: What data will I need? If we go down this path, where will it lead? The best and fastest teams often rough out the planning step of the process just to see where it will lead. They often try several approaches to determine which would be the most interesting and have the highest payoff. The best team leaders are willing to experiment, throw things away and refocus. The first few problems solved will be a major learning process. Trying to do it perfectly will only lead to frustration and dead ends.

SUMMARY

The implementation of TQM succeeds through teamwork—leaders, programmers, analysts, and managers. TQM demands a level of teamwork that most IS professionals will find uncomfortable at first because it will seem unfamiliar. After a while, however, it will become a more natural and more productive way of working together.

Quality succeeds through human interaction—relationships among people. Balancing behavioral issues and the problem-solving task is critical to the success of the team and TQM. Software engineers, because of their comfort with technology and discomfort with people, will find working in quality teams to be a challenge initially, and ultimately very rewarding. Respect for each individual and the team as a whole is one of the foundational principles of TQM. Only through engaging the wisdom of every employee can software organizations begin to climb the stairway to software excellence.

In the next chapter, we'll look at ways to define and measure processes. Once defined, we'll look at ways to identify the value-added and non-value-added functions, which will enable us to reengineer the process to streamline and eliminate waste and rework.

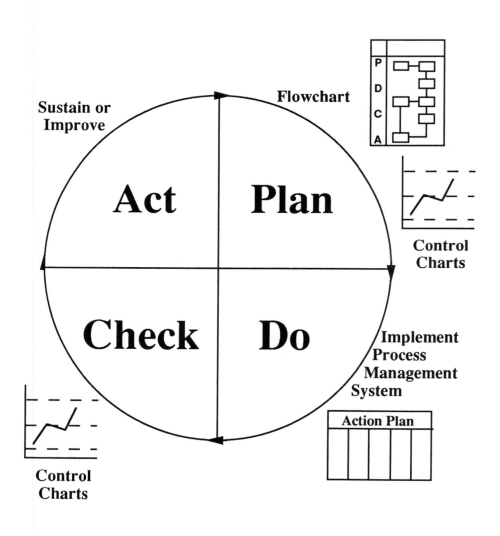

CHAPTER 10

Process Management—Doing Things Right

Process management focuses on all repetitive, cyclical, or routine work and its improvement. Process management ensures that daily work will be done in such a way as to sustain current level of productivity and quality. It also helps us identify opportunities to improve customer satisfaction and to reduce defects, costs, and cycle time. Process management defines processes, who owns them, requirements for those processes, measurements of both the process and its outputs, and feedback channels. Process management supports the quality problem solving process by laying the groundwork for improvement—the processes and measurements of SEI maturity level 3 and 4—and by identifying opportunities for improvement.

Process management begins by defining your most important processes as they currently exist—*baselining*. Like everything else in quality improvement, process management seeks to focus on the vital few processes that achieve the majority of your customer's requirements and satisfaction. Information Systems processes are only a small component of larger business processes. A process like *billing* covers much of the organization, from new product introduction to collections. Anywhere there is a key product, service, and customer, you have a key process. IS processes are usually one link in the chain of delivering that service or product. At a high level, most software processes involve business planning, software creation and evolution, software operation, and software operation (Figure 10.1). These processes can be developed into

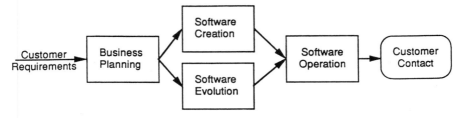

Figure 10.1   Main Software Processes

more detailed processes. Quality improvement will be difficult without ongoing definition of IS processes.

As the SEI discovered, 88 percent of all software departments are still lost in the initial stage of process maturity. Process management helps us define our processes and the measurements that evaluate them. Process management helps us climb through levels three and four of the SEI maturity framework. The steps to process management ask the following questions:

1. Who are our customers? What do they want from us? What is the most important thing we do? What is the order of priority of all the things we do? What measurements can we use to know how we are doing?
2. Who are our suppliers? What do they do for us? What is the most important thing they do? What measurements can we use to know how they are doing?
3. Who is the overall owner of the process and who owns the sub-processes?
4. How does the process work now? How do we want it to work?
5. Which portion of this process is the most "out of control?" What part of the process is causing our customers the most problem?
6. What does the customer expect from us and this process? How will we measure it? What are appropriate goals for improvement?
7. How can we begin to improve?

The old question is often asked: "Which came first, the chicken or the egg?" Quality teams came before process management, but it may not be useful to keep the two in that order. Process management grew out of the need that most teams experience—most software processes are ill-defined, poorly measured, and rarely owned by anyone. It is hard to improve a process that isn't defined, measured, or managed. In the cases where there is available data and a defined process, you can leap right into quality improvement. In cases where there is none, however, you will need to stop and define the process before initiating improvements. Process management is ultimately about giving control of processes back to the people who own them.

One of the advantages IS experiences with process management is that anyone trained in structured systems analysis will have a head start on defining and refining processes. Virtually everyone has some level of understanding of system design using flowcharts or data flow diagrams. This is a key element of process management.

Once everyone has had a minimum of two days training in quality improvement tools and techniques, and had experience on at least one quality improvement team, we can begin to use the quality tools in our daily work to ''PDCA'' how we're doing.

Programmers, analysts, project managers, and supervisors can all track and improve their work on a daily basis. Programmers, for example, could measure the number of compiler errors in their first and successive compilations, analyze their error tendencies, and seek to reduce them *each time* they compile a program. They could also track the kinds of defects they uncover in unit and integration testing, analyze these as well, and take action to prevent them in the future.

An analyst can track the types of user requirements discovered *after* the requirements phase, develop a Pareto of the most common types, and evolve the requirements process to ensure that these common requirements are captured early in the process. An analyst could also track the information loss that occurs between requirements and design, or design and code.

A project manager can track the types of requested changes and their impact on schedules. They might also evaluate the effectiveness of their estimation process against actuals and determine, over time, how to improve the accuracy of their estimates. If there is one thing a customer hates is to be told one time and price, and later discover that the cost is twice as much.

Since supervisors serve employees, they can have their employees evaluate their management style, analyze the root cause of their deficiencies, and act to improve their management and leadership styles. They can begin to track the timeliness and accuracy of the decisions they make.

Testing organizations can track the types of defects that slip through the testing process, analyze the root cause, and put countermeasures in place to catch the more slippery kinds of defects that the testing process misses.

PROCESS MANAGEMENT

The customer-supplier analysis discussed in Chapter 5 is one of the key elements of process management. By understanding who our customers are, what their valid requirements are, and how to work with our suppliers to achieve our own requirements, we can begin to meet and exceed our customer's expectations. The customer will always want us to be better, faster, and cheaper than we were before. Process management helps us define, measure, and improve how our processes are performing. It helps us identify weaknesses in any step and take action to move them dramatically in the direction our customer requires. Of course, this means that we will often make new and unusual demands of our suppliers as we change our processes to meet our customer's needs, wants, and wishes.

Customer-supplier models are much like the food chain in nature (Figure 10.2)—a cycle of connected elements that feed each other in an endless chain. Everyone is both a supplier of someone else and a customer of another. One complete ''process'' may encompass many of these chains. The software life cycle is only one component of many larger chains in a corporation, but as we have seen, it is an increasingly important one. Rather than dig into all of the ramifications of process management, let's just look at how to manage the software process.

The SEI Maturity Framework states that you have to define your software processes to move up to level three and measure those processes to move to level four, so we might as well look at ways to define and measure our process using process management.

THE PROCESS MANAGEMENT PROCESS

Process management follows the PDCA model directly (Figure 10.3). It employs the following process:

Plan

1. Identify the most important process for serving your customer
2. Flowchart the process
3. Identify where to measure the process

Do

4. Install the process management system—the steps and the measures

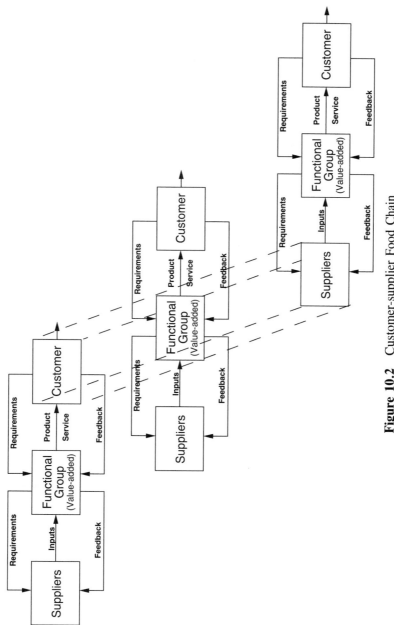

Figure 10.2 Customer-supplier Food Chain

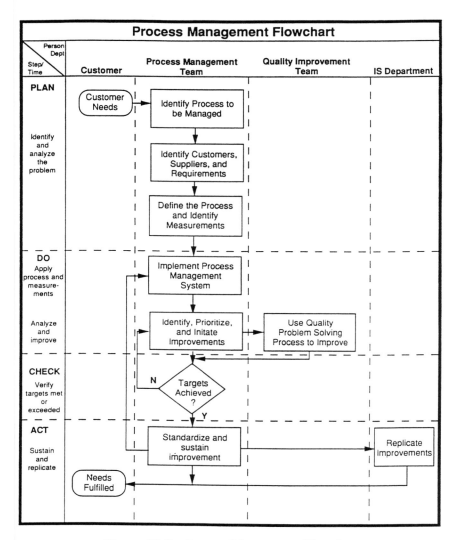

Figure 10.3 Process Management Flowchart

Check

5. Analyze the process:
   - Are the process measures stable and repeatable?
   - Are the output indicators meeting the customer's valid requirements? If not, change the process to achieve stability and meet their requirements

Act

6. Standardize, replicate, and continuously improve the process

Process management systems help new and existing employees learn what to do; it helps lay the groundwork for quality improvement teams; it maintains the gains from quality improvements; it provides a vehicle for replicating those changes across the organization to multiply their benefits, and it helps identify the key processes required for breakthrough improvement in quality and productivity.

Identify the Most Important Process

Like everything in quality improvement, we want to start with the most important processes first—Pareto's 80/20 rule again. The most important process may not be the most obvious one. The most important process will be the one with which your most important customer experiences the most dissatisfaction in regard to the delivery of a product or service. So, for example, a project manager might be doing an excellent job of managing a development project but a lousy job of keeping the customer informed of progress and jeopardy situations. In this case, the most important process might be a status communication process between the project manager and the customer.

A process is the step-by-step method you use to satisfy your customer's needs. To begin to identify the most important process in your organization:

1. Create a list of the most important customers. For each customer, list the most important products or services they receive and for each product or service, list the most important processes required to produce it.
2. Then ask: Where and how does my customer experience the most dissatisfaction with these products or services?
3. Identify the most important process with regard to relieving their dissatisfaction. Use consensus of the group and gather input from your customers to determine if you have actually hit their key frustration or not.

Flowchart the Process

Once you've identified the most important process, customer, and product or service, you will need to develop structured flowcharts of the process. This flowchart begins with the customer's valid requirements and ends with the customer being satisfied. It may involve people, tasks, methods, tools, materials, and environmental factors. Like any good system design, the first flowchart should be more general and describe the process at a higher level. More detailed flowcharts will be needed to document the more detailed, lower-level processes. At the highest level (Figure 10.4), there are business planning, software creation, evolution, and operation processes. Below this high-level flow, there are macro processes for each like the software evolution process shown. Below these, there are successive levels of micro processes.

To flowchart the process, gather the people who actually do the process now. Avoid using the flowchart in your software life cycle methodology because it is rarely how work actually gets done. Use it as a reference only. Other sources of process information will include job descriptions, procedures, standards, and any checklists that exist.

The structured flowchart (Figure 10.3) begins to evolve from the customer and moves into the actual process flow for delivering the product or service. The key players are listed across the top of the

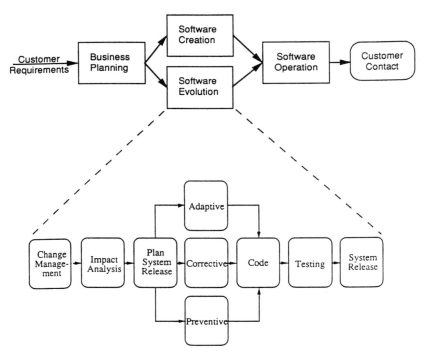

Figure 10.4   Macro and micro processes

flowchart and the major processes are listed along the left. If you don't know what to put on the left-hand side, use the PDCA steps because every process should include elements of them. Use a large white board and sticky notes, or a large pushpin board and index cards to lay out the first version of the flowchart. These can be easily moved around as the participants wrestle with how work *actually* flows through the department.

Once the major decisions and actions have been identified, use a graphical tool to lay out the entire process including arrows, boxes, descriptions, and so on. Review this flow with supervision and your customer.

You may discover ways to simplify the process flow just by looking at it. If so, and you can get agreement of all of the contributors, then change the process to its more simplified version now. This will help reduce the need for future improvements.

Identify Where to Measure the Process

Once we've flowcharted the process, we need to measure it to ensure that it is stable and capable of meeting customer requirements.

For any process, we need to determine the customer's valid requirements for the output of that process (see Chapter 4). The key to valid requirements is that they must be *measurable*. If they aren't measurable, there is no way to tell if we are meeting our customer's needs. Process management requires that we instrument the process in such a way that we can measure the output of our process to assess conformance to valid requirements, and measure the upstream "process indicators" that tell us whether the process will deliver the outputs we expect.

Output indicators determine the quality of the product or service delivered. There should be an output indicator for each of our customer's valid requirements. Output indicators include system availability, response time, timeliness, and cost. For many of these measures, such as system availability, we are already achieving greater than 80 percent conformance with requirements, so it is better to measure the *non-conformance*—system unavailability (Figure 10.5). The target is two percent unavailability—62 hours per year (3132 possible hours per year). This diagram shows that we missed the customer's valid requirements in two out of 12 months. So the process appears to be stable, but it is still incapable of meeting the customer's needs. Focusing on the customer's pain instead of their pleasure is an excellent way to focus the efforts of quality improvement. Once we begin meeting the customer's valid requirements, we know that they will want even better performance. So we

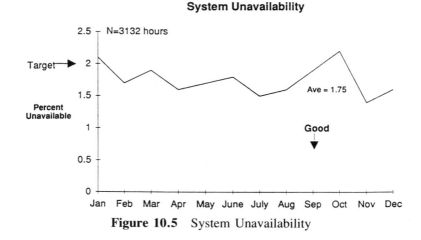

Figure 10.5 System Unavailability

will need to set targets perhaps a year or two out to reduce the system's unavailability to 1.5 percent, 1.0 percent, and eventually 0.6 percent. Targets for these indicators are based on our customer's needs, our own past performance, our competitor's performance, improving technology, and any other factor that might influence our process capability.

Output indicators help us determine whether we are meeting the customer's needs, but they are usually too far down the road to allow us to recover if there is a problem. Process indicators, on the other hand, measure upstream deliverables in such a way that we can determine if the process will deliver the results we expect. In the case of system unavailability, process indicators could include daily unavailability, failures during system test, and the magnitude of a system release (in Function Points). In a rapid prototyping environment, the growth of the system in lines of code, function points, and daily defect rates could all be process indicators of the successful evolution of a new software system.

Process indicators are best applied early in the process wherever some intermediate work product moves from one processor to the next, or from one step of the process to the next. The goal is to develop an early warning system of potential problems in the delivered product or service. These indicators should be tracked in a control chart so that we can determine if the process is stable.

Most software processes, however, are so poorly defined that there are huge variations in performance. Only through instrumentation and improvement can these processes begin to achieve the level of quality and productivity we desire. That's why a process management system is so important. It defines the process and tells us where to measure. The next step is to implement the process management system.

Implement the Process Management System

Once we've defined the flow of the process and where to measure it, we need to review it with our customers to ensure that we are indeed going after their valid requirements. Based on their input, we may need to revise the output or process indicators to ensure that they match the valid requirements and the targets we've set for improvement. Then we need to train all users of the process in the process management system how to collect the data and track it using control charts. We will need a clear action plan of who does what activity and when they do it. Like all quality activities, we will need to PDCA the implementation and make minor improvements as we standardize the process and its measurements.

Analyze the Process

Once the process is in place and we begin collecting data about the process, we will need a way to track and display the data in a graphical format that will help us analyze the process. To determine if a process is stable and capable of meeting our customer's valid requirements, we will need to use control charts to track the data. Control charts are nothing more than a simple line graph with statistically calculated limits for the data. Control charts assume that there will always be some variation in how a process performs, but that there will be predictable variation that is inherent in the process and special causes of variation that will occur from identifiable people, places, events, materials, or whatever. Control charts (Figure 10.6) calculate the upper and lower control limits from the data. 99.7 percent of all points will be contained within these two limits. Points outside of these limits indicate a process that is out of control. Each point outside of the control limits needs to be investigated and the *special causes* of process variation removed so that the process will become stable. What are special causes of variation? A flooded computer room might qualify, unless it happens frequently. A missed code inspection might qualify, unless they are avoided frequently. The incorrect installation of an old program might qualify, unless this happens repeatedly. Points within the upper and lower control limits vary in response to the *common causes* of variation—response time, processing volumes, and so on. Control charts help us identify and eliminate the special causes of variation and then reduce the common causes and improve the

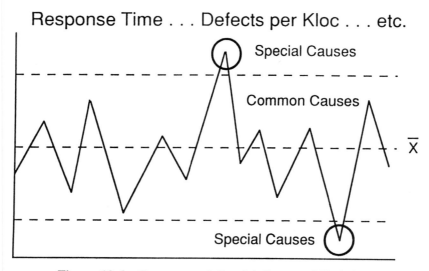

Response Time . . . Defects per Kloc . . . etc.

Figure 10.6   Common and Special Causes of Variation

entire process. Control charts improve our ability to plan and predict the delivery and performance of software, while giving us early warning signals of potential problems. To make our processes stable (Figure 10.7), we need to eliminate the special causes of variation. These special causes show up as data points outside of the calculated limits. They need to be identified and eliminated.

Then, we can begin to use the quality improvement, problem-solving process to begin to improve the process, reduce variation, and meet the customer's valid requirements. Once the process is both stable and meeting or exceeding the customer's needs, we can then say that the process is *capable* (Figure 10.7).

Initial **Chaotic** Process

Stable
(Special Causes Removed)

Capable
(Common Causes Reduced to meet
Customer Valid Requirements)

Figure 10.7   Process Evolution from Chaos to Stable to Capable

This is a simplified view of how to use control charts to improve software processes. There are many different varieties of control charts, depending on the data used—time, number of defects, percent defective, and so on. Since the discussion of control charts would make a book all of its own, please refer to the bibliography for excellent references.

Integrate, Replicate, and Continuously Improve

Once the process management system is installed, stable, and capable, we can standardize it for use within our own work group. Then, to maximize the benefit of this process, we need to replicate it across the organization to multiply its benefits. We've all heard of reusable code, and now we have a way to establish reusable processes. To succeed at replicating process management systems, we need to make them as simple as possible (but no simpler, as Albert Einstein would say); we need to train everyone in using the system; and we need to communicate the ''whys'' and ''hows'' to all employees.

One of the more obvious problems with replicating any thing is the NIH—not invented here—syndrome. To overcome the natural resistance to external forces, we need to:

1. Identify the appropriate places for replication. Who could most likely benefit from this process?
2. Give the supervisor in that area three to six months to implement the process management system. The group will need time and training to accomplish the objective.
3. Follow up to ensure that the system was either:
   - implemented as defined
   - adapted for the environment with data to support the changes
   - or a better system was already in place. Data and a process management system must be used to demonstrate superiority, not just ''gut feel.''
4. Quality improvement projects can then be aimed at improving the process to reduce cycle time, cut costs, improve reliability, or whatever the customer desires. **If it ain't broke, improve it anyway because it ain't perfect yet**.

Begin by investigating opportunities for improvement in each function: Is this task really necessary? Is it rework? Does it undo the work of someone else? Is it redundant? Could it be done in parallel with other activities?

Investigate opportunities at the interfaces between customer and suppliers, and between processes and functions. What elements are lost, revised, or misunderstood in between elements or activities? Are requirements and feedback communicated adequately? Are there unreasonable delays or costs or chances for error? Is there a more efficient or effective way to accomplish this interaction?

Rank the improvement possibilities—use a prioritization matrix (effectiveness, feasibility, impact on customer)—select the most effective and impactful improvements. Work on the vital few, not the trivial many.

SUMMARY

Process management is a valuable quality improvement tool that helps us document our process and figure out how to instrument the process and its outputs to meet our customer's valid requirements. Process management should come naturally to software engineers because the software life cycle focuses on requirements gathering and design of automated solutions to process problems. By flowcharting any process, we can begin to see its strengths and weaknesses and begin to correct them immediately. This can be especially useful in software creation, because we want to ensure that we automate the most effective and efficient means of achieving the customer's goals rather than merely automating the existing complex and wasteful process.

Once the process has been documented and refined, we can identify the output indicators that measure our conformance to the customer's valid requirements. This tells us if we are delivering what the customer wants. Also, we identify the upstream ''process'' indicators that will serve as an early warning network about our process and its potential success. All of these indicators are tracked via some form of control chart which enables us to tell if the process is stable and capable of meeting the customer's needs. If the process isn't stable, then we need to eliminate the special causes of variation. If it is stable, then we need to make sure that it is capable—meeting the customer's valid requirements. If not, then we need to initiate quality improvement teams to reduce the common causes of variation and begin to move the process through a series of targets aimed at meeting the customer's ultimate goals.

Only through defining the process (SEI maturity level 3) and measuring the process (SEI maturity level 4) can we build a stable platform from which to begin to continuously improve every aspect of software creation and evolution (SEI maturity level 5). Process management involves a level of structure that software engineers may find initially constrictive, but they will ultimately find that it frees them to be more successful, both in quality and productivity, than they have ever been before. It will create more time to investigate new technology and to explore what is possible through automation. Ultimately, process management will drive new levels of customer satisfaction and excitement. That is where the fun truly begins.

CHAPTER 11

Supporting Software Quality Improvement

There is nothing more difficult to take in hand, more perilous to conduct, or more uncertain in its success than to take the lead in the introduction of a new order of things.

> —*Nicolo Machiavelli*
> (The Prince)

Quality is not an act. It is a habit.

> —*Aristotle*

If you can't come, send nobody.
> —*William E. Conway (Deming 1986, pg. 21)*

Adopt and institute leadership.

> —*W. Edwards Deming*

Establishing Total Quality Management will reduce risk, costs, and cycle time, and increase productivity and customer satisfaction. To be successful, TQM must be viewed as a management *system* that replaces the existing management system over time. TQM is not an add-on to daily work, but rather the way work gets done from day to day and year to year. TQM is the most effective known way to deal with the size and complexity of the problems that occur in our global market. By serving customers more effectively and efficiently through TQM, we can secure our foothold in the market and begin to expand both market share and profits through better quality and lower costs. First comes customer satisfaction, and then profits. Focusing only on profits blocks the employee's view of why they are working. People rarely work just for profit, although Wall Street might have us think otherwise. People work for the satisfaction of fulfilling a need in the community. Focusing on the customer broadens everyone's horizon and with that panoramic view, opportunities appear and profits grow.

Through serving customers in better ways than anyone had ever thought possible, employees enjoy their work more than ever and continuously improve their commitment to products and services, which keeps customers coming back for more. Achieving this level of employee involvement happens through a management commitment to continuous training and education at all levels in the quality management system. Everyone needs to study the quality improvement methods, visit other companies to see what they are doing, try various improvement approaches, and learn from the mistakes that often occur on the way to mastery.

It is no use to exhort workers to "do better" or "do it faster" because most of the things that contribute to being "better, faster, and cheaper" rest in the hands of management—excellent training, tools, materials, process, and environment. Since TQM is a management system, it cannot be delegated to a quality department or group. Everyone from the executives to the administrative staff of the IS organization must participate in quality improvement, especially the executives. Of course, you will need a group to assist with the process of training, supplying materials, and measuring the progress of the TQM implementation, but they are not the keepers of the flame. If you make them the keepers, it will go out. Only senior management can light the torch of quality and keep it burning through their persistence. To date, no quality system has survived unless the management team supports it completely. Top management has to be convinced that quality is the right thing to do and that they are prepared to take the leadership role in initiating and implementing the evolution. Then they convince middle and line management.

IMPLEMENTING QUALITY IMPROVEMENT

There are five key stages of implementing quality improvement (Walton 1991):

1. Deciding to adopt continuous quality improvement
2. Incubation of the quality improvement paradigm

3. Planning and promotion to ensure success
4. Education of everyone, top to bottom, and ongoing
5. Continuous and never ending improvement

The decision to adopt continuous quality improvement can begin almost anywhere, but it will be most effective if the transformation begins at the top of the organization. The transformation often begins when top management hears about quality from their peers in other companies. Or sometimes they attend training that causes their "conversion." Some top managers travel to Japan to become quality converts. Others begin by reading articles about quality and slowly expand their understanding and interest in learning TQM.

The incubation of the quality improvement requires fundamental quality planning by top management. It would help if they got an advisor from Japan or an American company that has implemented TQM. To begin the planning process, top management must develop and continuously improve a mission, vision, and values. Figure 11.1 offers questions to help develop these key foundations of TQM. Our mission asks: What are we in business for? The vision asks: What will we look, sound, and feel like when we have become a quality-oriented company? And our values ask: What should we believe and value that will create a fertile environment for quality to grow? The toughest issue for top leadership is to understand quality so well and so far in advance of their employees that they can literally "walk the talk." Without the ability to demonstrate quality commitment, employees will know that leaders are only "talking the talk" and paying "lip service" to quality improvement. Little will happen until the leadership tries on the quality paradigm and becomes comfortable with it.

Planning and promotion are key elements of implementing TQM. Employees in most companies have become skeptical and almost immune to management "programs." So it will take time and effort to override their concerns. "How long will this one last?" they ask. Only our "constancy of purpose," as Deming describes it, can give them the answer. Top management can begin by setting world-class objectives for the organization, identifying the processes needed to get there, continually evaluating progress toward those objectives, and correcting course to ensure that we move toward excellence.

Education in quality is vital and then the training must be put to use. The training must involve everyone from the leaders to the clerical staff that support the programmers. The training must be continuous and ongoing. You can't just read a book, take a class, and be TQM certified. This book touches the surface of TQM. Like the blind men touching the

What is our aim?

Who are our customers?

What do we want to become?

How are we going to get there?

What are the barriers?

How will we know we are making progress?

What are our principal processes?

Which are the most in need of improvement?

Do our compensation and recognition systems further our objectives?

What business are we in?

What products or services do we supply? Present, past, future?

What human needs do we fulfill?

What is the prime purpose of the company? To serve the needs of the customer or
to make money?

Who are our customers?

What do they desire?

What is management's role and how do we go about carrying it ou;t?

What is the most important thing we do?

How will you measure our progress?

What are our goals?

What are our strategies?

Figure 11.1   Questions to Help Develop Values

elephant, it will take you many years to see the whole elephant and many
more years to fully understand and personify its many systems and
abilities.

And finally, we must develop a climate of continuous and never-
ending improvement. Managers become leaders who coach teams and
support the implementation of improvements. Everyone masters the
quality improvement process. It becomes part of the fabric of everyday
life and everyone's thinking. The company continuously invests in developing the ''core competencies'' of its people, especially quality improvement.

TOP EXECUTIVE SPONSORSHIP AND LEADERSHIP

Quality improvement requires an act of faith that having a quality process
will never cost money because TQM will always cause us to have lower
costs, better products, and more market share. Top executives must
believe this and operate from this belief at all times. IS leadership must
provide the resources, training and education required. A quality improvement staff provides the foundation to support the development of
quality. The employees at all levels engage in the improvement process.

TQM is not an "easy sell," however. Most software departments are still mired in the tar pits of the initial phase of the SEI maturity framework. There is an inherent distrust in such an environment—managers of technicians, customers of management, technicians of customers. Distrust, on all levels, is a key barrier to the successful implementation of TQM. In the beginning, many people regard quality improvement as an addition to or interfering with "regular" work. They will ask: "I thought we were already doing quality work. If we've been so successful at solving problems, why do we need this quality improvement process?" The answer is plain: we have always done well enough to get by as long as the competition was no better. If we've been so good at solving problems, why are there so many problems still around? Only through the support and encouragement of management can the quality improvement work weave its way into the "regular" work.

Perhaps the greatest challenge of establishing quality improvement in an organization is the sponsorship and leadership of the top executive in that organization. Without his or her participation, quality improvement will not succeed. Everyone, from the top down, must develop a clear understanding of the quality improvement process and, from working with the process, develop a commitment to its success. To begin your own personal transformation:

1. *Gather information.* Start to gather all the information you can about your customers and what they want. Gather data about how well you are meeting those needs and expectations. Gather data from other customers you want to have or customers you have lost. Gather data about the competition. From these various perspectives, the areas for improvement will pop out at you. Then set some "heroic" improvement goals and targets for their completion.

2. *Learn all you can about TQM.* Read books, take courses, visit Baldrige award-winning companies, visit Japan.

3. *Commit to TQM* as the management system of the future.

4. *Begin sowing the seeds of quality improvement* and cultivating them. Teach everyone the basic principles and tools of quality improvement.

Management has three key roles: maintain the current ability to produce products and services (process management); incrementally improve processes, people, materials, machines and environment (problem-solving); and achieve breakthrough improvements through innovation and quality planning to focus the problem solving efforts.

The essence of what we have to do to integrate quality more quickly will be to:

- *Develop a clear vision* of how the organization will look, sound, feel, and act under the influence of quality improvement
- *Develop challenging policies and objectives* for improvement of quality, cost, and delivery
- *Develop a fact-based, "common language"* for quality improvement that uses the seven original and seven new tools of quality improvement
- *Establish an evolutionary measurement process* to supply the facts
- *Define all software processes*—creation, evolution, documentation, and so on
- *Establish continuous, challenging quality education* at all levels
- *Commit to quality* as a way of life and personal excellence
- *Transform the recognition and reward systems*
  —From individual to team rewards
  —Formal and informal quality team recognition
- *Create the data collection systems* required

In the process of establishing these foundations, most companies follow the form, storm, norm, perform model of implementing TQM:

Form Early adopters say: "Okay I'll try it. I'm willing to do anything to change the way we work."

Storm After months (if not years) of trying to solve problems, employees and management seem to say: "It's not working! I'm frustrated!" Meanwhile, the "not-invented-here" people hold out, waiting for the process to go away.

Norm Ultimately, the CEO has to say: "We are going to do this, so get on the bus." If we could figure out a way to summon our peak performance *before* we get tired and mad, I think we could really move the quality process along. Maybe we need the "soft" approach to lure the early adopters, role models, and start-up community, and then have a plan in place to shake up the holdouts.

Perform With the dedicated commitment of the top management of the corporation, employees begin to say: "We can do this" and as they begin to succeed they come to the realization that: "This really works!"

To succeed at the implementation of TQM, we need to follow the metaphors of craftsmanship and mastery. Within the discipline of TQM, we have the uninitiated, the beginners, intermediates, and masters. To succeed at TQM, we need to rapidly develop 7 ± 2 people to the intermediate or master level. Training alone will not do this . . . only experience can. Select a TQM team, train the dickens out of them, send them to Japan, and get them involved for a few months at a Deming Prize-winning company or a Baldrige award winner. Have them work alongside the masters. It may seem like a significant investment, but it is nothing compared to starting quality teams and activities with only a beginner's level of knowledge. Seeking to start TQM with a few people going to one training course is like trying to perform brain surgery after reading a book about it.

Continue to develop these masters and, in turn, have them develop other masters until the skills weave their way into the fabric of the organization. In every exploration of new frontiers, there have been pioneers and people who have returned to lead others. These kind of systemic changes happen not by trying to get everyone trained at the same time, but by forging a path that others can follow.

MIDDLE MANAGEMENT

Above all else, middle management, like top management, must be involved in quality improvement. Middle management will want to:

1. Initiate, advise, and approve work on theme (problem/opportunity) areas
2. Approve suggested countermeasures and steps
3. Standardize and manage process improvements
4. Recognize and reward quality improvement activities
5. Attend quality team meetings to support, not interfere, with their work
6. Create a sense of urgency and stimulate interest

An enlightened middle management layer can greatly facilitate the quality implementation. An uninformed middle layer can kill it. For some reason, the top and bottom layers of an organization respond most easily to TQM. The middle management group, however, are rewarded for accomplishing business projects and resolving issues. They often view TQM as just another stone in their pack, not a way to deliver better quality products and services faster. The reward and recognition system for middle management needs to be one of the first to change to support TQM. They need the training to understand and help drive the process into the organization. Top leadership cannot do it alone. Neither can the workers, as evidenced by the rise and fall of quality circles. Get the middle managers on the side of TQM early in the exploration and its implementation will flow much more smoothly.

RECOGNITION AND REWARD

You get what you measure and you get what you reward. If you don't like the results you are getting, it is because the reward system is encouraging it. Most American reward systems encourage competition between individuals, groups, and departments. They also encourage individualism. TQM requires that we encourage cooperation among everyone in the company. TQM requires that we move toward rewarding teamwork to accomplish corporate objectives. While there is still room for individual contribution, it is not such a huge portion of the reward and recognition system under TQM. To succeed at implementing TQM, we must focus energy on one key element of the existing system:

- **Changing the reward and recognition system**

  Nothing else has the power to change behavior like a change in this system. Getting ahead of all of the recognition, reward, data collection, and customer-engagement systems required will also accelerate the process. Borrow these "honorably" from other successful companies (or work with your own internal customers—employees). The best way to go about it is to benchmark the reward and recognition systems in Baldrige Award and Deming Prize-winning companies and adapt the best of the best for your own company. Once the rewards are in place, we need to establish challenging objectives.

ESTABLISHING CHALLENGING OBJECTIVES

Quality companies set outrageous objectives and achieve them. Motorola is somewhat famous for its six-sigma program. They want to drive all of their products to a level of 3.4 defects per million. That means that everything, including their software will be 99.99966 percent correct by 1993. They began in the early 80s by setting 100-fold improvement goals. When they reached the first 100-fold improvement in the mid 80s, they raised the bar to another 100-fold improvement. When they reached that in the late 80s, they raised the bar again and set their six-sigma goal for 1993. Xerox set a four year goal to slash the cost of producing a copier by 50 percent while simultaneously improving reliability by a factor of four.

When everyone understands the problem-solving process and the company's objectives for improvement, dramatic improvements are possible and desirable. Top management needs to set "heroic goals," ensure their achievement through quality improvement, and "raise the bar" to ensure continued improvement.

Quality planning and competitive benchmarking will help determine where to set the goals in relationship to the competition and the corporation's ability to achieve these goals and targets.

MEASUREMENT

Like everything else in quality, the only way to observe management's commitment to quality is through measurement. The amount of time all management levels commit to quality improvement activities is a key indicator:

Management commitment = time allocated to quality issues / total time spent

In quality oriented companies, this percentage is usually 40–60 percent. In most initial quality efforts, management spends a token amount of time on quality. Let's say that they spend two hours a month on quality—meetings, learning, visiting teams, or whatever. Further let's assume that managers only work 40 hours a week for four weeks a month (160 hours):

Management commitment = 2 hours/160 hours/month = 1.25 %

Employees measure management commitment through actions they can observe. Clearly, one percent a month is not going to translate into observable commitment. In a TQM company, 64–96 hours will be commited to quality. Everyone can observe management's commitment to quality.

In comparison, employees in a non-TQM company can measure the fire fighting quotient—the amount of time managers spend responding to emergencies caused by poor quality. In a typical company, fire fighting is typically 60 percent of a manager's job:

Fire fighting quotient = time spent fighting symptoms / total time spent

In a TQM company, the fire fighting quotient drops below 20 percent. Reductions in administrivia and other wasteful activities account for the remaining time devoted to quality. Time management plays a key role in a manager's ability to commit to quality. The tyranny of the urgent must be constantly replaced with the achievement of the important. Fire fighters, especially ones promoted for their ability to put out fires, will not change over-night, but they will need to embrace quality or face their own extinction.

TRAINING FOR QUALITY

> *Total Quality Control starts with training and ends with training. To imple-ment TQC, we need to carry out continuous education for everyone, from the president down to line workers.*
>
> —*Kaoru Ishikawa*

Empowering employees to solve the problems of the business is the second largest investment IS will ever make and the best one as well. Most of the companies that go after the Malcolm Baldrige award spend a minimum of four days and about $1,400 per person to train employees in the use of the quality improvement process. Motorola has found that quality training delivers a 33:1 return on investment (Moskal 1990). Every Motorola employee must take a minimum of 40 hours of training each year (Heilig 1990). Every Motorola department spends 2.4–2.8 percent of its budget on training and they expect to double the amount of training by 1995 to sustain competitive advantage.

> *Competent* [people] *in every position, if they are doing their best, know all that there is to know about their work except how to improve it.*
>
> —*W. Edwards Deming (1986, pg. 143)*

John Hudiburg (1991) said that "the direct costs involved in TQM are devoted to education and training and are usually very small when compared to the overall operating expenses of a company. (At FPL these costs were never as much as 1 percent of the overall operation and maintenance budget.) The real issue is fear of change. . . . The most profound change that may need to be made is the willingness to trust every one of the company's employees: to come to realize that they can and will do an outstanding job of managing their own work if given the proper leadership and training. Only when you have top management sending a clear and consistent message of their commitment will their employees be willing to make TQM work.'' The investment required for training and application of quality improvement techniques is easily measurable; the results sometimes are not so easy to measure. All employees receive a minimum of five days of training a year.

The goal is to get at least 75 percent of employees involved in quality over the period of several years:

- Everyone will need an overview of quality to create awareness. (2–4 hours)
- Everyone will need to learn the PDCA problem-solving process and how to use it in quality teams and in their daily work. (2–5 days)
- Quality team leaders and facilitators will need in-depth problem-solving (5 days) and facilitation skills (5 days) to establish a beginner level of knowledge. Ongoing training and visits to quality companies are essential to develop intermediate and master level skills.
- Top and middle management will need to learn about quality planning and policy deployment (3–5 days). They will need to learn how to *lead* the quality improvement effort. Without their demonstration of the quality paradigm, nothing will change.
- Initially, key process owners and ultimately everyone will need to learn process management (2–3 days).

There are four key learning styles: *Doers* who just try things, *reviewers* who read all about it, *theorists* who just want the concepts, and *pragmatics* who want real life problems and subjects. Any IS environment consists mainly of people who have some background in software. Unfortunately, this means that any training will usually require a period of *unlearning* because it is impossible for people to learn what they think they already know. They must first unlearn before they can relearn.

The half-life of the knowledge of a new engineer is about five years.
—Gary Tooker,
President and COO - Motorola

Quality improvement is a management revolution, but it is not new. In 1950, W. Edwards Deming took quality improvement techniques to Japan. The techniques were developed about 30 years earlier at Bell Labs by Dr. Shewhart. Now, in the 90s, Japanese quality is highly regarded in many fields of endeavor. The 1990s will see an explosion in quality training as companies struggle to compete in the global village for a piece of the ever-expanding market. Unfortunately, much of this training will be focused on manufacturing and not on software—the black art. The Japanese, although trailing in software technology, have made great strides in using quality techniques on software. If the past is any indication, they will be a formidable software opponent in this decade.

No matter how hard Western nations try to engage in QC education, they may not catch up with Japan until the 1990s, since it requires ten years for the QC education to take effect.

—J. M. Juran

Every level in an organization needs a minimum of five days of quality training. Executives will require a slightly different approach than employees. Software developers will need custom training that will be somewhat different from that required by maintainers or operations. Training must begin at the top and then cascade down through the hierarchy. Top level management must train the middle, then the middle the line management. Team leaders train team members. Once companies complete entry level training in quality improvement, the training continues. "QC education has been conducted in Japan since 1949 without interruption," (Ishikawa 1985). "Formal education is less than one-third of the total educational effort. It is the responsibility of the boss to teach his subordinates through actual work." A behavioral example from a peer or a supervisor is worth a week of classroom training.

Companies that attempt to leap over the other developmental stages of software maturity to the highest level will experience significant pain and expense. To begin quality improvement, you must have the data that comes from measurements. To measure correctly, you must have a defined process with supporting tools. To have either of these, you need some basic project controls in place. Like human development, each stage—from infancy to childhood to adolescence to adulthood—must be experienced. Companies can't jump from infancy to adulthood; they must grow and evolve toward excellence. Throughout this evolution, training and education will assure the rapid growth of productivity and quality.

TQM requires a significant investment in time, resources, training, and travel. To successfully initiate TQM requires a management leap of faith and continuing investment and commitment. Recognize that you can begin by wading into the river of quality, but eventually you will have to immerse yourself in it.

ORGANIZING FOR QUALITY AND PRODUCTIVITY

To maximize productivity and quality, we will need to reduce the causes of poor quality: *procedures and methods, materials, machines, environment, and people.*

First, we'll need a process for working effectively, then we'll need tools that automate as much of that method as possible. We will need to train our developers and maintainers in the use of these methods and tools. Then we'll need a culture that rewards high quality and productivity. And finally, we will need measurements to determine if we are working effectively. This implies that we need five organizations:

- An executive quality council with subordinate quality councils
- A process/methodology group
- A training group
- A measurements council
- An environment council

The *quality councils* support high quality software creation and evolution. They develop the quality policies and deploy task teams to work on key improvement areas (Chapter 2). Their involvement will help ensure that we move constantly toward the top 5 percent of all software companies.

Process/Methodology Group

The *process/methodology group* continuously improves development and maintenance methodologies. The group works closely with the quality councils and measurement groups. The 10:1 difference in organizations is partially a reflection of the process used to develop and maintain software. Attention focused on this key element will maximize quality and productivity.

Why do you need a process group? Simple, 40 percent of software costs are spent on debugging—defect removal through inspections, walkthroughs, and testing. It typically costs three times as much to debug a program as it did to write it. And an estimated 60 percent of all enhancements correct *specification* bugs. Specification bugs also create the need for the replacement of existing systems. Our current methods of software development and maintenance have created a *debugging industry*. The cost of poor quality—of not doing it right the first time—is an estimated $100 billion.

W. Edwards Deming states that the cost of poor quality in U.S. industries is 25–40 percent of total expense. $100 billion puts software at the high end of this scale. "Well it's always been that way!" But companies with an emphasis on quality processes have found that they can achieve rates of five percent or less, *saving 20–35 percent of their total expense*. Would this make you more competitive? More testing isn't the answer.

If you had a report program that produced pages of defects, would you hire a staff of cutters and pasters to fix it? Unlikely, you'd fix the program. Similarly, you probably have a development process that produces software loaded with defects (1–3 defects per 1000 lines of code). Instead of fixing the process, we hire crowds of testers and debuggers and maintainers to cut, paste, and patch the product. Which would you rather pay for, someone to put in the defects and take them out again, or someone to fix the process to prevent defects?

In the best companies, quality is the rule! Ignoring the process is a recipe for *minimizing* quality and productivity.

Training Group

The *training group* ensures that our training stays abreast of our processes and technology. In this way, we can maximize the quality and productivity of each person by keeping the differences between individuals well below a ratio of 10:1.

To keep your corporation and employees ahead of the competition, you need to invest in employee quality through continuous training and retraining. Capers Jones has examined the data from thousands of corporations, and the leading-edge companies have 15 or more days per year of training for every employee. Tom Peters, in *Thriving on Chaos*, says the same thing. To be the best, we will need a training group to ensure excellence.

Measurement Council

"You can't manage what you can't measure!"

—Tom DeMarco

This is a basic engineering principle. And anything you're not measuring is getting worse. There are some excellent metrics of productivity and quality that have been validated over the years. But to be useful, they must be analyzed and *calibrated* to reflect your culture and environment. A measurement group can make this happen.

The **measurements council** collects and continuously refines productivity and quality measurements in support of continuous quality improvement. Top management will need a "dashboard" of quality indicators (Figure 11.2) that show how the organization is performing. These come from quality planning (Chapter 2). Without measurement, we cannot understand the impact of changes in technology, methodology, or culture. Using the Hewlett-Packard model for implementing a company-wide software measurement program (Grady 1988), form a Software Metrics Council, which will choose the initial set of productivity and quality measurements. Then manage the data collected. A metrics database will be required to facilitate analysis. The Metrics Council will update the measurements as required to meet the needs of the process organization.

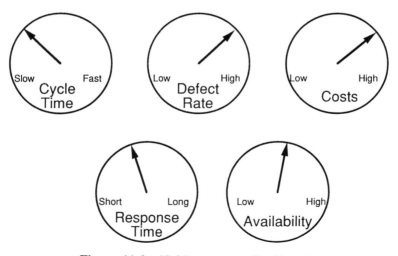

Figure 11.2   IS Measurement Dashboard

Train everyone in the application of the initial set of measurements. These will not be the micro measurements of lines of code, function points, or cyclomatic complexity. They should be a simple set of cycle time, defects, reliability, accuracy, and cost measurements.

Environment Council

The *environment council* uses the law of cause and effect to examine the results achieved and the environmental causes. The other half of the 10:1 difference between organizations is a *quality* culture.

Some organizations are more productive than others by an order of magnitude. We know from measurements that Hitachi and Toshiba have a 6:1 advantage over most other companies in productivity and quality. We are all using similar tools and similar methods. Something has to be different, and that something is culture. If you look at U.S. culture, we reward: the quick fix, hot, high-tech, new projects, and fire fighting. But we rarely recognize or reward: continuous improvement, teamwork, process and cultural improvements, teams that deliver on time and within schedule, teams that reengineer their systems to reduce maintenance costs, and fire prevention.

The results we're achieving from a faulty process that produces defect-ridden software are the direct result of our recognition and reward systems. To achieve high productivity and quality (because without quality, high productivity doesn't matter), we must change the way we recognize and reward employees.

The most important finding of DeMarco's (DeMarco 1987) and Boehm's study is that to maximize productivity and quality, employees need 100 sq. ft. of *enclosed*, private workspace, with 30 sq. ft. of desk area. This flies in the face of the furniture police and the blitzkrieg advertising of the nation's furniture vendors, but it has been studied and confirmed. In an open office cubicle, the average worker is interrupted every 11 minutes. This prevents them from achieving the *flow* so necessary to productive work. In the best companies, workers achieved 2–3 *hours* of flow in enclosed spaces as compared to 0–1 in the worst. The difference in performance is at least 3:1.

This, the authors contend, is a cultural issue based on short-sighted, next-quarter thinking. The additional cost of enclosed space is about $1300 per person to achieve a return of 3:1 on the total cost for the employee—salary, benefits, etc.

What about the Japanese, some people ask? They work on narrow tables, scrunched together. True! In a discussion with Tom DeMarco, however, the head engineer of Hitachi told him that if they could solve their space problems, especially in Tokyo, they would *bury* the U.S. software industry.

Can we afford to sink tens of thousands of dollars into hardware for each programmer and then leave them open to a non-productive environment for the lack of a few thousand dollars worth of walls and doors? Or should we make it easier on the furniture police when they need to change arrangements? In 1979, when I first implemented UNIX, a terminal on every desk was considered a ridiculous expense. Time and measurement have shown that workstations are an essential part of quality and productivity for the software professional; enclosed workspaces are no less important.

We need a cultural/sociological organization to see to these changes. If culture is the overriding characteristic of the 10:1 companies, we need to see that our culture remains in the spotlight for many years to come.

These kinds of far-reaching opportunities have traditionally been handled by management between budget views. They are best handled by quality teams, by putting the power back in the hands of the software professional.

VISIT A TQM COMPANY

Top management needs to be converted first. Start with a study mission to one of the top software organizations in America or Japan—Fujitsu or Hitachi. At FPL, this was called ''going to Japan for the operation'' (Hudiburg 1991). There is nothing like viewing a successful implementation of TQM to give management the faith required to make the investment required to implement TQM. Without such first-hand experience, it will be difficult to visualize the quality environment to be created and the steps necessary to get there.

SUGGESTION PROGRAMS

Quality improvements can also begin at an individual level. Suggestion programs enhance the quality process, but they can also be a drag unless they are used correctly.

When employees suggest an improvement, the most important characteristic is a fast decision and quick response back to the employee. At Milliken (Hudiburg 1991), supervisors must acknowledge a suggestion in 24 hours and have a response in 72 hours—even if it requires more investigation. Milliken receives as many as 18 suggestions per employee a year. FPL in 1989 received about 25,000 or almost two per employee. Fifty percent were implemented on the spot. Savings averaged $800 per suggestion in the first year alone.

Suggestions go directly to the supervisor. So supervisors must be trained to encourage employee participation, evaluate suggestions, and to respect employees, welcome their ideas, and reinforce this attitude. Management must truly want suggestions and demonstrate that they do in such a way that the employees will know it's true. There must be a system to approve or disapprove suggestions quickly and to see that they are implemented. Management should have a target for implementing suggestions. At Toyota, 95 percent of over 1.5 million suggestions are implemented each year. A suggestion can involve any savings down to a half a second. Is it any wonder it takes Toyota only 16 hours to manufacture a car and it takes most American manufacturers over twice this long?

Individual suggestions need to be recognized locally and throughout the organization. Top suggestion generators and top results generated need to be recognized and rewarded to ensure that the behavior continues. For most people, getting their suggestion implemented is reward enough, but informal and formal recognition as well as monetary rewards will expand and extend the suggestion process.

The number of suggestions will expand rapidly as people become familiar with the problem-solving tools and techniques of quality improvement. The reason for this falls under what I call the covert objective.

THE COVERT OBJECTIVE

The covert objectives of initiating quality improvement are: to establish a new management system; to create a common language for problem-solving, and to install highly effective problem-solving and planning processes in the minds of all employees. The goal is to establish a common language for problem-solving that extends through the whole organization. To some people this might seem odd, and yet it gives every employee a shared problem-solving strategy they can use at work, at home, in clubs, and in organizations. The other side of this issue is that the human mind will only accept programming that it perceives as being better than its old programming. So you can't actually install this problem-solving process without the person's active agreement to do so at either a conscious or an unconscious level.

The human brain works in three key modes: visual, auditory, and kinesthetic—sight, sound, and touch (Dilts 1991). The brain can remember and create images easily. If you don't believe me, try not to think of a purple elephant.

The quality improvement process is very visual, which matches our highly sensitized TV- and photo-like way of processing things. It teaches people to think in terms of graphs of data—linear trends (line graphs, control charts), bar-like comparisons (bar chart, Pareto chart, histogram), pieces of the pie, and relationships of two sets of data (scatter diagrams). It also teaches the law of cause-and-effect using the Ishikawa diagram so that we can begin to see beyond the symptom, back in time to the origin of a problem. Perhaps the only drawback at this time is that these graphical images are two dimensional, still, and usually black and white. The addition of color increases their impact and one day soon someone will figure out how to animate these otherwise still pictures to give a more movie-like rendition of the discovery process.

The process is punctuated by words and sentences (auditory) that define the problem and give us common ways of talking about the story—PDCA, countermeasures, root causes. Some are even highly descriptive of their visual counterpart: consider the fishbone diagram, pie or bar chart. Participants in the quality improvement process add their own excited tones to the words as they describe their process of discovery. They may even bring in terminals or papers to help you get a feel for what they uncovered in their analysis.

All of these pictures and words combine into a story. For thousands of years, all anyone has had to do to capture an audience's attention is say the words "Let me tell you a story . . ." and therein lies the power of the quality improvement story. Stories teach both the conscious and unconscious mind without interference. Often, stories entertain, surprise, and delight as they reveal themselves. The same is true of QI stories. These stories capture the folklore and wisdom of the business in ways that are accessible to all. The more you see, the more you understand the QI process and the more easily you can apply it.

The human mind learns quickly. A phobia, for example, was typically learned in one instance and usually during childhood. It can be unlearned almost as quickly using another mental process (Andreas 1989). The quality improvement process is no different; the faster you go through the process, the faster it becomes installed. The first time through may be slow, because people often need to unlearn a variety of old ways of doing business to make room for the new way. Then, it gets faster and faster. A first time team may take 80 hours to solve a problem. After a few iterations, they may do it in 10–15 hours. Over time, employees go from unconscious incompetence (they don't know that they don't know how to solve problems effectively) to conscious incompetence (they know that they don't know), to conscious competence (they know how, but still have to think about it), to unconscious competence (they don't know that they know how). The covert outcome of any quality improvement process introduction is to achieve unconscious competence. Most of you, for example, drive a car, which is an enormously complex visual-motor task, without even thinking about it most of the time. When employees achieve unconscious competence with quality improvement, they will begin to automatically resolve the root cause of problems in their daily work. The impossible problems of yesterday will become child's play for them today. The employee ''body'' will begin to solve and resolve problems before they even reach a state of nudging your customer's awareness.

So, this is our goal, to create an IS industry populated by men and women who are unconsciously competent at improving software quality everyday in every way. It is no simple feat to accomplish this, however. Every employee needs 4–5 days of training to establish the fundamentals of QI and dozens of hours of practice until it becomes second nature. The alternatives to this course of action, however, are bleak. Most information systems organizations are still mired in the tar pits of chaos or barely able to repeat a successful project. To remain on the competitive edge of information technology, all IS engineers will want to grab hold of the quality improvement process and learn to love processes, consistency, measurement, and continuous improvement. Without them, software will remain of poor quality, which invites our more aggressive competition to come in and displace our jobs, homes, and families. It invites other countries to become the dominant world powers of the next millenium. We cannot afford to wait and see what happens. In the quality improvement game, once you fall behind you stay behind.

Ensure your children's future. Embrace quality improvement *now*! The transformation from the old culture to a quality improvement culture cannot happen without the continuous, never-ending support of IS management. Once you decide to adopt TQM, it will need planning, promotion, training, education, and patience to move to the new level of excellence. Changing the supporting reward and recognition programs will help speed the transformation. Put the systems and procedures in place to support quality efforts and you will ensure its success. The more experience you develop in quality tools and processes, the more quickly your organization will begin to develop the unconscious competence to succeed in competitive global marketplace.

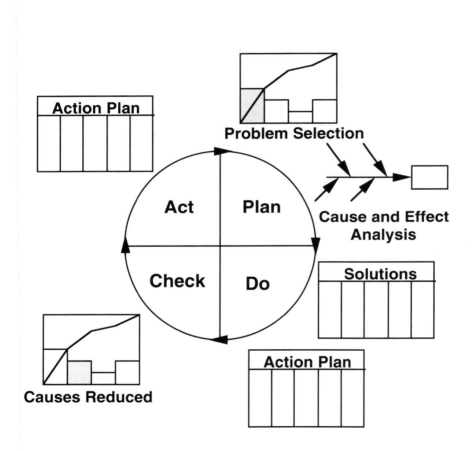

CHAPTER 12

Quality in Software Evolution

Too much of our precious software resource is tied up fighting fires in existing and freshly delivered systems. Testing and debugging software is an industry, not a simple activity. The question is: "How do we stabilize our process enough so that we can begin to improve it?" The answer lies in the SCORE model and the causes of problems. All processes have some variation in how they are done. There are two causes of variation in software processes that cause problems:

- **Common Causes** (variation in the process) 85 percent
- **Special Causes** (*assignable* to special events) 15 percent

The quality improvement problem-solving process has been applied widely to what has been called "common causes" of process problems. The quality improvement problem-solving process works *best* in situations where there are defined processes and measurements of those processes. In most companies, however, there are huge variations in how software is created (Figure 12.1). Essentially, most software processes are "out of control" with respect to quality, and a small portion of the total software system harbors the majority of the quality problems. Before you can begin to improve your software processes, you must first define your processes (process management) and then eliminate the *special causes* of variation. Then you can begin to use the quality problem solving-process more effectively to reduce the *common causes*

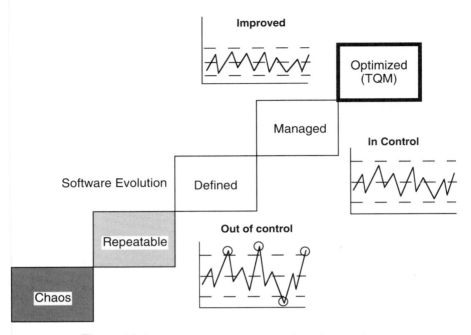

Figure 12.1 SEI Maturity Framework and Variation

of variation. In this chapter we will look at ways to use the problem solving process and quality tools and techniques to:

1. examine the root causes of special events—poor quality software projects and releases.
2. identify the 20 percent of the software that generates 80 percent of the waste, rework, and cost.

In any software system, there are software problems, most of which were created by the diversity of people, methods, and tools employed in software. A little-known secret of TQM is that these "special causes" of variation (Figure 12.2) can be identified and removed using the quality improvement problem-solving process. What were once called "post mortems" to examine software failures can now be more appropriately termed "quality reviews" to determine the root causes of software failures. This may seem like splitting hairs, but post mortems imply the patient is dead, while quality reviews imply that the software is living and can get better.

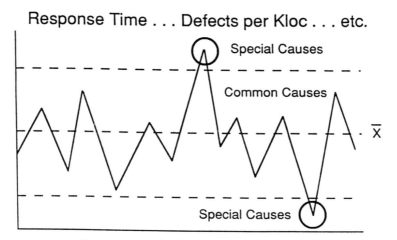

Figure 12.2   Common and Special Causes

One of the scariest metaphors of software is one of death. Most software systems have *dead*line for their delivery. Afterwards, engineers conduct a *post-mortem* to determine how the project went. Projects have *milestones*, which are often more like *gravestones* marking the exhaustion and burial of workers on the project. And if a project fails to deliver on its promises, then IS departments often punish the project manager. We figuratively *behead* the project by removing or demoting its director or project manager. Is it any wonder that so many projects that should be aborted are continued well beyond the discovery of their genetic defects?

The current language and behavior of software engineering is peppered with language and actions that presuppose that the delivered system will be diseased, decaying, or dying from the moment of its delivery. Notice how this would change if we decided that software is a living system and that it has *birthdays* and celebrations to measure its progress toward maturity. What if we viewed "failure" as *feedback?* Projects could be stopped at any point because we could *learn* enough to know that the system would be genetically defective and unable to care for itself. Think of the waste and rework we could prevent and the resources we could redirect to creating healthy, living software systems if we would only change our metaphor for software from death to life. Quality demands that we change all of our experiences from being ones of failure or success to ones of simple feedback. So let's look at ways to begin to bring our software processes under control using the problem solving process.

RESOLVING SPECIFIC CAUSES OF VARIATION

Since most IS departments are still mired in the tar pit of chaos or barely struggling up into the repeatable level of process maturity, the problem-solving process can be a powerful tool for quality improvement. By identifying and eliminating the special causes of defects, we can begin moving up the stairway of software excellence. There are other advantages to using the problem-solving process on special causes:

- People learn the quality problem-solving process more quickly
- Problems are automatically sized to an occurrence that can be solved easily
- Immediate success stories help drive the acceptance of quality improvement

The drawback to using quality improvement in this fashion is that programmers, analysts, and managers are well-trained fire fighters. They may use the problem-solving process as just another tool to put out software fires, but fail to begin using it to prevent them in the first place. Rewarding fire fighters often breeds arsonists. Recognizing the dangers and planning for them, a lot can be gained from employing PDCA on specific software problems—poor releases, program failures, major system outages, and so on. An entire example is shown in Figure 12.3. Using the standard problem solving process, we walk through all of it, beginning with planning.

Plan

When an occasional software release suffers the pain and torment of the user community, we can begin by looking for an indicator of their pain. If we have a fire control system in a fighter aircraft, then the number of targets identified within a certain range might serve as an indicator. A payroll system would measure the timeliness and accuracy of paychecks. Each of these software systems would have certain targets and goals for these indicators. If we have a billing system, for example, then an indicator of the user's pain might be the *percent of bills in error*. If less than one percent is our customer's valid requirement and, after a software release, we have a surge up to 35 percent (Figure 12.3a), then we would have a reason for improvement: *Reduce percent of bills in error*.

In many quality problems, customer dissatisfaction occurs after one of their indicators, real or imagined, has exceeded some threshold. One

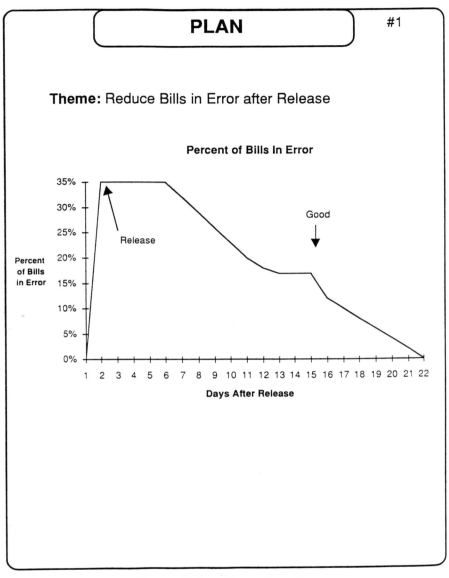

Figure 12.3a Theme Selection

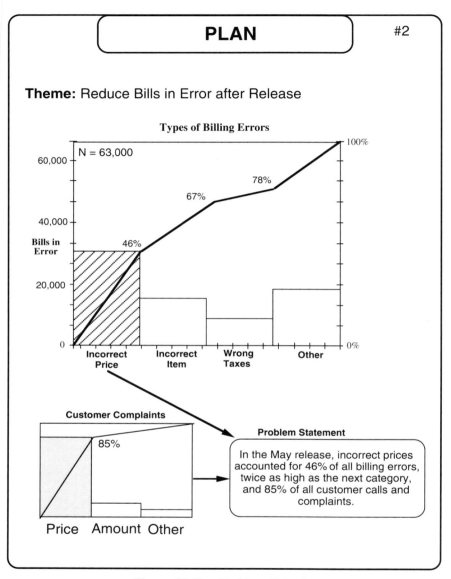

Figure 12.3b   Problem Selection

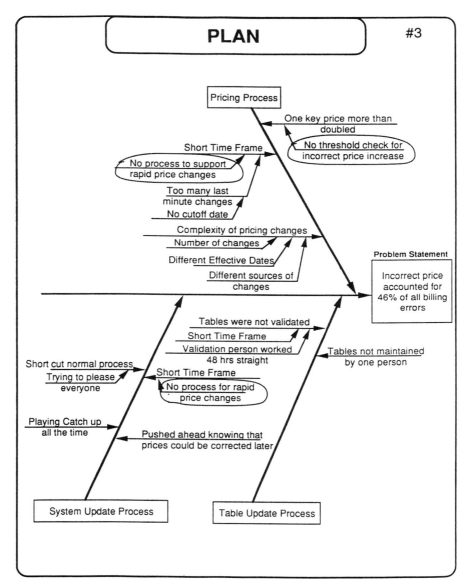

Figure 12.3c Root Cause Analysis

common quality improvement story involves the bull frog. You can put a frog in a cool pan of water and raise the temperature gently. As long as the frog doesn't notice a significant change in temperature, it will sit and sit until the water is very hot. Customers will do the same thing with their bills and the price they pay. The percent of bills in error may not matter as long as the price does not go up too much. In psychological circles, this is known as "threshold."

When it comes to pricing, most of the initial pain occurs when the cost increases by more than some threshold. We might discover that the customers were enraged about the cost of some services but not others. In this release (Figure 12.3b), 85 percent of all customer complaints involved exorbitant price increases on items that shouldn't have changed by more than 5–10 percent. On investigation, we discover that these costs were *incorrectly* increased by 50 percent or more. The customer's threshold for price increases is probably around 20 percent. Our problem would become: **In the May billing release, incorrect prices accounted for 46 percent of all billing errors and 85 percent of all customer complaints**.

So now we have two indicators: percent of bills in error and percent of customer complaints about billing errors. Using this problem, we could use the Ishikawa diagram to identify the root causes of these inflated prices (Figure 12.3c). The special cause of variation could turn out to be that the pricing table manager stayed up 48 hours straight to get the prices entered into the table, but the root cause was the continued acceptance of pricing changes right up to the last minute. Upon further investigation, we discover that all of the pricing changes that caused customer dissatisfaction were put in during these final 48 hours. This verifies the root cause. Now we can identify the countermeasures required to prevent future occurrences of customer dissatisfaction.

Do

Continuous, last minute pricing changes could be deemed to be invalid requirements. Two countermeasures are proposed (Figure 12.3d): establishing a cutoff date for pricing changes before a release and implementing edit checks on the pricing table. The edit checks on the pricing table will discourage pricing increases of more than 20 percent without some operator override. A series of edits or table comparisons could prevent a price table increase of more than 20 percent unless the person updating the table responds to a question like "Do you really want to increase this rate by 97 percent?" This is similar to a PC computer program that checks: "Delete this file?" Such an analysis could minimize the damage

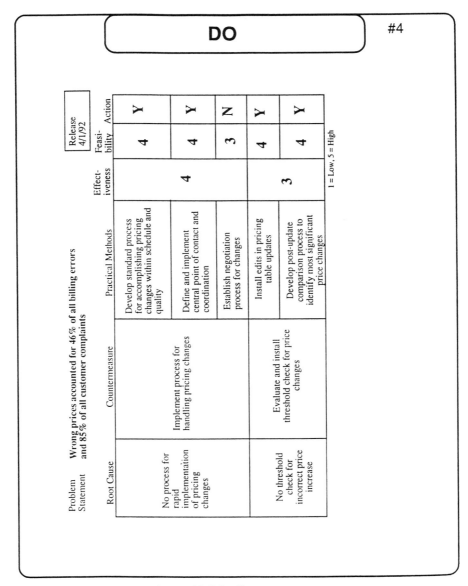

Figure 12.3d   Countermeasures

DO #5

ACTION PLAN

WHAT? (Objectives)	HOW? (Action steps & Structures)	WHO? (Accountability)	WHEN? (Start/Complete)	HOW? (To Measure Results)
Develop and track quality indicators of price change implementation quality	Backtrack to prior releases to establish baseline		5/1/92	Graphs and charts of quality indicators
	Develop measures		Ongoing	
	Develop standard process for accomplishing pricing changes within schedule and quality		6/1/92	Process developed and % bills in error tracked
Implement process for handling pricing changes	Define and implement central point of contact and coordination		5/1/92	Central point identified and operational
	Establish negotiation process for changes		6/1/92	Negotiated changes tracked as percent of total
Evaluate and install threshold check for price changes	Install edits in pricing table updates		7/1/92	Pricing updates installed and tested % of prices in error
	Develop post-update comparison process to identify most significant price changes		9/1/92	Table validation programs and processes established % prices in error

Figure 12.3e Action Plan

from faulty table updates. Another countermeasure would be to use process management (Chapter 10) to define and reduce the time to implement pricing changes. Figure 12.3e shows the resulting action plan formed by the quality review team.

Check

Following implementation of these two countermeasures (Figure 12.3f), customer complaints about prices fell to only 15 percent of total complaints, the percent of bills in error dropped from 35 percent to 26 percent after release. These solutions were then standardized and the "threshold" edit check was replicated to other financial systems—accounts payable, payroll, and so on.

Act to Improve

Although we reduced the percent of bills in error, we still haven't reached our target of less than one percent. So a task team was formed to continue diagnosis of post-release problems.

The investigation also identified problems caused by the pricing update form itself. Often confusing and rarely date-stamped, they could easily get shuffled and misinterpreted. A quality team was formed to establish a process management system for pricing changes.

The specific nature of this kind of problem enabled the team to focus on the special causes and work to prevent them in future releases. Having quickly learned the problem-solving process, the team was able to begin working other more complex issues involving common causes of variation. Pleased with the results of this special cause analysis, the supervisor was willing to encourage the team to continue on more complex problems.

The Quality Review Process

The beauty of the quality problem solving process is that it can be used on problems of almost any size, and it is especially useful on small, tightly-scoped problems like program failures or release problems—a quality review. In many software fires there are readily identifiable indicators of the customer's dissatisfaction. Using the quality improvement process tools and techniques—graphs and Pareto charts—we can begin to measure dissatisfaction through our customer's eyes. Then, we can use cause-and-effect analysis to identify the causes of the problem

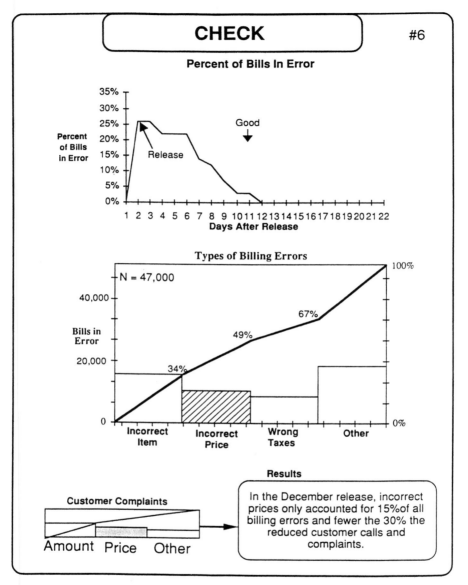

Figure 12.3f Comparing Results

and again use data to verify the root causes of the problem. Then, because of the scope of the problem, we can identify countermeasures, implement them, and begin measuring results of the implementation. This can be done by an individual on a program failure or by a group on a system or release failure. The quality review process uses the problem-solving process as a guideline:

- The indicators and problem statement are completed by project manager and quality improvement expert
- The team works through analysis and countermeasures
- Management tracks the implementation and results
- Management ensures the standardization and replication of the improvements
- A central coordinator tracks all "special" problems and improvements as a way to spot trends that imply problems arising from common causes of variation, not isolated events
- Quality teams pick up the other problem areas identified by the analysis team

The quality review process helps the team identify and resolve the *root causes* of the problem, not just the symptoms. This helps prevent future such "fires." In analyzing these isolated events, the team often uncovers problems in neighboring processes that need improvement. Quality teams spin off to resolve these issues. By fixing the root cause and not just the symptom, the team begins to stabilize the process so that measurements and quality improvement can succeed more easily.

Responsibilities of Review Leader are to: schedule reviews, prepare an agenda, put together the indicators and problem statement, and lead the meetings. Review leaders need to be trained on the quality improvement problem-solving process and on the specific tools used during reviews.

Responsibilities of the Quality Expert are to: assist review leader in leading meetings, help put together the quality indicator and problem statement, assist in cause-and-effect development, assist in identifying countermeasures and developing action plans, and help train the team.

Quality Review Process

1. Identify problem, project, or special event to be reviewed. (Extremely successful projects or releases should be analyzed as well to determine the root causes of success. These can then be

standardized and replicated. This is a mini-form of benchmark-ing.)

2. Review leader and quality expert meet to put together the quality indicators and problem statement. The quality indicators help us understand what *quality* means to the client and how to measure it. Begin collecting this information. In some cases, however, there will not be any readily identifiable measure of customer dissatisfaction. If you can't find one, begin with your best description of the problem from the customer's viewpoint. The problem statement should be as specific as possible. Once the indicators and problem statement are developed, they are distributed to the team members.

3. Review leaders schedules meeting(s).

4. During the meeting(s), the review leader and quality expert
   - Conduct mini trainings in quality improvement tools and techniques
   - Lead the cause-and-effect analysis
   - Help determine and verify the root causes
   - Help develop countermeasures and an action plan
   - Develop measurement methods to track action plan implementation.

5. Present project review team findings to IS leadership for review and approval.

6. Implement the countermeasures, monitor, and follow up.

7. Distribute and publicize results. Success stories help engage all employees in quality improvement.

Quality Review Summary

The quality improvement problem-solving process is a powerful tool to begin shifting IS awareness from the symptoms of problems back to the root causes of problems. By fixing not only the symptom but also the root cause, we can begin to stabilize the software life cycle to the point that measurement and process improvements become easier and more natural. The narrow scope of these problems helps everyone learn the problem-solving process more quickly and delivers tangible improvements in a timely fashion—something that our "quick fix" mentality demands. By matching our cultural demands for speed we create an understanding of the need for problem-solving. It also creates a need for further understanding and involvement in quality. Skeptical employees and managers who get involved with this process come out of it "born again" or at least willing to make time and resources available for training and quality teams. Quality team leaders and facilitators who do actually lead such an effort usually come away with a deeper awareness of the problem-solving process and many skills and abilities that they can use in their teams. The more journeys we take through the problem-solving process and the faster the trips, the more quickly and effectively it becomes part of our unconscious way of thinking.

Using the problem-solving process any time there is a program, system, or release failure will help everyone develop an understanding of quality improvement. Your processes will become stable enough to encourage breakthroughs in improvement.

Now let's look at ways to use the quality tools to identify the vital few programs, data tables, interfaces, hardware, or network systems that consume the majority of your software resources. Then let's look at ways to improve them to reduce costs and do more meaningful work for our customer.

PERFECTIVE SOFTWARE EVOLUTION

Why should you improve software that works? Wouldn't that waste time and money? These are questions maintainers often ask when a program works, but the quality could be improved. When software quality improves, costs shrink, programs become more maintainable and users satisfaction leaps. One reader of my metrics book (Arthur 1985) called to say that he worked on a system written in COBOL that cut metal parts for Navy ships. The metrics analyzer helped him spot a problem in one program that was causing the cutting machine to waste half a sheet of metal. That generated a lot of interest on the part of both management and other employees. They installed the metrics analyzer in the compiler stream and set objectives that everyone would reduce the complexity of every software component they entered by 10 percent, based on Mc-Cabe's Cyclomatic Complexity—a measure of decision complexity. Not only did the complexity decrease, but software failures dropped by half.

This broad effort to improve software quality was a cost-effective success. Using quality improvement techniques, the effort can be focused even more specifically. Pareto's 80/20 rule tells us that 20 percent of our software consumes 80 percent of our resources. Stop and think about systems you've worked on for a moment. Weren't there a few key programs or modules that consumed the majority of your time? Well, it doesn't have to be that way. There are techniques for identifying the vital few software components—code, data, or documentation—that need quality improvement. Pareto charts can help identify the vital few candidates for quality improvement to minimize the cost and maximize the effectiveness of reengineering. Cause-and-effect analysis can then help us identify how to improve these vital few software components to eliminate the root causes of waste, rework, defects and enhancements. Perfective software evolution includes all efforts to polish or refine the quality of the software or documentation.

Don't patch bad code, rewrite it.

—Kernighan and Plauger (1974)

Perfective software evolution includes restructuring poorly written code to make it easier to maintain; normalizing and restructuring data bases to simplify and increase reuse potential; and revising or rewriting documentation for ease of access and usability. Following restructuring, code *maintainability* and *flexibility* improve, reducing the cost of fixing and enhancing software.

It's widely known that software defects tend to cluster in a few programs, modules, or data bases. It is not unusual to find 50 percent of the defects in only four percent of the system's programs (the top 20 percent of the top 20 percent). An intensive inspection and correction of potential defects in these modules is perfective software evolution. It improves the system's *reliability* and reduces the cost of corrective maintenance.

Rewriting (in assembler language) or restructuring the most extensively used routine in the system (as identified by execution monitors) to maximize its *efficiency* is also perfective software evolution. Rewriting in assembler language, however, can reduce the software's *portability* and *maintainability*.

Upgrading documentation to a standard format and style will improve its *consistency, readability*, and *maintainability*.

Quality improvements can be as extensive as a complete redesign and rewrite of a program using structured design techniques, or confined to one line of code. The size of the improvement is not particularly important; it *is* important that each improvement reduce the system's evolution costs.

So, let's begin to look at the typical problems found in a software maintenance environment when perfective software evolution is not used. Then we'll examine the features and benefits of perfective software evolution. We'll also examine how to use Pareto analysis to select perfective software evolution candidates.

Using Quality Tools to Improve Software Quality

Figure 12.4 shows how perfective software evolution fits into the overall software evolution process. Perfective software evolution consists of two processes:

1. Identifying candidates using the quality improvement tools. This occurs before a system release is planned.
2. Analyzing and correcting identified quality problems to maximize the benefits.

Perfective software evolution includes all efforts to improve the quality of software, data, or documentation. It does not correct defects or change what the system does. Perfective software evolution focuses on improving expensive-to-maintain software.

Existing systems are profitable systems, but improper repairs tend to destroy the system's structure and increase the system's entropy. As systems are enhanced and repaired, more time is spent on repairing defects injected by previous changes. Eventually the repairs and chaos become intolerable and the system must be replaced. Because replacement is an expensive process, every effort needs to be made to slow the decay of system software. And that is the aim of perfective software evolution: to delay the day of unrepairable obsolescence.

When consistently implemented, perfective software evolution can provide the following benefits:

- Improved maintainer skill—With practice, maintainers develop skills in improving program quality which can be used throughout their careers to minimize maintenance costs and to develop new systems which maximize maintainability.
- Reduced exposure to risk—Higher quality programs reduce the risks of schedule and budget overruns and program failures.
- Reduced maintenance costs—By improving the 20 percent of the programs that consume 80 percent of the costs/resources, maintenance costs can be measurably reduced.
- More time for enhancements and new development—Perfective software evolution can reduce the number of hours spent fixing defects or making an enhancement. This newly available time can be channeled into implementing other enhancements and doing new development work.
- Enhanced system maintainability—With structure, modularity, and comprehensive tolerance of software faults, emergency corrective

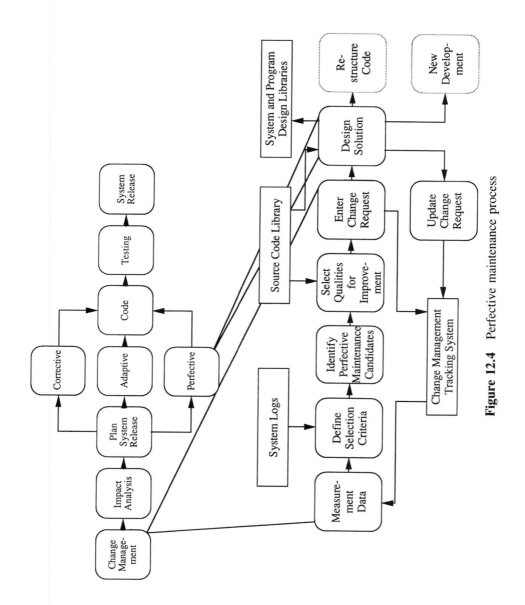

Figure 12.4 Perfective maintenance process

maintenance can be whipped. Thus, maintainers encounter fewer overtime hours and midnight calls, caused by hard-to-maintain systems.

SELECTING PERFECTIVE EVOLUTION CANDIDATES

Many software engineers seem to intuitively know which programs and modules need perfective software evolution. Intuition, however, can be inaccurate, and unsupported ideas are hard to sell. Therefore, to gain management and client support for perfective software evolution, it is important to document a case for quality improvement.

To select perfective software evolution candidates, we will need to establish the criteria for selection and the *data* needed to identify the candidates. Using the data and the criteria, we can develop a Pareto Analysis, which helps identify the "vital few" perfective software evolution candidates.

To document a reason for perfective software evolution we can begin by defining the selection criteria, gathering related data, analyzing the data, identifying the root causes, implementing a countermeasure, and reviewing the benefits and results derived.

Step 1 — Identify Candidates

- Maintainers or quality assurance personnel define the criteria from which perfective software evolution candidates are to be chosen. This normally depends on available data and location of "hot spots."
- Then, a Pareto analysis is conducted to identify perfective software evolution candidates.
- Then, based on the Pareto analysis, qualities for improvement are selected. Qualities can be maintainability, reliability, efficiency, or a variety of others covered later in this module.
- A change request is then entered in the change management system to track the perfective software evolution work.

As a first step, maintainers define the selection criteria for choosing perfective software evolution candidates (most failures, most defects, highest frequency of enhancement, etc.). Like everything else in the quality paradigm, the selection criteria should be based on customer requirements. Do they want a more responsive system? Focus on response time. Do they want a more reliable system? Focus on system failures. Do they want faster turnaround on their enhancement requests? Focus on time to enhance existing programs. Defining selection criteria focuses your attention on the customer's key problem areas and the data needed to document those problems.

This data varies by organization, but its purpose is always the same: to identify the best perfective software evolution candidates. Often, these are programs that perform critical functions, or require the most resources to maintain. Focusing on these modules would maximize the benefits of preventive maintenance. As you might guess, Pareto analysis is a fact-based, graphical approach. For it to work, you have to define ways to separate the beans—selection criteria—cycle time, defects, costs. Some examples of selection criteria are:

- Defect type—A defect is any failure to meet requirements. For example, programs with the most logic, computational, interface, or data manipulation errors. Another way to classify defects is by severity code.
- Defect costs—The costs of repairing defects. Costs can include dollars, time, or equipment usage.
- Cause—A cause is a proven reason for the existence of a defect. For example, storing the results of a multiplication in a field that is too small (i.e. storing the results of 10*10 in a field two digits in length).
- Failure rate—The number or frequency of failures can signal quality problems. This is also referred to as the mean time between failures (MTBF).
- Failure type—Some examples are dividing by zero and incorrect logic.
- Field performance—For example, slow response time, CPU hog, core hog, etc.
- Enhancement costs—For example total or average cost (in days, dollars, or CPU) per enhancement.
- Enhancement rate—Changes requested per year.

Having defined and chosen one or more of these selection criteria, certain reliable sources of data can be used to identify or document these problems. Reliable sources of data include the:

- Change request data base
- Historical change request logs

- Configuration management system histories
- Operating system logs
- Time reporting/project management system

A change request data base will contain most of the data needed to identify perfective software evolution candidates. The change request should contain the following data for each change to be able to support quality improvement:

- Systems affected
- Programs affected
- Modules affected
- Documents affected
- Estimated and actual time worked
- Type of change (i.e., corrective, adaptive, or perfective)
- Severity code

Historical data from the change request database or the configuration management system is best used to identify high-cost programs. After all, the more changes a system, program or module receives, the more it needs to be highly maintainable and flexible.

Operating system logs can be examined to identify programs that fail most often, the major reasons for program failure, (i.e., failure code), the mean time between failures and the mean time to repair. Reliability improvements should be made to those programs that fall in the top 20 percent of these categories.

Operating system logs can also highlight which programs use the most computer resources, such as memory, tape drives, disk drives, and other peripheral devices. This data can be used to select programs for efficiency improvements.

The time reporting, cost tracking, or project management system can be used to identify time and costs by program, module, task or any other factor by which time is recorded. Some of the key variances to look for are:

- Overtime worked by system, program, module
- Total time worked by system, program, module
- Time spent on adaptive, corrective, or perfective software evolution
- Overtime costs for corrective maintenance
- Total costs for corrective maintenance

Now that you know what data to collect and where to find it, you need a technique to analyze and interpret the data. Pareto analysis can be used to identify perfective software evolution candidates [Juran 1979]. Pareto analysis seeks to identify the 20 percent of the programs which consume 80 percent of the budget, costs, time, and personnel resources, or harbors 80 percent of the defects. Also known as the 80/20 rule, it is based on the principle of the *vital few* and the *trivial many*. In other words, the bulk of all programs (the trivial many), account for very little of the total effort. The vital few programs, however, account for the majority of the cost and effort. In a typical system, the top *four* percent of the system will account for as much as 50 percent of the total cost.

Pareto analysis uses a checksheet of information (Figure 12.5) as a basis to construct a Pareto diagram. Systems, programs, or modules are listed down the left side. Defects, failure types, time worked, or any other meaningful measurement data are listed along the top.

Once the checksheet has been constructed, we can use a Pareto chart to identify the vital few contributors of defects or enhancements. Candidates that produce the most defects or consume the most resources should be selected for perfective software evolution.

The following three checksheets show the data gathered from change request and time reporting systems. The first checksheet shows the failures, defects, enhancements, and time worked.

Based on the checksheet (Figure 12.5) and data below, we can construct Pareto diagrams of the vital few contributors (Figures 12.6 and 12.7).

PROGRAM LEVEL CHECKSHEET

Programs	Failures	Defects	Enhancements	Time Worked
Program A	1	3	15	20
Program B	10	17	2	15
Program C	0	1	1	2
System XYZ	11	21	18	37

Based on these Pareto charts, following programs should be selected for quality improvement.

- Program A to reduce the time spent on enhancements.
- Program B to reduce the high density of failures and defects.

Total Defects Checksheet

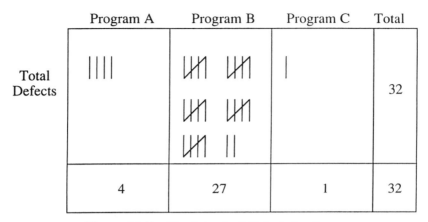

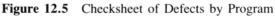

Figure 12.5   Checksheet of Defects by Program

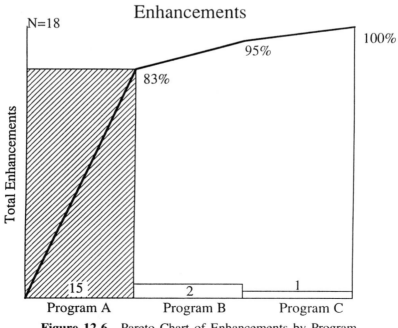

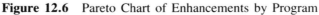

Figure 12.6   Pareto Chart of Enhancements by Program

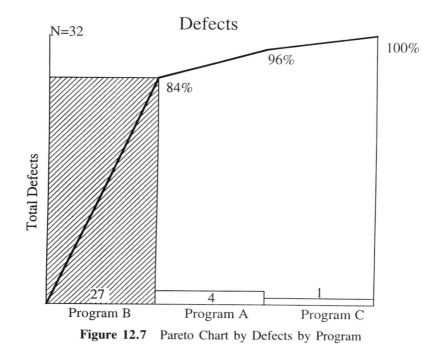

Figure 12.7   Pareto Chart by Defects by Program

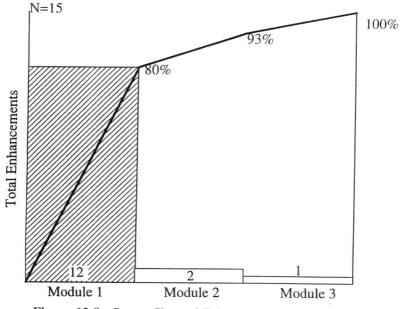

Figure 12.8   Pareto Chart of Enhancements by Module

Further analysis based on the following checksheets would show further stratification by *module* (Figures 12.8 and 12.9).

MODULE LEVEL CHECKSHEET

Program A Module	Failures	Defects	Enhancements	Time Worked
Module 1	**1**	**0**	**12**	**15**
Module 2	0	3	2	3
Module 3	0	0	1	2
Totals	1	3	15	20

MODULE LEVEL CHECKSHEET

Program B Module	Failures	Defects	Enhancements	Time Worked
Module 1	1	1	1	2
Module 2	**9**	**15**	**1**	**12**
Module 3	0	0	0	1
Totals	10	17	2	15

These Pareto charts indicate that two modules should be selected for improvement: module 1 in Program A to reduce the time spent on enhancing that module and module 2 in Program B to reduce the high density of failures and defects.

From this information, we can write problem statements to drive the quality improvement effort: Module 1 in Program A accounted for 15 days of enhancement work, five times more than any other module; Module 2 in Program B accounted for 12 days (80%) of all repair work, six times more than any other module. These can now be used in the Ishikawa diagram (Figure 12.10) to identify the root causes and counter-measures required to improve the enhancement- and error-prone modules.

Step 2 — Analyzing and Correcting Quality Problems

The quality problem-solving process is used to improve the quality of the evolution candidates. In summary this process:

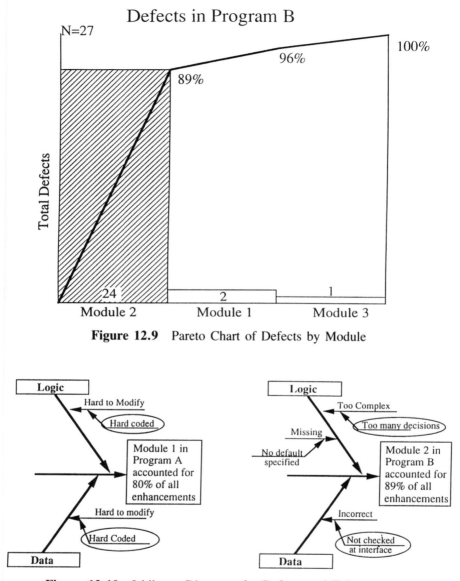

Figure 12.9 Pareto Chart of Defects by Module

Figure 12.10 Ishikawa Diagrams for Defects and Enhancements

- Defines the quality problem, identifies the root causes of the problem, and devises a solution.
- The system design, program design, and change request are then updated and replaced under control of configuration management and change management systems.

- Finally, code, data or documentation are either restructured or re-written to meet quality goals and objectives.

Having identified the candidates for improvement, we can use cause-and-effect diagramming to identify the root causes of these maintenance and enhancement problems. Using the data we've gathered already, we can verify the root causes and select the specific qualities to improve. Some widely accepted quality factors and their attributes are:

- Maintainability
  —Can you fix it?
  —Does it take little effort to fix it, or modify the defect?
  —Is it indented in a standard way?
  —Is it well commented with prologue and decision points?
  —Are the modules simple?
- Flexibility—Can you enhance it? Is the program free of unstructured "spaghetti" code?
- Reliability—Will it run and produce the correct results every time?
- Reusability—Can the system, program, or module be used in other applications to reduce development costs?
- Usability—Can the customer learn and use the system easily? Can operations run it?
- Efficiency—Does it run on your hardware as quickly as possible?
- Testability—Can you test it?
- Integrity—Is the application and its data secure from outside intrusion?
- Portability—Can the system easily move from one hardware and operating system environment to another?
- Interoperability—Can it interface easily with other systems?
- Correctness—Is the application and its data complete, accurate, and consistent?

The major alternatives for correcting quality problems are: a complete redesign and rewrite, complete restructuring, partial restructuring, or system retirement and redevelopment. The guidelines for implementing each one are listed below:

- Complete redesign and rewrite (using structured design and programming techniques). Use this approach when more than 20 percent of the program must be changed (e.g., the functionality of the program is radically changed by the user's requests) or the program is being upgraded to a new technology (e.g., from sequential files to data base).

Do not use this approach when the design and function of the existing program is not known. Rewrites will fail to include all of the existing functionality causing extensive corrective maintenance.

- Complete restructuring or overhaul of the existing code. Use this technique on high maintenance-prone programs. Choose a time when the program has minimal changes during a release. It will be easier to insure that restructuring does not compromise its functionality.

- Partial restructuring integrated with adaptive maintenance. This approach provides an orderly improvement of the program with each system release. In this approach, you never leave a module without making it better by reducing decision complexity or module size. Use a software metrics analyzer to compare the two versions.

  In one case, this kind of improvement reduced the number of programmers and analysts required on a key program from five full-time to one part-time. In another instance of two equally sized COBOL systems, partial restructuring in one eventually led to a maintenance staff of only three people. The other system grew to over 30 people.

  Software engineers can select modules for partial restructuring based on changes required within the module. In fact, maintainers can and should restructure every piece of code they enter when making a change, (i.e., A COBOL paragraph, FORTRAN subroutine, PL/I function).

- Retirement of the system and complete redevelopment. Retirement is the best solution when moving to a new technology or when the cost of maintaining the software *and* hardware exceed the cost of redevelopment.

SUMMARY

The quality improvement problem-solving process can be used to identify the "root causes" of chaotic "special events" that often arise in our immature software process—bad releases, program failures, data problems, and so on. Using the PDCA, problem-solving process offers the advantages of beginning to eliminate the special causes of variation from the software process while simultaneously helping employees learn the quality process more quickly. The skills they learn from rapidly solving these specific problems will carry over into their ability to use the improvement process to solve larger problems in quality teams.

Quality tools can also be used to identify and propose solutions to problems in existing system, program, modules, data, and documentation. Perfective software evolution uses Pareto charts and cause-and-effect analysis to identify candidates for reengineering or replacement. The key improvement activities are:

Plan
- Defining selection criteria
- Gathering related data
- Analyzing the data

Do
- Implement a solution

Check
- Measure the results of improvement

Act to improve
- Recommend further improvements
- Standardize the improvements so that they are built into future software

Perfective software evolution includes all efforts to improve the quality of software or documentation. Perfective software evolution focuses on improving only the most expensive-to-maintain programs. When consistently implemented, perfective software evolution can *reduce* risks and maintenance costs, and *increase* available development time, system maintainability, maintainer skill and user satisfaction.

Pareto analysis compares systems, programs, or modules to determine which ones consume the majority of resources. This analysis is used to determine what work to do, in what order, and for what reason.

We can use cause-and-effect analysis to determine a means for achieving the improvements. The solution may be a complete redesign and rewrite, complete or partial restructuring or retirement of system and new development.

This chapter has addressed one of the key success factors for using quality in everyday work—gathering quality data and using it to refine software. Perfective software evolution and the use of Pareto analysis can clearly identify candidates for improvement, reduce the root causes of software problems, and increase the time available for doing work that provides value to the customer.

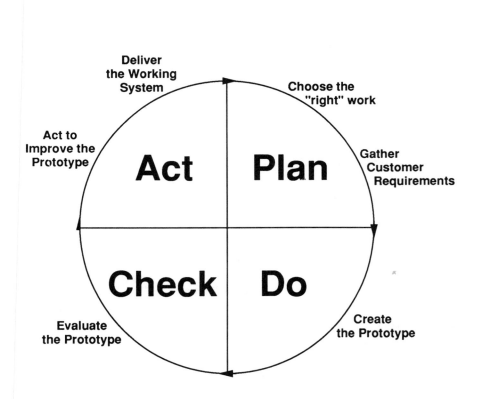

CHAPTER 13

Rapid Evolutionary Development

Do it badly, do it quickly, make it better, and then say you planned it.
—Tom Peters

To produce software quickly and correctly, we need a new model for software development and maintenance—Software Evolution. Software evolution focuses on software not as something you build or manufacture, but as a living system that grows and evolves. Achieving level 3 of software process maturity, the defined level requires that we have defined processes for software creation and evolution. In the absence of an existing methodology, consider using these two interconnected processes to lay the groundwork for software development and evolution. *Rapid Evolutionary Development* (Arthur 1991) and *Software Evolution* (Arthur 1988) describe the rapid prototyping and ongoing evolution processes needed to rapidly create and grow software. With these processes in place, you can begin to actively measure and improve software quality and productivity. In this chapter, we'll look at the basics of Rapid Evolutionary Development and in the next, we'll look at Software Evolution.

In the Christian ethic, everything began with Genesis. God created the world in six days and rested on the seventh. Everything else occurred through evolution. Genesis is an excellent model for Rapid Evolutionary Development because we want to create a deliverable, functioning prototype in as short an amount of time as possible, take a deep breath, and begin the endless series of additions, changes, and deletions required to keep the system in balance and evolving to meet the needs of the business.

Notice that in Genesis, God didn't create a prototype, show it to the users, and then tell them that they would have to wait 15 million years for the real thing. God created the basic working model which contained largely pairs of opposites—heaven and earth, ground and water, light and dark, man and woman—which provided balance. God obviously had a very binary mind. In Genesis, the earth was created quickly, and then gradually evolved into its current state.

> *We should focus on solutions that will bear fruit quickly, within a manager's 12-month planning horizon.*
>
> *—Brad Cox (Cox 1990)*

Rapid Evolutionary Development relies on speed, simplicity, and a shared vision to create a desired product. In Rapid Evolutionary Development, prototypers create a basic working system which does not contain all of the infinite variety the customer ultimately desires, but which does work and provides the essential initial elements of the system. To continue the organic analogy, a baby has all of the bones, muscles, and organs it will ever need, but none are full-sized or fully-developed. Once this basic working system is installed and turned over to the customer, a series of step-wise improvements—evolutions—turn the system into the customer's desired Garden of Eden. Sounds like a utopian fantasy doesn't it? And it's much more likely to occur this way than through construction. Can you imagine what would have happened if God had tried to specify the requirements for this earthship and then build it from scratch, with all the bells and whistles? It would take 150 million years just to get started. Instead, God chose to rapid prototype the initial version in seven days and grow it from there.

Rapid Evolutionary Development flies in the face of almost everything we believe about setting and achieving goals and objectives. Rapid Evolutionary Development demands that we embed the decision-making and direction-setting in the fabric of the ongoing processes of creation and evolution. Paul MacCready, inventor of the ultralight Gossamer Condor aircraft, put it this way (Insight 1990): "If it's worth doing, it's worth doing badly. If you can make it crudely, you can make it fast and it doesn't cost much. You can test it easily . . . fix it crudely." He insists that this approach maximizes the *speed of learning*, and I agree; the same applies to software.

Unlike the traditional development life cycle, speed is required more than direction. Once you're rolling, you can change course at will. If you're not moving, you have no feedback to guide your first steps. For those of you who know how to ski or have ever thought of learning, you can't position or turn the skis until you are moving. The faster you move, the *easier* it is to turn. At too slow a speed, skis are rigid and inflexible and it takes just plain work to direct them anywhere. Just like skiing, Rapid Evolutionary Development requires that we point our skis downhill and build up some momentum before we start setting directions and goals.

BENEFITS

Compared to standard development processes, Rapid Evolutionary Development offers several benefits. Rapid Evolutionary Development:

1. *Achieves more effective communication* because the embryonic systems demonstrate what is happening, rather than represent it. Designs are maps of the world. Prototypes are the territory. Prototyping simplifies demonstration, evaluation and modification of the growing system.
2. *Reduces risk* by eliminating uncertainty. The initial system is often created with fewer people in less time. Cycle time to proof of concept is dramatically reduced.
3. *Increases the ability to deliver desired* functionality. Customers continuously refine their needs by using the prototype and offering feedback. This reduces the need for maintenance and enhancement when the system is delivered. They don't know what they want and can't know exactly what they want. They learn along with IS as the system develops. Changes in direction are accomplished easily.
4. *Incorporates a learning process* into the development process. Since we know that we are operating on *incomplete knowledge* whenever we start a development process, Rapid Evolutionary Development encourages us to learn as we go, backtracking and changing things until we get them right. It encourages change rather than stifles it. Frozen requirements cannot reflect the dynamics of the organization or market.
5. *Encourages discovery and serendipity* in the development of desired functionality. If we learn as we go, there is a much greater chance of discovering opportunities along the way that will shape the course of the system and possibly the course of the company.

6. *Chops cycle time* from concept to delivered product by a factor of four or more. Since we are only creating the 20 percent of the product that provides 80 percent of the value, the infant system comes into the world with incredible capabilities. "80/20 solutions . . . have a great deal to recommend them—80 percent of the ideal result, achieved through 20 *percent of the effort* that might have been expended. Companies can gain strategic advantage . . . through 80/20 solutions, when aggressive company-wide efforts are judged to take too long and cost too much (Ernst 1989)."

Software evolution (Chapter 14) then expands and enhances these capabilities to quickly converge on the desired solution, even though we couldn't see it when we began the journey. Rapid Evolutionary Development allows information systems to be created quickly and effectively at low cost. (Kraushaar 1985) suggests that the cost of a micro-based system can be as low as $10,000 to 50,000 for a three to twelve month effort. Rapid Evolutionary Development also permits early availability of a working system to begin exploiting the opportunities in the market.

7. *Reduces defects* through continuous testing and evaluation of system components during the initial prototyping and ongoing evolutionary phases. User manuals and training can be developed *using* the working prototype to ensure accuracy.

8. *Encourages the creation of evolutionary systems* that are easy to grow and evolve because every step of development is an evolutionary step as well.

9. *Continuously involves users in the solution*, which encourages ownership and commitment, and a level of cooperation rarely experienced. It also encourages product acceptance. The marriage of IS and users creates a healthy environment for the system's growth and development.

The "objective" is to nudge forward the process of discovering goals along the way to induce the largest number of people possible to quickly engage, to try something; to maximize the odds of serendipity.

—Tom Peters

" 'Having goals' and 'making plans' are two of the most important pretenses." But they are dangerous in that they prevent us from getting into the thick of things and discovering the "real goals" and needs of our customer. Our customers don't often know for sure what they want, specifically, but they know it when they see it. Our job is to help them discover what they're really after as quickly as possible.

In (Davis 1988), the authors observed that user needs are always changing and that software, by nature, is always late and falls short of the user's expectations. Evolutionary prototyping, however, minimizes delay and shortfall when compared with conventional, incremental, or throw-away prototype development approaches.

Attempts to establish software factories have often failed, largely due to a failure to understand the nature of the methods and tools required. In many cases, software factories need a toolsmith to create the tools and bridges to support the team. In other cases, managers mistakenly believed that their staff didn't want to change, when what the staff really wanted was to clearly understand the new process and tools. Managers often tend to view new methods and tools as a quick fix, but fail to train their personnel in even the basics of using the methods and tools. Most managers are looking for microwave solutions, not the kind of steadfast, consistent attention to employee training and development required to create an environment that fosters rapid evolutionary development.

Effective evolution of the software development process across an IS organization requires sustained management attention. Where the Hawthorne effect can create some initial improvement using CASE tools and new methods, it can take years to bring about the complete culture shift required to make Rapid Evolutionary Development a way of life. Yet management continues to be seduced by the siren call of vendor-promised solutions to complex problems.

What upsets software professionals more than anything is to have some new laborious paperwork process foisted on them in the guise of a great new methodology. Rapid Evolutionary Development, however, tends to minimize paperwork because the system grows organically. Rigorously documenting a changing structure and functionality is unnecessary. There are so few people involved in the project that communication of changes can be handled informally. Only the bare essentials of documentation are required. The prototyping team should create its own standards for depth of documentation and then follow them.

CRITICAL SUCCESS FACTORS

In Rockart (1988), the authors describe the critical success factors of an executive support system (ESS), which, oddly enough, are also the essence of succeeding at Rapid Evolutionary Development:

1. A committed and informed executive sponsor.
2. An operating sponsor—a champion.
3. Appropriate IS staff.
4. Appropriate technology.
5. Management of data.
6. A clear link to business objectives.
7. Management of organizational resistance.
8. Management of system evolution and spread.

At Hitachi (Cusumano 1989), management found that it needed: a disciplined and standardized approach to development, an effective way to visualize and control the production process, a consistent way to specify requirements, an integrated set of tools, portable computer languages, and reuse of components. Rapid Evolutionary Development encompasses all of these things.

We could talk at length about these critical success factors, but I think they speak for themselves. Next, an organization must put aside its internal struggles for power and focus on the ecology of the whole organism to:

1. Identify the most strategic application required.
2. Create and grow the application to the desired level.
3. Evolve the application to maximize its benefits and sustain competitive advantage.

The executive sponsor can help manage the internal battles for funding and systems, and provide help prioritizing the applications to be completed. The first application chosen for rapid development should be of medium priority and then as the prototyping teams develop the skills to handle increasingly complex projects, the applications selected should be ones that can influence the corporation's survival or dramatically impact the bottom line. Once a project is chosen, the prototyping team can begin working with the customer to create the first working version of the system, which is then delivered into production. From there, the prototyping team can continue to grow and evolve the system toward the customer's desired solution. In essence, the system continues to grow indefinitely unless an innovation occurs that pushes it onto a dying branch of the evolutionary tree.

RAPID EVOLUTIONARY DEVELOPMENT

Imagine walking into a car dealer's showroom and seeing that perfect red sports car that you've always wanted. The salesperson takes you for a test drive and it feels like a dream. It corners like it's on rails and the acceleration is second to none. You know that in this car, you'll feel unstoppable, on top of the world. This car is everything you've ever wanted. You say, "I'll take one" and the salesperson says, "I'm sorry . . . this is only a prototype, but I can have one ready for you in 24 to 36 months." How would you feel? Disappointed? Angry? Would you take your business elsewhere?

This is the common mistake most prototyping projects make using the construction paradigm. They believe that the customer will stand still, waiting while the IS staff redevelops the "production" version of the system based on the prototype's demonstrated requirements. If you can show it to them, they'll want it and you had better be ready to deliver, or there will be hell to pay in terms of customer relations and lost credibility.

If you are going to create a prototype, it must be a deliverable prototype that can then be evolved to meet the customer's desires and expectations. It is much easier to manage the momentum of a system in operation than it is to shout "STOP!" when the prototype is completed and start building the production system.

One way to look at Rapid Evolutionary Development would use a logical view of what happens:

Grow (initial prototype)   **Creation**
Until (replaced)   **Evolution**
    Grow (expanded version)
enduntil
Grow (system)
    Until (converge to a solution)
        (**Plan**) Analyze the customer's needs
             • people
             • processes
             • machines
             • materials
             • environment
        (**Do**) Create a demonstrable system
        Check closeness of fit (with the customer)
        Act to improve
    enduntil
    Deliver the system
End (Grow)

First, we create and grow the initial working system. Then, until the system is replaced by a younger one, we continue to expand and grow the system from infancy to maturity using PDCA. Amazing things can happen using this approach.

"At DuPont, the use of an iterative development approach, coupled with heavy user involvement and CASE tools, has produced more than 400 new programs with no failures and helped reduce maintenance by 70 to 90 percent (Moad 1990)."

"TransWorld Airlines Inc. completely rewrote its IMS-based frequent flier program in a relational database system. The project took 15 months using a data-driven methodology and integrated CASE tools. Users can now add new functions to the application in four to eight hours. In isolated cases, users reported fivefold productivity gains in new product development (Moad 1990)."

Despite the success stories, few Information Systems organizations have undertaken the job of transforming the development and maintenance processes to one of an evolutionary nature.

PROCESS

History has shown us that large, cumbersome methodologies will only fit a certain size of project, not all projects. These heavy methodologies also generate masses of paper and require extensive paper support systems which further impede productivity.

A flexible, evolutionary prototyping methodology lays out the fundamentals of software creation and evolution using PDCA. It can significantly improve productivity and quality. The methodology works like the expansion unit in a personal computer: the application creation or evolution team can choose the specific *methods* (expansion cards) to customize the prototyping methodology to match their application.

Using a flexible, evolutionary methodology, we can then integrate software tools with the *methods* to create an integrated, *technology platform* to automate the software processes. The technology platform will then support all of the activities of software creation and evolution.

The creation process for Rapid Evolutionary Development is simple (Figure 13.1).

Plan the Project

1. **Choose a project that requires fast delivery and is not well understood**. This means that there must be rapid growth and

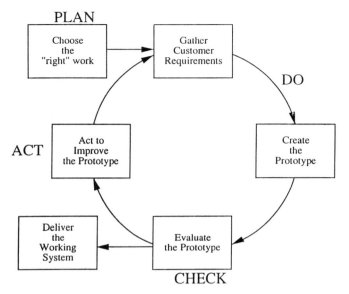

Figure 13.1   Rapid Evolutionary Development

evolution of the requirements and the whole product during its development. Iteration and evolution will occur whether it is planned for or not. Planned evolution before the product escapes is better than unplanned evolution after a failure in the field.

2. **Gather and define customer and market requirements**. It is useful at this point to begin framing the user's expectations of the creation process. We will focus on their *needs*, not their *wants or wishes*. We will require many rounds of mutual negotiation, participation, and feedback to create an embryonic system that can be used effectively. This repeated assessment of the customer's and market's requirements will insure rapid convergence on the best possible solution.

3. **Begin the analysis of the customer's process**. As we gather requirements, we need to begin sorting and chunking the customer's requests into needs, wants, and wishes. We need to begin anticipating the evolutionary path of the system as it grows. Process management (Chapter 10) can help IS guide the technical evolution. Will the system be a plant, rooted in one place, or a more mobile system which can move quickly to attack various markets?

Create the Prototype

4. **Create a prototype or model**. The prototype plays a key role in the success of the software mission. A demonstrable, behavioral model provides so much feedback that you can't help but come up with better products. Static, two-dimensional representations (i.e., design documents) of dynamic software systems that are supposed to move and grow and process information cannot help but be incomplete.

Check Closeness of Fit

5. **Evaluate the prototype using customer feedback**. Given a working, demonstrable system, customers can tell you how far or how close you are to their goal. They can give you better feedback about how to make the system better.

Act to Improve

6. **Act to improve the prototype**. Using customer and prototyper feedback, identify the next steps required to ecologically grow the fetal system to the next step in its evolution.

RELATIONSHIP MODEL

Another way to look at Rapid Evolutionary Development is being like human courtship and family development:

Courtship

First, you have to choose the right mate. Initially, there's a lot of courting as the software developer and customer romance each other. Eventually, they decide to ''get into bed'' together. A prenuptial agreement is often a great idea.

Pregnancy

Prototyping is much like pregnancy—creation of an embryonic system that can survive in the real world. First, the customer conceives an idea.

Together, the software developers and the customer work together as the fertile nucleus develops into the initial version of the system. This pregnancy is accompanied by tremendous enthusiasm and growth.

Notice that mothers never ask fathers "How many corners do you want me to cut in the construction of our child?" Software systems with birth defects usually carry them for the rest of their life unless a highly skilled software surgeon makes the necessary repairs. Lots of prenatal care will prevent such problems.

And notice that fathers never ask "How long will this take? Couldn't you deliver it in four months instead of nine?" Because everyone knows it takes nine months, no matter how many people you put on the task. Children born prematurely need a lot of care, most of it expensive. Children born too late are a burden on the mother and cause endless anxiety. It's best to let the prototyping process take its natural course and deliver the baby when it's ready.

During this period, the parents must prepare a loving environment to receive the new child. Everyone has to be trained in child care, feeding, and so on.

Birth

Finally, the system is formed sufficiently to live in the world. The initial version (a small one) is "delivered" and installed for use. Like most newborns, it will wake us up in the middle of the night with all kinds of problems—it can soil itself, it can get sick, it can get hungry. Brand new systems need a lot of initial care. Parents don't say "When is this child going to be able to take care of itself?" because they know it will take time for the system to reach a level of maturity where it can do things for itself.

The Terrible Twos

The system needs a lot of care and feeding in its first few years as it continues to grow. Like expectant parents, the software developers and the customers continue to care for its needs. The rampant enthusiasm of the pregnancy yield to a feeling of confinement. A lot of preparation and work must go into any outing with the new system. The infant system continues to grow organically and naturally—no new hands, feet, or organs are added.

It is a good idea at this point to immunize the system against all of the childhood diseases.

Childhood

Look who's talking! At this point the system is fairly well mannered. It continues to grow and learn at a reasonable rate. Customers and IS both enjoy this period of working together to help the system develop.

Adolescence

The system will continue to grow, gain weight, and learn. At this stage, changes in markets or organizations can cause problems. The software may develop some wild hormonal urges that will test the mettle of the developer and customer. The software may need braces for its teeth or strong guidance to set its path.

At this point, the system may get the urge to spin off some children of its own. JUST SAY NO!

Adulthood

Maturity develops. We can no more create a mature system than we can create a mature person. As the system matures, however, it will provide increasingly more benefit to the customer and require less support and attention from the developer.

At some point in their life, systems may put on some extra weight and need to reduce some of the flab—both data and processes. Some systems will opt for plastic surgery and various cremes and balms to postpone the aging process. This is okay! No one likes ugly, old systems; we appreciate elegant, mature ones. Through good nutrition and balanced effort, the system can stay younger longer than we perhaps ever thought possible.

Old Age

Through proper exercise and diet, software can thrive. It can live a long and healthy life and retire, or it can develop all kinds of health problems and require expensive medical care. All of this depends on how it was treated during its lifetime. Rapid Evolutionary Development demands that we examine the overall ecology of any change in the system during its life.

I prefer this metaphor of courting and childbearing to the more algorithmic model offered previously. The question on your mind now, however, might be: "How do I begin to use the model?"

SOFTWARE EVOLUTION

Unlike a car that rolls off an assembly line or a house ready for occupancy, software systems continue to expand and change over time. The next step of Rapid Evolutionary Development delivers the system into everyday use. From here on, the freewheeling accelerated growth of the prenatal system slows. The system grows and evolves in a more carefully orchestrated and focused process of Software Evolution (Arthur 1988).

The software creation process can be used throughout the system's life to create major enhancements and extensions of the systems knowledge and abilities. Using the Software Evolution process described in Chapter 14 and the Rapid Evolutionary Development process, prototypers can continuously improve and enhance the system as the environment changes around it. The system, however, is not the only thing that needs to evolve.

Evolution of the Methodology

One of the problems with most "construction" or "manufacturing" methodologies is that they rarely evolve to meet the changing needs of the business or technology. When a methodology does change, it is typically too little, too late. The methodology and technology must evolve to match the needs of the customer. The PDCA process described in Chapter 10 will assist you in keeping the process and technology up-to-date with the evolutionary life forms created using Rapid Evolutionary Development.

SUMMARY

In this chapter we've explored the benefits, critical success factors, and process of Rapid Evolutionary Development. By using the metaphor of evolution, we can drop the constraints of the "construction" paradigm and discover new ways to quickly grow working systems that can surprise and delight both users and IS personnel. We've also looked briefly at the other evolutionary processes that support continued growth of the software, software processes, and technology that support it. In the next chapter, we'll look at ways to evolve the system.

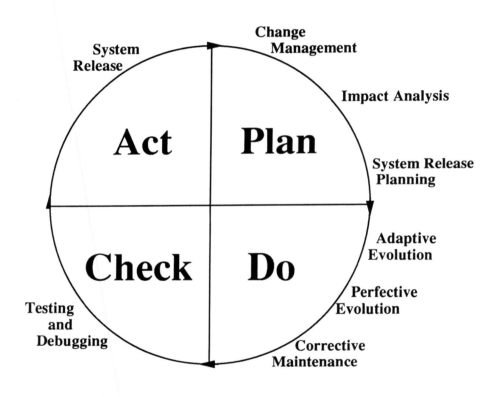

CHAPTER 14

Software Evolution

In *The Mind and Nature*, Gregory Bateson's central theme states that evolution is a *mental* process. In essence, software is a reflection of the mental process of our customers and programmers. Software Evolution involves both the physical and mental growth of the application system.

A third to half the programming population is occupied maintaining and enhancing old code (DeMarco 1990). This explosion of evolutionists might be viewed as an overall success in achieving our initial mission—application creation. Successful automation is bound to increase the proportion of existing code to new.

Traditional manufacturing thought processes have produced five to eight years as an expected average lifetime for software, but most large, established companies have millions of lines of code that are 15 years or older. From this we must infer that through growth and evolution, software systems secure their niche in the corporate environment. Once entrenched, replacing these systems becomes difficult and expensive, if not impossible.

Rather than cut the cost of software creation, we should increase the investment in software creation to reap significant decreases in evolution costs. Creating durable, reusable software is more expensive initially, but less costly over the long haul.

Once the initial version of the system has been created, there must be a way to evolve it toward the customer's ultimate goal. In this chapter, you'll discover the proven steps to software evolution that will allow you to take the system from infancy to adulthood. This process of continuous evolution is described in more detail in *Software Evolution—The Software Evolution Challenge* (Arthur 1988).

In many ways, software *maintenance* fails to describe the daily activities of the hordes of programmers and analysts who work on existing software. They constantly change software to meet the evolving needs of the business, the application, and technology. In a typical environment, these people spend less than ten percent of their time actually fixing defects. They spend the majority of their time on enhancements—software evolution. Maintenance means to preserve from failure or decline. Evolution means a continuous change from a lesser, simpler or worse state, to a higher or better state. Given a choice, would you rather improve software or merely preserve it?

Because most organizations depend heavily on existing software systems, software evolution is a critical function. Supporting these systems is the mission of the software evolutionist. To help you accomplish this mission, this chapter will:

- Explain the functions and flow of the software evolution process.
- Define the three types of software evolution: corrective, adaptive, and preventive.
- Identify the factors critical to successful, productive evolution and evolution of software.

FIRST STEPS

IS departments spend money on software creation and evolution in approximately the following amounts:

30 percent Creation
70 percent Evolution

So, if you want to reduce your costs, you must initially focus on the place with the most potential for gain—Evolution. Some people mistakenly believe that once you replace a system that you will eliminate the burden of keeping the system up-to-date with its environment. Ridiculous! You simply substitute a larger, more complex system, with higher evolution costs for the old one. What you need is a strategy for improving, reengineering, or replacing systems that optimizes the company's return on investment. Your goal should be to move all systems from a lesser, simpler or worse state, to a higher or better state.

CHANGE MANAGEMENT

Perhaps the key tool for both creation and evolution is a change management system. Think of it as the purchase order system that drives all work. The business is constantly changing; you must have a mechanism to support that evolution. Evolution projects most commonly need to manage their growth and evolution. Prototyping projects often experience continuous change in requirements and design that occur *after* the project has begun. Rapid Evolutionary Development helps manage this change and change management can assist the process.

Change management is also a strategic tool for client satisfaction. Open the system to clients so that they can directly request changes, check on the status of their requests, and contact application gurus directly via electronic mail. By linking customers directly to IS, as Tom Peters suggests, you can win their confidence for years to come.

Change management also collects all of the information necessary to identify the *20 percent of the programs that generate 80 percent of the costs*. It is key to a successful evolution strategy.

The major concern of software staffs today is how to maintain the existing portfolio of programs. Consider the following evolution problems. Most computer programs are difficult and expensive to maintain. Software evolution costs $300 billion per year worldwide and demand is rapidly increasing (Martin 1983). In the past 15 years the budget for evolution has increased from approximately 50 percent of the resources expended on application software to 70 to 75 percent. Each new creation project adds to the evolution burden. "Add little to little and you have a big pile!" End user applications on micros, minis, and information centers will require evolution. Demand for evolution already exceeds the capabilities of most IS organizations. In business, the user department is programming many of their new applications. If evolution is not managed and improved, demand will easily exceed available programming resources, IS professionals and end users.

Software changes are poorly designed and implemented. Design documents are rarely examined and updated to reflect changes to the system. A carelessly planned system takes three times as long as estimated to complete; a carefully planned system takes only twice as long. Difficult-to-maintain systems are ultimately rewritten at great expense. The two years following the release of a new product are spent implementing enhancements to bring the system up to the user's *expectations*. And, most major enhancements are so poorly understood and implemented that several additional releases are necessary to clean up the enhancement. The repair and enhancement of software often injects new bugs that must later be repaired.

To resolve these problems and manage the growing software inventory, improvements are needed in the skills and productivity of maintainers, and in the quality and effectiveness of their work. This text focuses on helping you accomplish these goals.

To begin with, programmers, analysts, and managers should recognize that:

- Not all system maintainers are created equal, but they can be educated to equivalent skill levels.
- The difference between the best and worst performers is at least an order of magnitude.
- The reason for this disparity is a difference in the level of knowledge and skill, often referred to as *breakthrough* knowledge.
- The best performers can perform the key software evolution activities more effectively than their counterparts.
- No single activity or area of expertise accounts for the differences.
- The key to evolution productivity is to do most things a little better or faster (Peters 1985).
- A little more knowledge and skill multiplied over many activities produces striking differences in performance.

Providing maintainers with the latest knowledge, skills and techniques to achieve their mission by performing the key software evolution activities a little better will reap significant productivity and quality improvements.

Software evolution consists of the activities required to keep a software system operational and responsive after it is accepted and placed into production. These activities include:

Correcting defects (maintenance)
Enhancing software functionality (evolution)
Improving the quality of existing software (evolution)

In general, these activities keep the system in sync with an evolving, expanding user and operational environment. Functionally, software evolution can be divided into these three categories: corrective, adaptive, and preventive.

THE SOFTWARE LIFE CYCLE

The software life cycle covers the period from conception to retirement of a given software product. There are many definitions of the software life cycle. They differ primarily in the classifications of phases and activities. For many large software systems, only one-fourth to one-third of all life cycle costs are attributed to software creation. The lion's share of the effort and costs are spent in the operations and evolution.

While many activities related to creating and evolving software are similar, software evolution has unique characteristics of it own, including:

- *Constraints of an existing system*—Software evolution is performed on an existing production system. Any changes must conform or be compatible with an existing architecture, design, and code constraints. Typically, the older the system, the more challenging and time-consuming the evolution effort becomes. We need to understand how to prevent software extinction.
- *Shorter time frames*—Software creation may span one or more years, while evolution may span a few hours to cycles of one to six months.
- *Available test data*—Software creation creates all test data from scratch. Software evolution can use this existing test data and perform regression tests. Thus, the challenge is to create new data to adequately test the changes and their impact on the rest of the system.

Software evolution can, and should be a structured process. It involves many different people and groups. Figure 14.1 illustrates the software evolution process and its relationship to the PDCA model.

THE EVOLUTION PROCESS

The evolution process begins when a request for change is initiated by a user. (Note that a user is defined as anyone who uses or interacts with the system, including systems engineers, IS personnel, data processing, operations, or marketing personnel.) It ends when the system passes testing, is accepted by the user, and released for operation. In between, a variety of activities involving maintainers, quality assurance, configura-

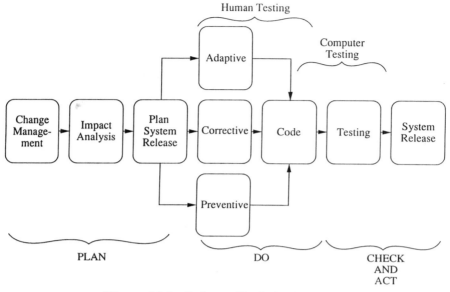

Figure 14.1   Software Evolution Process

tion management and test personnel must be planned for, coordinated, and implemented. These activities should be coordinated by use of change management.

Change Management

The basic objective of change management is to uniquely identify, describe and track the status of each requested change. A change request provides the vehicle for recording information about a system defect, requested enhancement, or quality improvement.

The major change management activities are:

1. Entering change requests—Maintainers receive a request for some type of change (i.e., defect, enhancement, quality improvement), analyze the change, and generate a change request.

   —In this text, a system is defined as a group of programs (business environment) or configuration items (DOD environment).

   —A program/configuration item is an executable piece of software made up of many modules or units.

—A module is equivalent to a unit. It consists of object or source language code that, under the precepts of structured programming, implements a single function.

2. Tracking change requests and provide regular and exception reports on the status of change requests.
3. Providing an audit trail of changes.
4. Providing input to project management and quality assurance systems.

Impact Analysis

Once a change is initiated, an analyst has to evaluate its impact on the existing system and estimate the resources needed to complete the change. The overall objective of impact analysis is to determine the scope of the requested change as a basis for planning and implementing it.

The major impact analysis tasks are:

1. Evaluate change requests for potential impacts on existing systems, other systems, documentation, hardware, data structures, and humans (users, maintainers, and operators).
2. Develop a preliminary resource estimate.
3. Document the scope of the requested change and update the change request.

System Release Planning

Once these changes have been analyzed, they can be grouped together as a scheduled evolution release. This requires planning. The principle objective of system release planning is to determine the contents and timing of system releases.

The major system release planning tasks:

1. Rank and select change requests for the next release.
2. Batch the changes by work product and schedule the work.
3. Prepare a system release planning document (Version Description Document for the DOD) and place it under control of the configuration management system.
4. Update approved change requests.

When system release planning occurs varies depending on whether you work in a contractual or non-contractual environment. When evolution is done under contract, the contents and timing of a system release are negotiated and agreed to before any major work is begun, unless the contract is a "level of effort" contract.

Naturally, to agree on a contract, some level of analysis must be done to determine the scope of the changes and the resources required. When evolution is done without a contract, (i.e., in-house), a release is planned after the change requests have been analyzed and the scope of work is clearly understood.

Once a release is planned, maintainers can design the change.

Making Changes

Corrective maintenance focuses on healing the system—fixing the defects. Using the construction or manufacturing paradigm, people who fix defects are *mechanics* or *maintainers*. This often demeaning title implies that programmers who maintain software like to "get dirty." They tend to "work with their hands" and they are often under educated.

If we use the evolutionary metaphor instead, we notice that the people who fix living systems are doctors. Doctors are typically highly trained, highly skilled men and women who work with their heads *and* hands. Doctors are usually well paid for helping their patients live a normal, productive life. Changing the metaphor of software will change how we view virtually every aspect of software creation and evolution.

Like living systems, software defects indicate that the system is not performing as originally intended, or as specified in the requirements. There are a variety of situations that can be described as corrective maintenance. Some of them include:

- Correcting a program that fails in the field or during testing (failures).
- Correcting a program that produces incorrect results (faults).

Corrective evolution is usually a *reactive* process. Defects generally need immediate attention. As most doctors will tell you, however, it is the excesses of our live-for-today lifestyle that cause most problems. Like living systems, we have the option to help our software systems lead a more balanced life that will help the system live a long time.

Adaptive evolution includes all work related to changing how the software functions to meet the demands of its environment. Adaptive evolution includes system changes, additions, insertions, deletions, modifications, extensions, and enhancements. Adaptive evolution is generally performed as a result of new or changing requirements. Rapid Evolutionary Development can be used during the adaptive phase of Software Evolution to rapidly prototype major new enhancements to the system.

Some examples of adaptive changes include:

- Rearranging fields on an output report.
- Changing a system to support new hardware configurations.
- Adding a new function.
- Deleting a function.
- Converting a system from batch to on-line operation.

Making a program more efficient does *not* affect its functionality. As a result, this type of change should be considered as part of preventive evolution.

Perfective evolution (Chapter 12) includes all efforts to improve the quality of the software. These activities can include restructuring code, creating and updating documentation, improving reliability or efficiency or any other qualities. Some specific examples are:

- Improving efficiency, maintainability, or reliability *without* changing functionality.
- Restructuring code to make it more maintainable.
- Tuning a system to reduce response time.

Although these three types of work are discussed separately, much of the work is performed concurrently. For example, enhancements and quality improvements are often worked and tested together. Design of one program's changes will overlap the coding of another's. All of these activities occur during the Software Evolution life cycle.

Coding

The objective of coding is to change the software to reflect the approved changes represented in the system (logical) program (physical) designs. The major coding activities are:

1. Implement and review all changes to code.
2. Restore or place the source code under control of the configuration management system.

3. Update the change request to reflect the modules or units changed.

Testing

The next step in the evolution process puts the revised designs and code to test. The primary objective of testing is to ensure compliance with the original requirements and the approved changes. An incremental, evolutionary testing strategy will work the best. This kind of testing process weeds out bugs along the way, not when most of the work is done. The major testing activities are:

1. Human Testing:
   —*Walkthrough* or *inspection* requirements, designs, code, and data.
2. Computer testing:
   —*Unit test* all code changes by module or unit.
   —*Integration test* the interfaces between each module of the program and the program as a whole.
   —*System test* the interfaces between programs to ensure that the system meets all of the original requirements plus the added changes.
   —*Acceptance testing* where the user approves the revised system.

System Release

Once a system has been thoroughly tested and accepted, it can be released for use. The objective of system release is to deliver the system and updated documentation to users for installation and operation.

The major activity associated with releasing a system is to package the release and send it to the user. System release packaging organizes all of the products of the evolution project—user manuals, software, data definitions, and job control language—for delivery to the client or user. System delivery methods vary from mail to floppy disks to telecommunications.

SOFTWARE EVOLUTION

Software evolution has been presented as a series of linear or sequential steps. There are, however, a number of activities which require overlaps and iterative loops. Some examples include recycling emergency repairs through the scheduled release process, returning change requests for clarification, additional analysis and estimation after an impact analysis, and additional design and coding changes after testing discovers bugs. Usually, these processes occur synchronously throughout the evolution staff, (e.g., systems analyst works on program design B while programmers revise the code in program A.).

Although they may be handled loosely in some less crucial environments, the following factors are critical to effectively conducting software evolution:

- Develop and adhere to a well-defined and structured software evolution methodology. Know when and how to tailor it to fit your environment.
- Use structured design and coding techniques.
- Control changes and software products with change and configuration management systems.
- Conduct an impact analysis of all requested changes before agreeing to do them.
- Establish scheduled releases and batch change requests to maximize productivity and quality.
- Gather quality assurance data and use it to refine and improve software creation and evolution practices.
- Use incremental testing to improve the quality of delivered software.
- Introduce and use modern, automated tools to improve quality and productivity.
- Obtain management's support for software evolution.

SUMMARY

It is no secret that billions of lines of code execute every day in computers around the world. These systems are our cash cows, we've invested in their creation, we change them to meet the needs of the business, and they will be needed for years to come.

Existing systems have reached their position through evolution. Under the law of the jungle, existing systems have an advantage: all of the knowledge about the business is embedded in their logic. Replacement systems must rely on humans for this knowledge.

Where did these existing systems come from anyway? In business, they started as a seed to replace a manual procedure. Over the years they grew, extending their roots into the heart of the business. Their shade and fruit nourished the business. Other systems sprang up to consume their data. Existing systems live in ecological balance with the decisions support systems they feed and their neighboring systems.

Replacement systems have no such support. Few software developers can build a replacement. Existing systems continue to grow and evolve while the replacement is being built. The replacement system does not have this advantage. Its requirements and designs are cast in stone. If the creation process takes longer than six months to a year, the replacement emerges from the swamp only to discover that it is already obsolete, on the verge of extinction. Even if the replacement succeeds in suddenly replacing the existing system in a flash cut, it may harm or kill the rest of the environment. Successful replacement systems usually grow and evolve from a new seed. Replacement systems can also be purchased from vendors and transplanted into your environment.

Software reengineering is an evolutionary process which educates software technicians, identifies candidates for reengineering, genetically and structurally reengineers them, and then sustains the improvements.

Software evolution consists of the activities required to keep a software system operational and responsive after it is accepted and placed into production. The key differences between evolution and creation are that:

- Rapid Evolutionary Development focuses on the fast creation and growth of an initial working system. Evolution continues the growth at a slower, more manageable rate.
- Creation happens in 7 ± 2 months. Growth and evolution occur over the life of the system.
- Creation rapidly creates a working prototype or infant system. Software evolution ensures that it grows up in a rich environment safe from harm. Evolution consists of three key activities:
  - Corrective maintenance—fixing defects
  - Adaptive evolution—enhancing existing systems
  - Preventive evolution—improving software quality
- Creation freewheels through a fast, five-step PDCA process to create the system. The evolutionary process uses a longer, seven-step PDCA approach to changing software safely and ecologically. Those processes are:
  - Managing change

- Analyzing impacts
- Planning system releases
- Making corrective, adaptive, or preventive changes
- Coding changes
- Testing changes
- Releasing the system

Like having children, giving birth to a software system is only a small portion of the challenge. Keeping the system alive and growing to adulthood is a unique and interesting challenge that will consume most of the resources ever spent on the system. It pays to do it well.

CHAPTER 15

A QI Story

Author's note: I've often observed that some people have a hard time digesting information about quality improvement or any other more technical issue unless it is put in the form of a story. The Japanese often use little parables to teach the concepts of quality improvement. The following story teaches quality improvement from just such a perspective. Not all of the hundreds of technicians who have read it found it useful, but the majority did. I offer it as a way to begin teaching your mind the quality problem-solving process.

There once was a wise King and Queen who ruled over a vast Kingdom, but they were troubled. People came from around the land bearing problems. It seemed that no sooner would the King and Queen solve one problem than others would spring up in its place. They felt obligated to help the Kingdom prosper and felt only limited success.

So the rulers sent their sleek, black carriage pulled by six white steeds to fetch the wisest man in the land. The wiseman's modest home was two days ride from the castle. It seemed almost a part of the landscape setting back into a lush green hillside which kept it warm in the winter and cool in the summer. Leaves on the surrounding trees were golden brown and a few carpeted the path to his door. Having heard the rumble of hooves and the shouts of the driver's voice, the wiseman stood waiting in the open doorway when the carriage arrived. His bearing gave him stature, yet his softness made him seem as flexible as a willow. Like the red-tailed hawk, his eyes were sharp, yet his beard was full and grey. It took but a few minutes for him to gather a few necessities and enter the soft leather confines of the coach.

When he arrived at the castle, the wiseman followed a guard cloaked in red and black livery through the long broad halls, listening to the clack of their heels against marble. The sound of servants singing filled the halls as they cleaned nearby chambers.

Two massive oaken doors nearly twice his height stood open as the wiseman and the guard swept into the throne room. The air smelled of flowers.

"Sovereign Lord and Lady," the wiseman said, bowing, "How may I be of service?" He noticed that the King and Queen wore robes of yellow and gold that matched the festive change of seasons. The King wore a lattice-like crown that held many fine gems. His hair was sable in color and his beard the same. His left hand grasped a sceptre of fine gold. The Queen wore a more simple gold crown that peaked in the middle over her forehead and swept back around her fine auburn hair. Her face was relaxed and a hint of a smile played at the edge of her mouth.

"Oh wisest of men," the Queen began, her voice melodious like a nightingale singing, "problems lie upon the land in ever increasing numbers like the onslaught of some plague. For every problem we solve, it seems that two leap up to take its place. They multiply like rabbits in the field. What can we do?"

"Problems?" he asked. "How do you know they are multiplying?"

"Why, we keep a log," said the King, his voice rumbling across the room like summer thunder. "Every year the problems increase and though we solve as many as possible, more come forth like termites in the woods."

"What kinds of problems, specifically?" probed the wiseman.

The King twisted his sceptre as he thought. "Problems lie in all directions. In everything from agriculture to finance, from bakers to shoemakers, from armies to textiles."

The wiseman nodded and shifted his weight to the other foot as he spoke: "As I was coming through the castle, I was impressed as always by the immenseness of the building. There are many rooms in the castle, are there not?"

"Dozens," said the Queen and then, noting the King's annoyance, she asked "But how does that apply?"

"It's been so long since I've come to visit. Please indulge my curiosity for just a moment." The wiseman watched as the Queen nodded and the King shrugged his shoulders and began tapping his ring against the sceptre in an audible flutter. Inwardly the wiseman chuckled, for it had long been his observation that people miss the best opportunities for learning because they would not remain open long enough to notice the gifts laid before them. ''As I came though the castle I noticed servants cleaning the rooms. There did not appear to be enough servants to clean the whole castle every day . . .'' he paused and glanced at the Queen who shook her head. ''So how do you decide which rooms to clean?''

''Easy,'' said the Queen, ''we always clean one of the smaller, dirtier rooms first.''

''And what does that do for you?'' he asked softly.

''There's a sense of accomplishment from quickly completing such a task and it propels the servants through the task of cleaning the other, larger rooms that are even dirtier. I often hear them singing.''

''Ah ha!'' exclaimed the wiseman with such force that the King jerked back from his revery. ''You see my lord and lady, the answer lies here in the simplest of truths.''

''What?'' they asked almost simultaneously.

''Think of your Kingdom as your castle and problems as the dirt in every room. The two of you cannot clean the whole Kingdom by yourselves. And by solving only the problems put before you, you cannot know if they are the biggest and dirtiest ones in the land. Furthermore, by working with problems of unknown value, you cannot get the same sense of satisfaction you would get from solving the most important ones. You can, however, conquer both of these issues by cleaning one of the larger, dirtier rooms in the Kingdom—a significant problem area—can you not?'' The wiseman watched as the King and Queen digested his words.

''It seems too simple,'' the King grumbled.

''Of course,'' said the wiseman, ''the best approaches are always simple . . . as simple as possible but no simpler. Complexity is a trap to be avoided at all costs. Now let me ask you, what are the biggest and dirtiest problems in the Kingdom?''

The King and Queen bent their heads together, speaking softly for a few minutes. The wiseman watched their unconscious communication of gestures and looks. When they nodded in agreement, he glanced away as if distracted by the room, but from his peripheral vision he noticed the King about to speak.

''One of the biggest problems has always been growing enough food for our increasing population. For the last three years, production has been falling. Nothing we have tried seems to stop it.''

The wiseman thanked the King and called for some parchment and a pen. When they arrived, he began to write and speak at the same time. "I always find it best to work my problems out on paper. Our problem is that we have a problem growing enough food for the Kingdom and production has been falling for the past three seasons. Instead of an entire Kingdom to repair, we have a much smaller problem area and a measurable reason for working on it." He turned the parchment to the King and Queen and showed them what he had drawn:

Annual Food Production

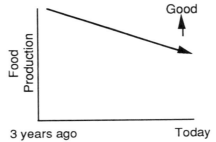

Problem Area: *Increasing growth of crops as measured by annual production.*

The King and Queen began to sit up and take notice.

"So," the wiseman continued, "we've begun to isolate a specific area where we can make the greatest contribution to the Kingdom, but the area is still too wide to do much about. We must search even farther to find something specific."

"I would guess that although the King still hunts for sport, his efforts also serve to feed the castle, am I not right?" The King and Queen nodded. The wiseman noticed them leaning forward slightly. "Let me ask you great King, there are many herds of deer and elk in the land. After you've chosen which herd to hunt, how do you decide which animal to bring down?"

The King slowly twisted the sceptre as he thought for a moment. He had never before examined his choices. They all seemed so instinctive. "I normally aim for one of the largest animals and invariably my arrow finds its mark."

"And why do you choose one of the larger ones?"

"Because it will feed more people. I would need to shoot two smaller ones to get as much meat."

"So, another principle springs to mind . . . *Aim for the largest problem in the herd!*" The wiseman noticed the King's head begin to nod. "Fixing one big problem will provide more benefit than fixing two smaller ones and it often requires less effort. To find our mark we must set our sights on only one problem in the herd."

"When the servants clean a room," the Queen said, nodding her head, "they always focus on the biggest mess first, whether it's the bed or the floor."

"Precisely," said the wiseman. "So tell me, what is the biggest problem in the area of agriculture?"

"Maize," said the King. The Queen nodded in agreement. "It feeds the whole Kingdom. Our livestock live on it and we grind it to make our bread."

"Maize," said the wiseman thoughtfully. "How do you know that it is the most important crop?"

"Have the accountant bring our tallies," commanded the King. A few minutes later a thin, pale man appeared, loaded with heavy leather-bound ledgers. "I've seen the tallies," said the King, "and maize crop is the largest of them all."

The wiseman looked over the records for a few minutes and then began to draw. When he finished he showed his sketches to the King and Queen:

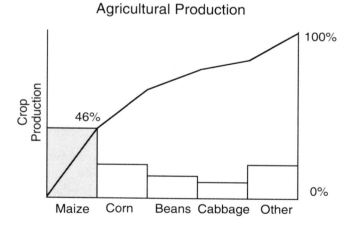

"So, maize accounts for 46 percent of the total agricultural production," said the wiseman. "But how do you know it's really the biggest problem?"

The Queen settled herself with her palms in her lap and said: "We store the grain in winter silos. For the last three years the silos have been less and less full."

"By how much?" asked the wiseman.

"By seven to ten percent," rumbled the King. "If it falls much farther we shall certainly face a famine."

"So," said the wiseman, "we can now state the problem in such a way that it focuses our efforts like an arrow in a bow and together we can set a target for improvement. How much would we need to increase production to achieve a state of not just sufficiency but abundance?"

The King and Queen conferred. "By 30 percent or more."

Nodding his head in agreement, the wiseman began to write, and when he was done he held up yet another sheet of parchment:

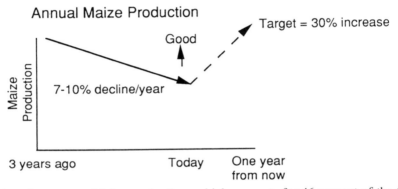

Problem Statement: Maize production, which accounts for 46 percent of the total agricultural output, has been falling at a rate of 7–10% per year for the last three years and must increase to support our growing population.

Target: 30 percent increase in maize production

"Now," the wiseman said, "we have a specific problem and a target for improvement. Now the fun begins.

"What are some of the causes of poor maize production?"

"The rains have been less the last few years," offered the King.

"Rain is a gift of the gods," said the wiseman. "We cannot influence the rain, but a great river runs through the Kingdom, does it not?" The monarches nodded their royal heads. "So perhaps it is not the rain, but an absence of water that restrains the crop?" The wiseman noticed nods of approval and continued.

"What else might cause such a decline in production?"

The King and Queen talked again, but shook their heads. "We do not know."

"Of course," said the wiseman. "How could you? Do you till the soil, plant the seed, or harvest the crops? No! Of course not. Let us summon the best farmers from the four corners of the Kingdom to join us. Send your fastest riders for them. Then, after a good meal and a night of rest, we will resume our analysis of the problem.

"I expect that you have found this time well spent," the wiseman said, "have you not?" And to the their surprise, the wiseman spun about and swept out of the room.

Later the next day, farmers arrived from the four corners of the land: north, south, east and west. When the wiseman heard they had arrived, he made sure they were rested and well fed before joining the King and Queen. As they prepared, the wiseman told them of the previous day's activities and all agreed that the maize crop was dwindling. Together, the five entered the throne room to continue the analysis of the problem. The King and Queen seemed anxious to begin.

Without wasting a word, the wiseman began to speak: "I've informed these farmers of the problem. Now the question continues: What is the cause of the declining maize crop?" Noticing the forward posture of the farmer from the north, the wiseman asked him to begin.

"I think it's the soil. We can plant a crop of maize in a field for a couple of years and then on the third year it begins to decline."

"Yes," agreed the farmer of the south. "We've noticed that the soil needs to lie fallow for a few years to rebuild its strength before we can again plant a crop of maize."

The wiseman noticed that the farmer from the east had something to say, but was shying away from speaking in front of his lord and lady. So he asked the man directly, "What light can you shed on this issue?"

"Well," began the man hesitantly, "we've found that we can rotate maize and our bean crop and both produce well."

"Fine for you," said the farmer from the north, "but we only plant maize. All of our fallow fields are under production. What can we do?"

The wiseman interrupted: "One issue at a time. First the causes and then the solutions. Although we already have one solution—rotating bean and maize fields.

"What else?" he asked.

The farmer from the west began to scuff one of his shoes against the floor. The wiseman walked over to him and pulled him gently forward. "What causes have you observed?"

"I think it's the seed. I've got one kind of seed that produces the biggest heads of maize you've ever seen. I got some others that produce good-sized heads, but nothing like the best seed. Either crop, however, will decline after a couple of years in the same ground."

"Good," said the wiseman. "Anything else?" He studied the farmers

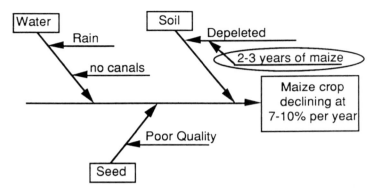

as they cast about for other causes, but noticed no more forthcoming. "Good," he said again and began again to draw.

In a few minutes, he turned to show his work to everyone:

The wiseman smiled and began to speak: "Problems are like weeds; they will not die unless you can get at the root of the problem. This diagram shows the various causes of the maize crop decline. There may be a number of minor causes, but the biggest one seems to be the depletion of the soil by repeated plantings of maize."

"Fascinating," exclaimed the Queen.

"Yes!" the King rumbled.

The wiseman observed the farmers nodding in agreement. "Let us now put our minds together then and think of the various measures we could put in place to remedy the root cause of the problem. We already know two: rotating bean with maize crops seems to work as does planting fallow fields."

"But," cried the farmer of the north, "that will do us no good. All of our fields are planted in maize. It is too cold to grow beans in our colder climate. What can we do?"

The wiseman looked around and noticed the farmer of the west scuffing his shoe again. "What is brewing in that fertile mind of yours?" he asked the man, pulling him forward.

"Well," he said slowly, "I don't know if this is of any help, but I raise some livestock too. I've been shoveling the barn and piling the waste outside by the back corner. I don't know how it happened, but some kernels of maize must have fallen in with it. I've got four or five stalks of the biggest, tallest maize you've ever seen growing up around the pile."

"What could that have to do with our problem?" grumbled the King.

"Sire," said the wiseman, "the cattle eat the maize. Perhaps the vital elements of the maize pass through the animals and back into their waste.

Everything is a cycle. Perhaps the waste is the key to returning energy to dying fields.''

"Yes," said the farmer of the north. "Now that you mention it, I've seen similar shocks of maize growing vibrantly near dung piles."

"Ah," said the wiseman, stroking his beard, "now we're on to something. I take it there are plenty of animals in the north?" The farmer nodded. "Then we can identify animal waste as a countermeasure to the root cause—depeleted soil."

The wiseman turned to the King and Queen who were smiling broadly at him. "Your majesties, if I may be so bold, let me recommend a course of action that I believe will begin to set the crops aright. First, let us send these four men back to their respective communities and have them till the available waste into the fields before winter arrives. Then, we will have them plant maize crops in the spring and see how they grow next year. Those who can rotate crops from field to field will continue to do so, since that seems to work as well. Once we've determined the results, we'll then act upon what we've learned to improve the following year's crops.

"I call it the plant, grow, check, and act cycle."

"Yes," rumbled the King. "We will decree it throughout the land."

The Queen sang her agreement and the men returned to their provinces to begin the work. Before the wiseman returned to his home, the King and Queen requested his attendance once more.

"Why," the Queen asked, "did you not pursue seed and water as options?"

"My Queen," he replied, "if we had done all three, how could we have known which one worked and which one didn't. Besides, building massive canals would strain the treasury and I doubt that even plenty of water would have made the maize grow in tired fields. The other seed, however, is an interesting question. It will be interesting to see how it grows next year and what dimensions it takes. If the crop is still better than the others, perhaps we should have a contest to see who can grow the best maize and then use that seed to sow more of the Kingdom every year."

"Splendid idea," she said. "We will wait and watch expectantly."

And so the wiseman returned to his home.

Almost a year later, he returned to the castle and was again led before the King and Queen and the four farmers.

The King stood and stepped down to meet him. "Your analysis was correct. Maize fields throughout the land have far surpassed anyone's expectations. The farmer of the west has brought the finest heads of maize I've ever seen. Using it for seed will increase the harvest even more.''

"How much has the crop increased?'' the wiseman queried, smiling, for he knew it had been a banner year.

"By over 35 percent,'' the Queen sang as she moved to join them.

"Excellent,'' said the wiseman. ''We met our target effortlessly.'' And so saying, he began to draw:

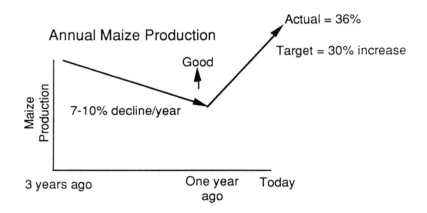

"The result of applying our countermeasure,'' he continued, ''was a significant increase in the maize crop. Now we have but a few more things to do.''

"Yes?'' questioned the King. ''What?'' asked the Queen.

"We must set a standard for all to use to maintain this improvement throughout the land. We must set a process in place to insure that we continue to replenish the soil.''

"It will be done,'' said the King.

"And we must decide where we can duplicate this increase.''

"I've already begun,'' said one farmer. ''My beans are huge this year.''

"Let all the fields be replenished,'' crooned the Queen.

"Excellent,'' said the wiseman, sensing the pride and accomplishment of everyone involved. ''And now we need to decide what to do for next year. I suggest that we begin to examine the issue of the seed. We know that one breed of horse can be better than another. It seems obvious that there must be finer breeds of seed. Let us have the farmer from the west begin to test and develop the best seeds in the land. Once developed, we will plant many acres and spread the seed throughout the land.''

Again the King commanded it done. He also called for a celebration to recognize and reward the farmers for their work and the wiseman for his deeds. The meal and entertainment lasted well into the night.

The King and Queen stood to retire when the festivities had ran their course and were surprised when the wiseman turned as if to say good night.

"I'll see you early in the morning," he said.

The King and Queen looked at him in a puzzled way.

"We've taken care of the agricultural problem," he said humbly. "And now," he said, the glee barely hidden in his voice, "it is time to decide which room to clean next!"

BIBLIOGRAPHY

Anderson, Duncan M., "Time Warrior," *Success*, Dec. 1991.

Baumert, John, "New SEI Maturity Model Targets Key Practices," IEEE Software, Nov. 1991, pp. 78–79.

Brassard, M., *The Memory Jogger Plus +* ™, GOAL/QPC, 1989.

Deming, W. Edwards, *Out of the Crisis*, MIT Press, 1986.

DeMarco, Tom, "Software Development: State of the Art vs. State of the Practice," ACM Sigsoft, 1989.

Dilts, Robert B., *Walt Disney—The Dreamer, The Realist, and The Critic*, Dynamic Learning Publications, 1990.

Hammer, Michael, "Reengineering Work: Don't Automate, Obliterate," *HBR*, July-Aug. 1990, pp.104–112.

Hudiburg, John J., *Winning with Quality*, Quality Resources, a division of the Kraus Organization Limited, 1991.

Imai, Masaaki, *Kaizen*, Random House, 1986.

Juran, J. M., *Leadership for Quality*, 1986.

Kernighan, B. and P. J. Plauger, *The Elements of Programming Style*, McGraw, 1974.

King, Bob, *Better Designs in Half the Time*, GOAL/QPC, 1989.

Leonard, George, *Mastery*, Penguin, 1991.

"Schwarzkopf on Leadership," *Inc.*, Jan. 1992, pg. 11.

Shewhart, Walter A., *Economic Control of Quality of Manufactured Product*, Van Nostrand, 1931; repr. ed., ASQC, 1980.

Sirkin, Harold and George Stalk, Jr., "Fix the Process not the Problem," *Harvard Business Review*, July-Aug. 1990, pp. 26–33.

Walton, Mary, *Deming Management at Work*, Putnam, 1991.

Weinberg, Gerald M., *The Secrets of Consulting*, Dorset House, 1985.

Xerox Corp., *A Guide to Benchmarking in Xerox*, NTIS, Springfield, VA, 22161, 1990.

Choosing a Process

If your process is	Then
defined and measured	use 7-step, problem-solving process to improve
measured but not defined	use process management to flow chart the process and begin using 7-step, problem-solving process to improve.
defined but not measured	use process management to identify and begin control charting measurements of the process.
not defined and not measured	use process management to describe the base line process as it exists today. Establish and control chart measurements of the process. Look for wasy to improve the process to reduce non-value added activities.
new, never done before	use the 7 management and planning tools to define the product or service, and the process that will produce it. Use process management to layout the new process and measurements. Once the process is functioning, stable, and capable, then start using the 7-step, problem-solving process.
fully optimized but not meeting customer expectations	use the 7 management and planning tools to reengineer the existing process. No further improvements are possible without significant redesign of the process.

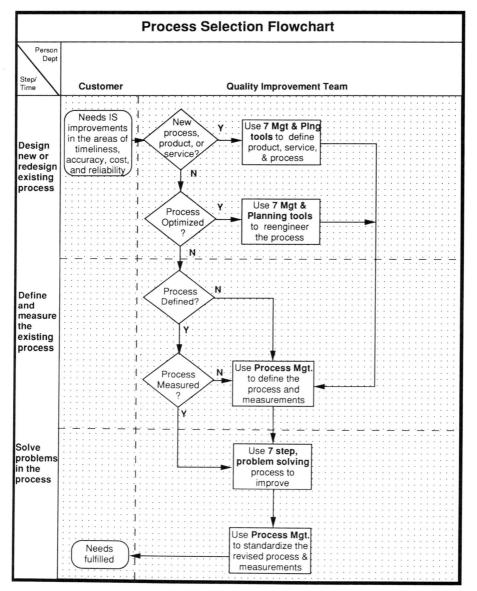

Process Selection Flowchart

ABEND Stoppers QI Story

QI TEAM PLANNING WORKSHEET		

Theme (Problem Area)	Reduce job failures in Billing application
Team Work Location	Denver, CO
Team Name	ABEND Stoppers
Duration	Mo./Yr. (8/91) through Mo./Yr. (6/92) Total Months (10)

TEAM MEMBERS

Team leader	Facilitator	Team Information
Member 1		
Member 2		
Member 3		
Member 4		
Member 5		

MEETING

No.	Date	Hours	Att.	No.	Date	Hours	Att.	No.	Date	Hours	Att.
1	8/21	2	88%	6	10/15	2	88%	12	1/19	2	88%
2	8/28	2	88%	7	10/29	2	88%	13	2/3	2	88%
3	9/10	2	88%	8	11/13	2	88%	14	2/17	2	88%
4	9/17	2	88%	9	11/23	2	88%	15	3/2	2	88%
5	10/1	2	88%	10	12/6	2	88%	16	3/16	2	88%
6	10/15	2	88%	11	1/5	2	88%	17	3/29	2	88%

OUTLINE OF ACTIVITIES

Schedule (☐ Projected ■ Actual)

Comments (How each step was done.)

Mo. & Yr.	A	S	O	N	D	J	F	M	A	M	J
Plan Analyze the Problem and Root Causes											
DO Implement Counter-measures											
CHECK The Results											
ACT - To Improve											

* Signifies Presentation Date

PLAN

Theme: Reduce job failures in Billing application

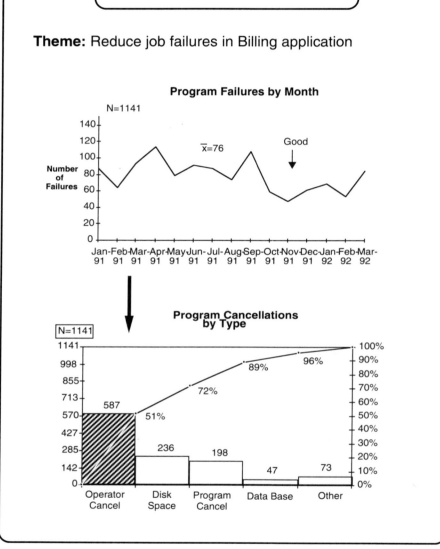

Program Failures by Month

N=1141

$\bar{x}=76$

Good

Number of Failures

Program Cancellations by Type

N=1141

PLAN

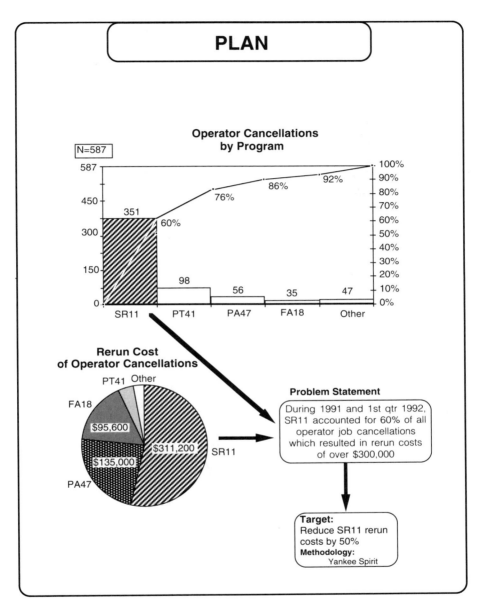

Operator Cancellations by Program

N=587

Rerun Cost of Operator Cancellations

Problem Statement

During 1991 and 1st qtr 1992, SR11 accounted for 60% of all operator job cancellations which resulted in rerun costs of over $300,000

Target:
Reduce SR11 rerun costs by 50%
Methodology:
Yankee Spirit

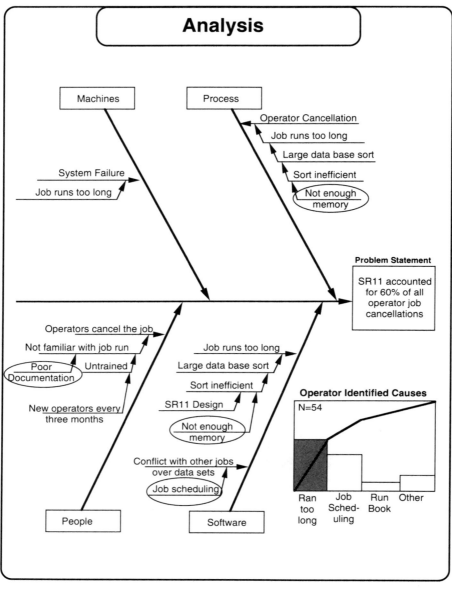

DO

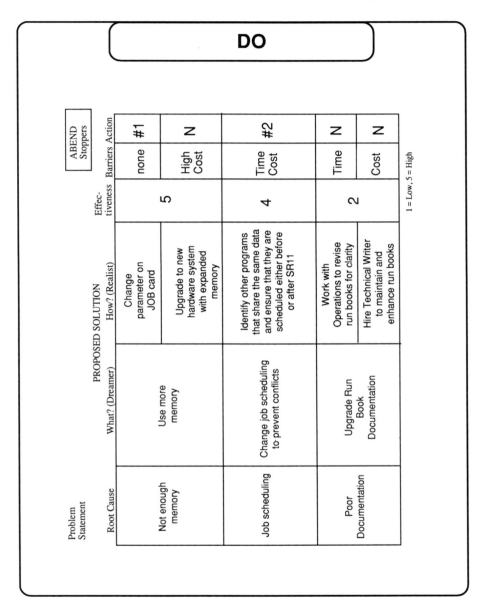

Problem Statement

Root Cause	PROPOSED SOLUTION		Effectiveness	Barriers	Action
	What? (Dreamer)	How? (Realist)			
Not enough memory	Use more memory	Change parameter on JOB card	5	none	#1
		Upgrade to new hardware system with expanded memory		High Cost	N
Job scheduling	Change job scheduling to prevent conflicts	Identify other programs that share the same data and ensure that they are scheduled either before or after SR11	4	Time Cost	#2
Poor Documentation	Upgrade Run Book Documentation	Work with Operations to revise run books for clarity	2	Time	N
		Hire Technical Writer to maintain and enhance run books		Cost	N

ABEND Stoppers

1 = Low , 5 = High

DO

ACTION PLAN

WHAT? (Dreamer)	HOW? (Realist)	WHO? (Accountability)	WHEN? (Start/Complete)		INDICATOR? (To Measure Results)
Use more memory	Change parameter on JOB card	Operations Tech Staff	4/1/92	4/1/92	Run Time with more memory and SR11 Job Cancellation
Change job scheduling to prevent conflicts	Identify other programs that share the same data and ensure that they are scheduled either before or after SR11	Application and Operations Staff	5/1/92	5/1/92	Conflicts identified and SR11 Job Cancellation

CHECK

Program Failures by Month

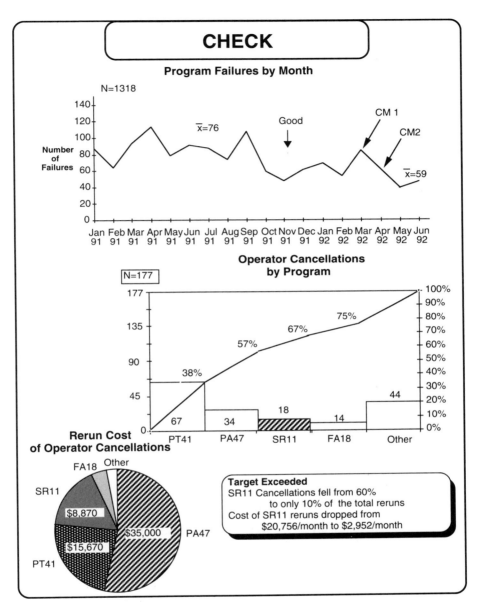

N=1318

Number of Failures

x̄=76

Good

CM 1

CM2

x̄=59

Jan Feb Mar Apr May Jun Jul Aug Sep Oct Nov Dec Jan Feb Mar Apr May Jun
91 91 91 91 91 91 91 91 91 91 91 91 92 92 92 92 92 92

Operator Cancellations by Program

N=177

38%   57%   67%   75%   100%

67   34   18   14   44

PT41   PA47   SR11   FA18   Other

Rerun Cost of Operator Cancellations

FA18   Other

SR11

$8,870

$35,000   PA47

$15,670

PT41

Target Exceeded
SR11 Cancellations fell from 60%
           to only 10% of the total reruns
Cost of SR11 reruns dropped from
           $20,756/month to $2,952/month

ACT TO IMPROVE

ACTION PLAN

WHAT? (Dreamer)	HOW? (Realist)	WHO? (Accountability)	WHEN? (Start/Complete)		INDICATOR? (To Measure Results)
Standardize Large Sort Parameters	Identify all large sort jobs by decreasing run time and revise parms	Operations Tech Staff	7/1/92	8/1/92	Run Time with more memory and Job Cancellation Rate
Standardize Job Scheduling Process to include conflict checking	Initiate Process management team to document current scheduling process and improve	Application and Operations Staff	7/1/92	10/1/92	Process flowchart and measurements in place / Cancellation Rate
Begin investigation of PA47 Cancellations	Continue Story starting with root cause analysis on PA47	ABEND Stoppers QI Team	7/1/92	1/1/93	PA47 Cancellation Rate

Index